Paul Simper's career in pop journalism began after a fortuitous encounter with Spandau Ballet in a Tiger Bay nightclub in 1980. Writing for *Melody Maker*, *New Sounds New Styles* and *No.1*, he spent the best part of the rest of the decade interviewing the new generation of pop stars who took over the world, before having his own crack at the charts as one half of the ill-fated disco duo Slippry Feet.

He has published one other book, the 1960s cult TV tribute *The Saint: From Big Screen to Small Screen and Back Again*. Paul Simper lives in north London.

POP STARS IN MY PANTRY

A Memoir of Pop Mags and
Clubbing in the 1980s

PAUL SIMPER

Unbound

This edition first published in 2017

Unbound
6th Floor Mutual House,
70 Conduit Street, London W1S 2GF
www.unbound.com

Lyrics from 'Maureen' by Sade reproduced by kind permission of
Sade/Paul Denman/Andrew Hale

Lyrics from 'I'll Be There' reproduced by kind permission of Nile Rodgers

Text Designed and typeset by Ellipsis, Glasgow

A CIP record for this book is available from the British Library

ISBN 978-1-78352-387-0 (trade hbk)
ISBN 978-1-78352-388-7 (ebook)
ISBN 978-1-78352-386-3 (limited edition)

Printed in Great Britain by Clays Ltd, St Ives Plc

1 3 5 7 9 8 6 4 2

Dedicated to:

The Crimpers, my dearest darling Crowther and Molly-Jean;
here's one I made earlier.

Geoffrey, for trusting your little brother with your
precious record collection.

Jacqueline, for risking putting on those oh so slippry feet.

And Mrs Simper, aka Mother, who will disapprove of much of this, but
without whom none of it would have been possible.

'No, I don't want to live in the past. But it's a nice place to visit'

Nile Rodgers and Chic, 'I'll Be There'

Dear Reader,

The book you are holding came about in a rather different way to most others. It was funded directly by readers through a new website: Unbound. Unbound is the creation of three writers. We started the company because we believed there had to be a better deal for both writers and readers. On the Unbound website, authors share the ideas for the books they want to write directly with readers. If enough of you support the book by pledging for it in advance, we produce a beautifully bound special subscribers' edition and distribute a regular edition and e-book wherever books are sold, in shops and online.

This new way of publishing is actually a very old idea (Samuel Johnson funded his dictionary this way). We're just using the internet to build each writer a network of patrons. At the back of this book, you'll find the names of all the people who made it happen.

Publishing in this way means readers are no longer just passive consumers of the books they buy, and authors are free to write the books they really want. They get a much fairer return too – half the profits their books generate, rather than a tiny percentage of the cover price.

If you're not yet a subscriber, we hope that you'll want to join our publishing revolution and have your name listed in one of our books in the future. To get you started, here is a £5 discount on your first pledge. Just visit unbound.com, make your pledge and type **pantry5** in the promo code box when you check out.

Thank you for your support,

Dan, Justin and John
Founders, Unbound

CONTENTS

PROLOGUE

It is one of eighties pop music's lesser known facts that Bananarama's second album – the one with 'Cruel Summer' and 'Robert De Niro's Waiting' – was at one time to be titled *Tea at Mrs Simper's*.

This followed a weekend jaunt in January 1984 by two of the Nanas – Sarah Dallin and Keren Woodward – and their best pal (and honorary fourth member) Mel O'Brien, to The White House, my mum and dad's home in the tiny, publess village of East Grafton in Wiltshire.

Bananarama vs. Mrs Simper was always likely to be a lively encounter. In the one corner: council-tenanted pop stars Keren and Sarah plus their gold-toothed mate from Bethnal Green, all three prone to piss-taking, eye-rolling and in-joking, lovers of *Blind Date* and *Brookie* and capable of drinking their own body weights in vodka.

In the other, the very just-so lady of the manor, Mrs S, an inveterate snob, falling somewhere between *The Good Life*'s Margot Leadbetter and *Keeping Up Appearances*' Hyacinth Bucket, queen of her colonially decked-out domain, lover of the *Antiques Roadshow* and *Last Night of the Proms*, partial to a dry sherry and the occasional (fairly lethal) Wiltshire cocktail.

Bristolians Sarah and Keren were at least on nodding terms with the countryside and country ways. Mrs S, on the other hand, who approved of only two records I'd ever owned –'Turning Japanese' by The Vapors, to which she would dance dementedly round the dining room like one of the three little maids from *The Mikado*, and Bowie's 'The Jean Genie', because it had her name in the title – had not the slightest idea who these rather unruly girls were, or of what they sang.

She had, though, been reliably informed by the teenage off-spring of one of her mates that these new pals of mine had been on *Top of the Pops*, which at least granted them a BBC air of respectability. Hence they were feted with the best china and ushered into the big sitting room – normally reserved for landmark birthdays and Christmas.

If Mrs S took to any of Bananarama, it was Keren who, perhaps with a premonition of her future life shacked up in a Cornish country pile with Wham!'s Andrew Ridgeley, appeared the most at home in these surroundings. There's a photo of the whole ensemble, including old family friends, St Mary's convent girls Giulietta and Bella Edwards, and my brother Geoffrey, taking afternoon tea, and Keren, standing by the mantelpiece, is the only one with an air of 'Sure this is my gaff, what of it?' Meanwhile Sarah and Mel muck about with the family teapot and Mother plasters on a smile and waits for everyone to return to venerating her Victoria sponge.

Needless to say, Mrs S was not impressed by the girls' general tomfoolery or the lack of a single skirt, nail varnish or lipstick between them. All of which only added to the air of barely suppressed hilarity as far as the Nanas were concerned.

Soon after arrival, Sarah and Mel struck gold when they discovered a small knitted frog in their bedroom, which they immediately christened Mrs Simper. This accompanied us to Savernake Forest after we'd been shooed out from under Mrs S's feet because of our constant tittering. The rest of the afternoon was spent with the girls going through their repertoire of exotic bird calls as they waggled the knitted Mrs S about on a pointed stick and sang old Cher hits whilst running from (non-existent) gypsies, tramps and thieves.

Due to the dearth of pubs in the village, we spent the Saturday evening in the public bar of the Royal Oak, Wootton Rivers, where the locals proved about as welcoming as *An American Werewolf in London's* Brian Glover and Rik Mayall when their game of darts is interrupted at the Slaughtered Lamb. Being the days before camera phones, and clearly unaware of the maxim 'take a picture, it'll last longer', various welly-clad, twine-belted characters ambled over to inspect the girls at extremely close range, as you might a new breed of heifer. The girls were not impressed.

Sunday was again spent taking to the great outdoors, walking up Martinsell Hill to do a few Beatles' 'Help'-style poses (possibly the inspiration for their 1989 *Comic Relief* Lananeeneenoonoo collaboration with French and Saunders?) and visiting my dad's herd of cows up Dursden Lane, which proved to be a poor substitute for the horses Sarah and Keren assumed we'd have knocking about somewhere out back.

I'd say the weekend was over all too quickly but as we bade our farewells and headed back to The Smoke there was (for me at least) a sense of relief that we'd all got through it in one piece. The glower from Mrs S when Sarah gleefully declared that her London living abode was 'council' has stayed with me to this day.

And yet, mortifying though much of it had been, there was also something thrilling about seeing these two worlds unfeasibly collide. Like Woody Allen's *The Purple Rose of Cairo*, where various on-screen characters magically burst free from the celluloid to enjoy a Madcap Manhattan Weekend in 1930s New York, here were shiny *Top of the Pops* stars I'd watched devotedly on our telly suddenly spilling out into the Simper household, supping cups of tea in our kitchen, popping upstairs for a quick wee or being tutted at by my mum for coming down late for breakfast.

Bringing a pop star back to the country – the place that as a teenager I'd been so desperate to leave – was, strangely, in some way the ultimate confirmation of how lucky I'd got with this wholly improbable career of mine. Not only was I being paid to interview and party with these sexy, funny pop people in the big city, they were even taking the time to hop on a train and meet the folks.

Not that it was always such a smooth ride. No pop journo memoir would be complete without a few stories of outraged stars wanting to string you up for one reason or another. We'll return to those. For the most part, though, the early eighties was a pretty glorious time to embark on writing about all things pop, especially living and working in London.

Nightclubs were young, thrilling and fun; packed to the gills with a new generation of pop stars set to take over the world and more than happy to be written about whilst they did it. New technology heralded the dawn of MTV and colour-printing presses – big-budget, glossy pop videos (and lifestyles) and big-budget, glossy pop mags. At its peak, fortnightly song words magazine *Smash Hits* sold half a million, a 7-inch single like Adam Ant's 'Goody Two Shoes' a million.

But for all the fancy trappings of this brave new world there was much at the start of the eighties that was reassuringly analogue. Records were played and reviewed (then frequently sold on for a tidy sum) on vinyl. Pop stars were not on conference call, electronic press kit or buffered by an army of publicists. They were there in person. You might not get to know them well enough to pop round their houses, but chances are they'd be up for a pint. With the bounteous array of home-grown talent emerging from the new clubland scene, we were often sharing the same dance floors and anything else that made for a good night out.

For those of a delicate disposition, be warned: it does get messy.

Let's not jump the gun, though. For now, it's back to the all-important task of naming that second Bananarama LP. To their credit, the girls pushed hard for *Tea at Mrs Simper's* to become its title. In the end, though, London Records plumped for something they considered more impactful.

They called it: *Bananarama*.

1

EVE GRAHAM'S TOAST RACK

It's 1972. A seminal year for pop on the telly. For many it will be that arm drape on *Top of the Pops*, one heady July evening, as Starmen Bowie and Ronson set off their cultural comet. But for me, 1972's most palpitating night of telly pop had already passed some five months previous, when all my hopes and dreams were focused on another BBC musical event – and one with a global audience.

Coming live from Edinburgh's Usher Hall and presented by Moira Shearer, this was the big one. The UK was hosting the *Eurovision Song Contest* and my absolute favourite pop group of that moment, The New Seekers, were red-hot favourites to win with their rollicking piece of bubble-gum pop 'Beg, Steal or Borrow'.

I'd been glued to my TV set since the thrilling process of picking our song for Europe had begun. Every Saturday night for six weeks, on *It's Cliff Richard!*, The New Seekers had offered up a different ditty for the great British public's careful consideration. My personal choice to get the job done was 'One by One', a tale of the Creation sweetly sung by Lyn Paul, but 'Beg, Steal or Borrow' ran away with it and, to be fair, it was a stonker.

All the signs were good. The New Seekers were already on something of a roll thanks to their chart-topping adaptation of the Coca-Cola theme tune (artfully changing 'We'd Like to Buy the World a Coke' to 'We'd Like to Teach the World to Sing') the previous year.

Allied with the UK's then rock solid Eurovision track record – Sandie Shaw winning in 1967 with 'Puppet on a String', Lulu tying in 1969 with 'Boom Bang-a-Bang' and Cliff's 'Congratulations' only being pipped at the post in 1968 by one vote – who could possibly deny them?

I still find it hard to revisit the events of that night. Back then it had all unfolded in slightly foggy black and white (our first colour telly didn't appear till the Queen's Silver Jubilee and Boycott's 1977 Ashes) but watching it now on YouTube in eye-popping (save for the beige stage) colour makes it all the tougher to bear.

The New Seekers had it in the bag. Spurred on by the BBC orchestra and cheered heartily by a partisan crowd (Eve Graham was from Perth) they gave it their all. Singing so sunnily, so winningly (that moment where Lyn Paul crinkles her nose adorably) and ending with a look so triumphant that even though there were thirteen more acts still to be heard, I was already anticipating their glorious air-punching moment of victory.

There are times, though, when pop goes wrong. That disastrous *Smash Hits* Poll Winners Party of 1993 when Take That's perfect trio of 'Pray', 'Relight My Fire' and 'Why Can't I Wake Up with You' tragically split the vote and the Fresh Prince snatched the Best Single award from their deserving grasp with 'Boom! Shake the Room' is one that's never truly healed.

Tears were shed by a fully grown (fairly pissed) man that fateful Sunday afternoon round my mate Sue Tilley's. And so it was for the nine-year-old me, some two decades earlier. Wide-eyed and over-brimming with optimism – yet in truth still hopelessly unprepared for the injustices of the entertainment world.

Vicky Leandros, representing Luxembourg, was the penultimate act to take to the stage with her ballad 'Après Toi'. It was good, solid Eurovision fare. Plenty of emotion and a stirring chorus and Vicky looked very nice in her floor-length black dress. But come on! Winner?! Where was the pizazz? Where was the likeability that Mr Cowell would later teach us was an essential of any singing contest winner? Where indeed was the X factor?

In the end fourteen points separated the two. It was neck and neck all the way and because our bodies tend to protect us from life's more traumatic moments, my mind has erased the memory of which fucker cast those final, decisive votes.

The recovery process was a long one. In my Letts Schoolboys Diary for that year, four weeks pass and then on the Wednesday of an otherwise unrecorded week I have scratched the words EVE Grahame [sic] in a handwriting that I can't even recognise as my own. There is not another entry for the next twenty-two weeks until I finally break my mourning by playing with my Action Man.

It is possible that that one curiously misspelled entry was the day on which I decided to make Eve a toast rack. I can't entirely fathom the reasons for this. Was I using basic arts and craft to repair my broken heart? Was it intended as some sort of consolation prize for Eve for not getting to lift that Euro trophy? Or was it a gift with which to woo her?

Cards on the table, between the two of them, I actually fancied Lyn Paul more. But many a fruitless game of playground kiss chase had taught me not to play the favourite.

On reflection, this is a fairly harsh call on the Graham. With her almond eyes twinkling with allure from beneath her dark fringe on the back sleeve of my album *We'd Like to Teach the World to Sing*, Eve is undoubtedly a hottie and deserving of far more lavish gifts than my D-minus effort.

All the same I parcelled it up and posted it off to Polydor Records. After which, big surprise, it was never seen or heard of again.

Many years later, I phoned into Danny Baker's weekend Radio London show to share this story and he was much taken with the idea of me imagining Eve sitting at her breakfast banquette, nibbling on a slice of toasted Nimble from my little rack and thinking fondly of Young Paul from Burbage.

If only she could have trusted herself to date a nine-year-old.

Still, though my young heart had taken its first battering at the hands of pop, there was much to be thankful for. I had discovered the buzz that went with it. Soon I would be gobbling up all manner of predominantly 7-inch vinyl from Glam to Disco to New Wave (I was too much of a wuss for Punk). My only trip to London in the 1976 summer of Anarchy involved me visiting the National History and Science museums and buying a copy of *Mayfair* and *Oui*.

With each new phase would come fresh agonies and ecstasy. The thrill of owning 'Metal Guru' in its beautifully branded red-and-blue sleeve with Marc and his corkscrew hair staring up at me as he chased himself around the turntable. Counterbalanced by the misery of discovering that the copy of T-Rex's *Tanx* – that I got off my cousin Gerald for the price of a conker – had warped when I casually left it exposed to the heat of the midday sun in the back of the family Renault 12.

Later, when I took to the dance floor of Tunisia's Sahara Beach Hotel, there was the giddy combination of my first holiday romance and my first earful of Chic's 'Dance, Dance, Dance (Yowsah, Yowsah,

Yowsah)'. Only to be followed by the crashing disappointment, on returning home, of realising that there really had been no romance and that the object of my fanciful desires (who lived down the road from my dentist) couldn't even be arsed to come to the phone let alone cut a rug again to Nile Rodgers and Bernard Edwards.

At first the records themselves were more than enough to be getting on with, but as I moved up through my teens, a thirst for information about all my latest chart obsessions led me to the music press.

Every Wednesday the *New Musical Express*, *Melody Maker*, *Record Mirror* and *Sounds* would bring me that little bit closer and make me that little bit more fascinated with these unreachable idols. Dropping in on them whilst they recorded their latest album, being invited backstage at their gigs, even flying to faraway lands with them for a bit of a chin wag. Imagine – just imagine – having a job like that?

2

50P NEW ROMANTIC

Seeing your name in print for the first time is a thrill. Not as cool, I'd imagine, as hearing your record on the radio or looking up at yourself on a movie screen, but a thrill nonetheless. There it is on the newsstand, an inky version of you, jumping up and down with a little loudhailer, shouting: 'Here's what I think of this mob!'

When I made it into the hallowed pages of the *Maker* in March 1981, I must have read my Stray Cats review pretty much all the way from Cardiff to London. Fellow NCTJ student Jane Moore – now illustrious *Sun* columnist and broadcaster, then fellow course mate living in a dodgy bedsit on the Newport Road opposite a funeral home – reckons she was more impressed by it than I was. 'It was like a big, proper grown-up thing to do.'

Still, my diary entry for the following Monday, when we were both back in college, belies any cool I might have been affecting.

'Just felt like a great day,' it breezes. 'Generally bounced around the place receiving congrats for the article.' You'd have thought it was me who'd played the gig.

There had been one false dawn before my ticker-tape parade. My first commission by *MM*'s features ed, Colin Irwin, for Bad Manners had arrived at my digs in Cyncoed by telegram (yes, really; that old) two weeks previous. After waving it around like Lord Chamberlain under the noses of my fellow course mates, I strode off to the city's

Top Rank that evening to cast a critical eye over Buster Bloodvessel giving it a bit of 'Lip Up Fatty'.

All went well, complimentary press tickets (my first!) were waiting, notes were taken (steady at 80 wpm Teeline shorthand) and there was even a bit of drama when the Manners' set was brought to an abrupt end by some local skinheads and their impromptu stage invasion – pretty standard for ska revival gigs circa 1980/81.

Unfortunately, copy written, what this wet-behind-the-ears cub reporter neglected to do was file it down the phone to the subs the very next day. Instead, I entrusted it to the Royal Mail and it eventually arrived on Colin's desk at much the same time as the weekly edition of the paper it was meant to be in.

Anyway, second time lucky. There I was in black and white, 350 words of 'more assured' this and 'vastly improved' that, covering half a page thanks to a live smudge of lead bequiffed Cat, Brian Setzer, leaning into his mike and sweating up a storm.

It had arrived on a propitious day. After much gabbing about it, fellow course mate and pop fanatic Gary Hurr and I were bound for London. We'd talked about little else since a chance encounter with Spandau Ballet the previous November that had set all manner of thoughts and dreams in motion.

I'd arrived in Cardiff in the autumn of 1980; a New-Wave-loving, just-turned-eighteen, nightclubbing novice. I had not the slightest inkling that a new game-changing youth movement was growing and that it was happening not only up the M4 in London, but right under my very nose. I'd not even heard of the band (just about to release their first single) that was at the vanguard of it.

I'd only made it to Cardiff by the skin of my teeth. My mother had presented me with a cutting from the *Daily Telegraph* advertising five courses across the UK run by the National Council for the Training of Journalists. I'd replied with the required essay on 'Why I Want to Become a Journalist' (apparently funny) then made the day trip to London for my half-hour interview with a three-member panel of editors and senior journalists, and sat the General Knowledge exam (apparently the worst they'd ever seen).

So here I was with Jane, Gary and twenty others at the South Glamorgan Institute of Higher Education on Colchester Avenue, studying libel and slander, public admin, practical journalism (how to structure a story) and 110 wpm shorthand with the supposed intention of doing indentures on a local newspaper for a subsequent two and a half years, before working one's way towards Fleet Street.

Except there was this clothes shop. A very trendy-looking clothes shop in the centre of town called Paradise Garage on Queen's Street. So fearfully trendy, in fact, that I'm not quite sure how myself and Gary convinced ourselves we were cool enough to step inside. Actually, I don't think we did. Jane Moore and course mate Ann Ashford were with us, and they just walked straight in.

The guy who ran the place, Mark Taylor, was tall, dark, immaculately dressed in some sort of leather long-coat and sporting 1940s Clark Gable shades. I didn't know it but he was part of the Welsh Taffia who, in the shape of Chris Sullivan, Steve Mahoney and Steve Strange, had already relocated to London and begun to revolutionise the way the capital went about its nightclubbing with their Soho and Covent Garden one-nighters (run by the kids for the kids): Billy's, Blitz, St Moritz and Hell.

I'm sure Mark didn't even notice us boys as we tried our best to look nonchalant in front of a rail of clothes that we palpably couldn't afford (thirty-five quid for a pair of trousers was a whole term's grant!). But he took a shine to Ann and that was when he pointed to the tiny poster on the wall.

It seems wholly appropriate that my first contact with Spandau Ballet should have been via a clothes shop and a nightclub. Their debut *Top of the Pops* appearance for 'To Cut a Long Story Short' two weeks before was the first I'd really heard of them. Now Mark told us they were playing that Sunday afternoon at Casablanca's, a disused church in Tiger Bay. Why not come along?

In fact Clark Gable could do even better than that. Not only would we see this hot new group, playing only their second ever show outside of London, but we could also interview them the night before at Mel's – Cardiff's most painfully trendy club – for our college rag, *Fuse*.

Mel's was an adventure in itself. Up to this point most of our course socialising had been conducted in traditional large boozers like the Philharmonic near the station or the more modest Poet's Corner which was closer to college. Mel's, on the other hand, was in Tiger Bay – these days a bustling docklands redevelopment, but back in 1980 a dangerous, dark, faraway place that appeared to be only reachable by foot and which escaping from depended on one very unreliable night bus, allegedly bound for Ely.

We had never ventured that far but on this Saturday night – spurred on by a second Spandau *TOTP* appearance as 'To Cut a Long Story Short' surged to Number 5 – we made it.

What happened next, I can now appreciate, was a classic Spandau hit-and-run. The notion that there really were other New Romantic scenes (that dreaded term, but it had stuck) sprouting up outside London was one that the band had only really road tested earlier that week when they'd presented their first out-of-town show in Birmingham.

On the Thursday, a coach-load of pissed-up, tripping Blitz Kids (another term bandied about) had descended on the Midlands, danced to Spandau at the Botanical Gardens – the city's most preposterous live venue – run up a massive bar bill at the one trendy club – The Rum Runner – compared notes (and competitive sideways glances) with the scene's own aspiring band (a bunch of no-hopers called Duran Duran who they'd refused as their support act) and a few style-conscious fellow-travellers, before piling back to London.

By the weekend, it was Cardiff's turn for similar treatment. Except this time, it was myself, Gary and Jane having our ears bent as Spandau's affable but astute manager, Steve Dagger, laid out both the scene's and the band's manifesto accompanied by his classic Young Americans wedge haircut. We were about to be a part of something very now – this new decade's update of the mid-sixties Swinging London club scene with contemporary designers, DJs, models, artists and photographers – and this band that was now standing in front of us – 'the applause for our audience', as they referred to themselves – representing it.

Within minutes of entering Mel's, we'd all three been paired off with the efficiency of a speed-dating service. I was given a comprehensive dissertation on the history of London club culture, courtesy of Gary Kemp. Gary Hurr got the low-down on contemporary wardrobe from Steve Norman and Jane Moore had half an hour of Tony Hadley on his *Mastermind* specialist subject, The Life and Works of Frank Sinatra, with a Bowie and Roxy bonus round.

By the time Spandau actually got around to playing the following afternoon, in the sweaty arches of a disused church called

Casablanca's, it was a done deal: this was a party I didn't want to leave. There were terrifyingly gorgeous girls painted like dolls, extremely drunk lads who could really dance and a top table musical feast from DJ Rusty Egan of Roxy, Bowie, Kraftwerk, the B-52s and Gina X that made my New Wave diet of Boomtown Rats, UB40 and The Police suddenly seem sorely undernourished.

There was even drama. Slipping backstage after the show, I was just in time to see a well-oiled and garrulous Robert Elms berating *Melody Maker*'s Steve 'Sticks' Sutherland as Steve tried to interview the band in their dressing room.

'Where were you when this all started?' scoffed Elms.

I couldn't have cared less. Marching up the road with Jane brandishing one of John Keeble's drumsticks, I was busting to tell everyone on the course what we'd just seen. Not only had the curtain been pulled back on a whole new way of life, there was even the possibility I'd been afforded a shortcut round the hard slog of local newspaper journalism.

From that weekend on it was nightclubbing all the way. Our New Romantic radar on high alert, we discovered all sorts in the city. Along with Mel's there was The Floorshow every Wednesday at Lloyd's by the railway station, Nero's – with new live acts like Shock and Depeche Mode – on Saturdays and Xanadoos – with its precipitous raised dance floor of flashing disco squares – on Tuesdays.

Lloyds was mine and Gary's favourite haunt. Mel's was a little too up itself and, truth be told, still a little too intimidating to enjoy week in week out. But for 50p, Lloyds had the lot.

Our compère and DJ was Anthony, a friendly David Sylvian lookalike who leaned towards the electro pop end of the spectrum – Visage's 'Fade to Grey' and 'Mind of a Toy', Landscape's 'Einstein

A Go-Go', Simple Minds' Moroderesque 'I Travel', Orchestral Manoeuvres in the Dark's 'Enola Gay' and 'Electricity', Ultravox's 'Vienna' and 'All Stood Still', and, naturally, as he pouted with rouged cheeks from beneath his bleached, flicked fringe, Japan's 'Quiet Life' and 'Life in Tokyo'.

Gary had a penchant for The Skids so was always lobbying for 'Into the Valley' and 'Working for the Yankee Dollar', whilst, card-carrying party member that I'd already become, I was always on at Anthony for the Spandau 12-inch of 'To Cut a Long Story' and 'The Freeze'.

There was naturally plenty of Bowie and Roxy. The obligatory 'Heroes', 'Sound and Vision' and the three *Scary Monsters* singles: 'Ashes to Ashes', 'Fashion' and 'Up the Hill Backwards' for the former; and thrilling back catalogue 'Pyjamarama', 'Editions of You' and 'Do the Strand' telling us of fabulous creations and danceable solutions for the latter.

Highlight of the night would be the moment when Anthony would slow things down with Roxy Music's 'Mother of Pearl'. Two Ferry lookalikes – the Two Bryans, as we called them – would take to the floor in dinner suits and play out the whole number: lighting each other's cigarettes, striking the poses, double clapping after 'even Zarathustra' and sticking it out through the torch song's numerous false endings (four of them) before enigmatically departing the now fairly empty dance floor on the final finger click. Once, one of the Bryans exited one round of finger clicks too soon, leaving Gary and me in fits for the rest of the night.

My wardrobe had also had a suitable makeover. Gone were the baggy Geldof jumpers and jeans and Sting-style stripy T-shirts and raincoats.

'Shone in my clown outfit,' reads one fashion-conscious entry from my February 1981 diary. 'Gary had his great mercenary outfit on.'

'Stunned and outshone all at Mel's in my plus fours,' reads another. I was doing a lot of shining.

My father was less impressed with my sartorial choices. When he came to pick me up from the M4 turn-off for Marlborough and saw the daring bleached motif in my hair – courtesy of Jayne, one of the trainee hairdressers also at Colchester Avenue, and a fellow Lloyds frequenter – his first instinct was to keep on driving.

You'd have thought the plus fours might have gone down a storm in Wiltshire but headbands and tablecloth-sized neck scarves with pixie boots were about as New Romantic as it ever got (and even that was a year or so off yet).

Back at college, Gary and I were not over-enamoured with the opportunities being presented to us. Jane, being far more sensible, already had her sights set on Fleet Street and was playing the long game. But with mine and Gary's coursework reading matter consisting as much of *NME*, *Melody Maker* and *Record Mirror* as NCTJ text books, we were keen to see what the music press had to offer.

In the summer of 1980, I'd entered a *Melody Maker* competition to review five favourite albums with the prize being that your work would be published in the paper. *Ziggy Stardust*, *My Generation*, the first Beatles album, *Regatta de Blanc* and AN Other were my five. I hadn't heard a peep.

But since our fortuitous Spandau encounter, I now had a better in. The tiny detail that I hadn't actually realised I was conducting my first exclusive interview with a bona fide pop star when I was propping up the bar at Mel's with Gary Kemp (and subsequently hadn't made a single note) luckily didn't deter me from writing 800 hastily remembered words about it.

With this and a couple of gig reviews of The Skids ('Exuberant highland whoops') and The Blues Band ('Layin' it down with good humour, energy and skill') at the local Top Rank as my calling card, I printed off and posted two copies to the *NME* and *Melody Maker*, offering my services as a thrusting young thing with access to the hot new bands that they had only just become aware of.

Three months later and there laid out in front of me, next to our bars of chocolate and mid-morning British Rail crappy coffees, was my first reward. 'The Cats Who Licked the Cream' was the headline. I was practically purring myself. Here we were bound for this new eighties version of Swinging London and me a published music journo.

Everything was in place. I had a foxy friend, Darling from Ludgershall, who had a swanky pad in South Ken, and Gary had a mate who worked at the BBC in Ladbroke Grove (wherever that was). All we needed to do was hook up, dump our bags, then hot-tail it to the West End – the epicentre of all that was hip and happening on a Thursday night – and let the japes begin.

At least that was the plan. Unfortunately, bearing in mind my recent Bad Manners *Melody Maker* fiasco, I was beginning to learn that letters – particularly the posting of and now the correct addressing of – were not my forte. When we eventually made it to Darling at her (West) Ken residence we discovered my letter had unsurprisingly never reached its destination and there was no room in her inn for two smelly, galumphing blokes.

The day wasn't a total washout. Earlier we'd happened across Robert Fripp engaged in some sort of record promotion at the Virgin

Megastore on Tottenham Court Road for the launch of his *Let the Power Fall: Frippertronics* album. Then, with the sound of his 'challenging' guitar art still jangling discordantly in our ears, who should we spy strolling down the other side of Oxford Street but Steve Dagger?

Of course, we were bound to see him. This was Dagger's and Spandau's London. These guys owned this city. No doubt before the day was out we'd see the Kemp brothers quaffing a cocktail in some suitably trendy establishment and perhaps Tony Hadley buying a Russian peasant's tabard in Soho.

Frustratingly, like many new to the city before and since, we couldn't make head nor tail of which side of Oxford Street was south and which north and although Gary knew Spandau's Reformation offices were on Mortimer Street (not a clue), Dagger had disappeared back down his hole like the White Rabbit before we could hail him.

The rest of our two-night London invasion was spent cadging sleeping berths, catching new movies (*Raging Bull*, *Alien*, *The Long Good Friday*) and singularly failing to get involved with the throbbing new clubland scene in any shape or form. Clearly there was more legwork to be done.

3

BANK HOLIDAY RONDO

Naturally Gary and I bigged up our London trip as soon as we made it back to Cardiff, but we both knew it hadn't lived up to expectations. Apart from the three movies, Dagger spot and burst of Fripp, our most exciting encounter had been with the doorman of Leicester Square's Empire cinema who was built like Joe Bugner but with the voice of Larry Grayson.

My final four months in Cardiff rolled by pleasantly enough with more nights at Lloyds and plenty of gigs. Echo and the Bunnymen (or to be more exact their philanthropic manager, Bill Drummond, later a chart-topper in his own right as money-burning founder of The KLF) treated me and fellow course mate Sam to a post-show curry. At Nero's, I spent a few mortifying (but sort of thrilling) minutes sitting in the dark with a very young 'Dreaming of Me'/'New Life'-era Depeche Mode after I wangled my way backstage, only for Gary Hurr to turn the dressing room light off for a lark.

There were two more reviews published. New Romantic dance troupe Shock, led by wild man Robert Pereno and girlfriend Lowri-Ann Richards, who I declared to be 'not just a diverting sideshow, but the main event' (they folded within the year) and Toyah, who had made the leap from *Sheep Farming in Barnet* punk fringe attraction to pop star, thanks to the squeaky, belligerent ear worm that was 'I Wanna Be Free'. 'The most beautifully crass pop lyrics since Gary Glitter's "Leader of the Gang",' I reckoned. Oh dear.

All too soon my year in Cardiff was over and I was confronted with the sticky problem of converting three £17 live reviews into enough funds to get me to the big city. Pressure from home suggested now was the time to knock this music press nonsense on the head and either go to university or get a job on a proper newspaper, like the *Reading Evening Post*.

To show willing, I had already gone for an interview at the *Post* but it hadn't gone well. When they asked me how I felt about doorstepping, I lied through my teeth that I would have no problem rapping on someone's front door after they'd just lost their only child in a house fire. The truth is, I couldn't think of anything worse. My journalistic reading matter up till that point had consisted of the music papers, *Film Review* and *Photoplay* (the mainstream movie mags of the day), *Continental* (European arty films with a sprinkling of tits and a bit of bush) and *The Cricketer*. I had not a single news-reporting bone in my body.

The only other alternative was to go to work for my Uncle Peter at his fruit-machine depot in Bath, save some money and then hope to somehow find my way to the capital. That summer, McEnroe bagged his first Wimbledon, Botham won the Ashes on the Beeb and Roger Moore's Bond went back to basics in *For Your Eyes Only*, save for a comedy coda involving Margaret Thatcher impersonator Janet Brown and a parrot.

And then the 1981 August bank holiday happened.

It started with a phone call from Gary Hurr. Did I want to go and see Blue Rondo A La Turk playing one of their top-secret, one-off gigs in Bournemouth?

I'll be honest, I wasn't entirely sure who or what Gary was on about. Since Cardiff, the closest I'd got to the constantly evolving

London club scene had been purchasing the thrilling 12-inch of Spandau's 'Chant No. 1 (I Don't Need This Pressure On)' as the summer of 1981 saw everyone binning the arty poses and diving feet first into a riot of funk.

I was getting most of this second-hand from my weekly *NME* where staff writer Adrian Thrills, formerly of punk fanzine *48 Thrills*, was enthusiastically reporting back from the sweaty frontline of the scene's latest place to be – Le Beat Route, as immortalised by Gary Kemp's 'Down down pass the Talk of the Town' rap. It was Thrills' singles column, busting with exotic sounding 12-inch imports purchased from Greek Street's Groove Records – Was Not Was, Bits and Pieces, Dr Buzzard's Original Savannah Band – that was keeping me at least marginally in the loop. But Blue Rondo A La What? Gary had to fill me in on this one.

Like Spandau, Blue Rondo had risen from the original Billy's/ Blitz scene, fronted by fellow club runner Chris Sullivan (Hell, St Moritz, Le Kilt) and key face Christos Tolera. They boasted some bona fide Latin and African heavy artillery in the form of a rhythm section that included Kito Poncioni – bass, Geraldo D'Arbilly and Mick Bynoe – percussion, and a dazzling dancing trio of Sullivan, rhythm guitarist Mark Reilly (later of Matt Bianco) and saxophonist Moses Mount Bassie (real name Tony Gordon), whose steps had been honed on the country's Northern soul dance floors.

To date, they'd played four gigs, including a South American music festival, coincidentally just down the road from me in Salisbury, where chief town crier Bob Elms had been refused a round of lager, cider and blackcurrant on the grounds that he would fiendishly combine them to make a snakebite.

Now Blue Rondo were to play at the Exeter Bowl Hotel in

Bournemouth, just up the hill from the Winter Gardens, and we needed to be there. Gary had been speaking to the band's manager, Graham Ball (like Dagger and Elms, another LSE graduate) who had already made himself known to us backstage in Cardiff. We were on the door.

The only snag was I'd already bought tickets to see Siouxsie and the Banshees that same weekend in Oxford. Banshees or Blue Rondo? A quick call to Colin Irwin at the *Maker* sealed the deal. This was the first Rondo show that the music press had got wind of and miracle of miracles I had the only in.

The key question – and one that, not for the last time, I should have probably given more thought to – was what to wear? I had gathered from Martin and Gary Kemp's immaculate posing on the *NME*'s 'Soul Boys of the Western World' cover earlier that summer (from the movie of the same name, coming your way in thirty-three years' time, folks) that zoot suits were the order of the day. But Prohibition-era bespoke tailors were few and far between in Burbage so what I actually wore was a tweed jacket and some sort of khaki baggy trouser.

If Spandau at Casablanca's had unveiled a whole new world, Blue Rondo in Bournemouth was the clarion call to hang all consequences and get properly stuck in. As Gary and I stepped down into the heaving subterranean ballroom, the strangest thing was the feeling we were walking back into a party that we'd only nipped out from for a breath of fresh air. Yet in that short space of time anything and everything had changed. The whole scene had gone from monochrome to Technicolor in the blink of an eye – or to put it in calendar terms, about eight months.

The one thing we did immediately understand – possibly at the behest of an attentive Graham Ball – was the need to get down the front. On a steamy bank holiday Sunday night, without any other prior knowledge of what these Bournemouth soul weekends were all about (funk, Pils, sex, stimulants), it was evident that everyone was more than ready to lose their shit.

Like Spandau, Blue Rondo knew a bit about creating a sense of drama. The club crowd were already familiar with Elms and his infamous poem that used to usher Spandau on – 'The dance of perfection – The Spandau Ballet!' – to stark, Fritz-Lang-inspired lighting. But if Spandau were Hollywood-matinee-idols-meets-German-Expressionism, Blue Rondo were more of a rumble.

There was a bit of Brando's *On the Waterfront* with a dash of *Raging Bull* about them. Moses in particular (he'd been a boxer) cradling his instrument like he was ready to go twelve rounds. It's possible that some of the slow, menacing build may have been more down to the haphazard nature of this notoriously unmanageable bunch of mavericks (as Graham Ball earned his keep propelling them stagewards) than any grand plan; but either way it was mighty effective.

Starting slow, building fast, at the sound of a high trumpet, the whole thing erupted into a mass of delirious, flailing limbs. Blue Rondo barely drew breath again till they departed an hour later leaving us punch-drunk and drenched.

Soon after, I'd get all fired up by the projected passion and conviction of Kevin Rowland and his Dexys Midnight Runners, but the unbridled mayhem that Blue Rondo created live was equally something to behold. Sure, their biggest UK hit ('Me and Mr Sanchez') would only get to Number 40, plus, they never came remotely close to filling Radio City Music Hall or six nights at Wembley Arena –

unlike some of their contemporaries. But of that era, along with Madness, Blue Rondo were about the most fun you could possibly stick on a stage.

Gary and I weren't the only ones to be bowled over that weekend. After a chilly night spent in Gaz's Mini Mazda in the top car park opposite the venue, we returned the following lunchtime to the scene of the crime for a second show laid on specifically for the benefit of Virgin supremo Richard Branson (with an audience of substantially more hungover soul boys and girls) who had arrived too late for the Sunday festivities.

It's not every day that the head of a record company schleps across the country to see an unsigned act, but with Spandau still riding high, the labels that had missed out on them were desperate not to let the next act from London clubland slip through their fingers. As with Spandau, Phonogram, in the shape of Roger Ames and Tracy Bennett, were pressing hard but Branson even more so.

'There were a couple of other companies that were interested,' says Graham Ball, 'but strangely enough Richard had kind of made his mind up that he wanted this. He was desperately trying to expand Virgin. They had The Human League but *Dare* was yet to be released. Blue Rondo was a hot group.

'Simon Draper, Virgin's head of A & R, was very objective about it and pointed out all the pitfalls: it was a fashion-based event; they were unproven in the studio; seven-piece groups are never easy. But Richard seemed very determined. Roger Ames and his label were still very keen but Richard is a persuasive individual and Virgin at that time quite appealed. So that bank holiday weekend built to this crescendo. Richard was at the show; the show was very good. I remember looking at him and thinking: "That's about right. Let's just roll with this." I spoke to Richard. He said he didn't really know what he was doing in Bournemouth on a bank holiday Monday so he was going to fuck off back to London. But he said: "I'll ring you. I want to do business with you.'"

While Graham began to do the dance with Branson, for me it was just a mighty relief to be back in *Melody Maker* after a couple of nervy months' absence. My lead review was most notable for a great Janette Beckman snap of Christos, Moses and Chris Sullivan sweating their socks off, which led to a surprise reprint in the *NME*. In a street-fashion spread in the paper it was pinned to the wall of a stall, Marvellette in trendy Kensington Market, where peroxide blonde store runner Sandy expounded 'the stylish ethics of selling past-present' in front of an array of period bow ties and guitar-shaped earrings.

Best of all, it finally put me on my long-hoped-for fast track to London.

If I'd been a bit reticent before about taking up either Dagger or Graham Ball on their offers of a sofa to kip on, I wasn't now. Within a month of Bournemouth, I was heading their way every Friday till Christmas, the rest of the week simply spent accumulating more funds working for Uncle Peter in Bath.

Messrs Dagger and Ball both did a grand job of introducing me to all the principal players in the scene. Dagger, in particular, was the perfect guide to all that was happening in London in the early eighties. Both living it and loving it, he somehow managed to remain sufficiently detached to provide the all-important third-person commentary.

Dagger's narrative was a lot like the Henry Hill voice-over in *Goodfellas*, but with Adam Faith rather than Ray Liotta doing the honours. He would introduce you to the great and the good of the clubland scene and then, as soon as they'd gone, provide you with the perfect thumbnail sketch detailing that person's role and including any personal eccentricities that he thought might amuse you.

Names like Sulphate Paul, Valentine, Carpethead, Barry the Rat, Pinkietessa, Wigan Jill and Sally Seagull-head swirled around me whilst I bumbled along, having a fine old time and doing my best to keep up. Because, despite having two fully qualified trendy London guides, these trips still tended to be as haphazard as mine and Gary's first sortie to the capital.

I was never very good at nailing down the finer details. Where were we meeting? Who was I staying with? What were we doing? Up I'd come with my little brown suitcase and head for some designated spot in Soho or Covent Garden that I'd either never heard of or been to only once and had not a hope in hell of remembering how to get to again. Somehow, having walked round and round in circles for an hour or so, my nose stuck in an *A–Z*, our agreed meeting place would miraculously appear and off we'd go. Sometimes to Rumours on Wellington Street for cocktails on Saturdays, or upstairs in the Cambridge at Cambridge Circus on Fridays. Followed the next morning by a most welcome cup of tea and a plate of crumpets from Dagger's mum, Alice, delivered to my resting place on their sofa before we turned on *Tiswas* and *Saturday Superstore* to check whether the latest Spandau promo had made it on.

The main event, though, was always Friday nights at Le Beat Route. As luck would have it, I couldn't have arrived in London at a better time. If Billy's and Blitz (and their mushrooming provincial equivalents) had been all about the art of the pose, Le Beat Route was very much 'fuck art, let's dance'.

'Suddenly there were a lot more people on the scene,' said Dagger. 'All those early disparate elements had been drawn together – disaffected soul boys, disappointed punks, art school people and anybody else who now thought, "That's for me". The word was out that people weren't standing around posing any more; people were partying.'

As a venue, Le Beat Route was all my nightclubbing dreams distilled into one.

Not that I dared say it out loud, but *Saturday Night Fever* had made a very big impression on me. Quite why a bouffant-haired, gabardine-clad, pizza-eating youth from Brooklyn strutting his stuff to the Bee Gees should speak so completely to a lad from Wiltshire I have no idea. But the first time I saw it – my top lip sporting a hastily applied coal moustache to help blag my way into the Savoy Andover for my first X certificate – my world shifted seismically on its axis.

One scene of Tony Manero and his cocksure cronies had particularly stuck with me. It's Friday night and Tony and the gang arrive at 2001 Odyssey, the hottest local disco spot. Bobby C, Double J, Joey and the rest are tooling about in the usual fashion. But as they push through the doors and descend the stairs, Tony admonishes them, telling them to shape up because they're the 'faces'.

I understood that none of my new-found friends needed to hear about my London visit in 1978 to get some 'genuine' Tony Manero gabardine trousers from that key retail point for all things Brooklyn street fashion, Harrods (with my mum). But, as anyone who's watched Spandau's 'Chant No. 1' video will know, there's something of the *SNF* 2001 Odyssey experience about entering Le Beat Route.

The thrill of being plucked from the crowd, wending one's way along the long corridor, making it past original Blitz Kid Fiona Dealey on the cash desk, and down into the sweaty cauldron of soul boys and girls was all my big-screen thrills of John Travolta descending into Brooklyn's 2001 made real.

The only thing missing from *Saturday Night Fever* was Ollie O'Donnell. Ollie was one of the first people that Dagger introduced me to, which was just as well because if Ollie didn't know me I wasn't getting in. Ollie was Le Beat Route's extraordinary gatekeeper, a hairdresser of Irish origin with an engaging lopsided smile, a six-inch carrot quiff and a fondness for tartan zoot suits that could be seen from space.

Ollie's approach to manning the door was, I discovered, quite different from Steve Strange's (who was yet to cast an eye over me). Whereas Mr Strange would tend to dismiss you outright, with Ollie there was room for negotiation. Dagger described Friday nights on the pavement outside Le Beat Route as a sort of New Romantic Speaker's Corner. Ollie's style was that people would be told why they couldn't come in – and then be given an opportunity to put their case forward as to why they felt they should be. For those who didn't manage to sway the gatekeeper there was then the option to walk around the block a few times and try their luck again. The less patient would sometimes try to mount a direct assault on the doorway, which was where the baseball bats tucked beneath the cash desk and accompanying muscle would come into play.

'The people that wound me up were aggressive straight guys,' said Ollie. 'But I could feel a vibe off people very quickly as to what their attitude would be like once they were in. As a club, it was mixed sexually and it was mixed ethnically and that's what I wanted. If anyone was gonna come in to disrupt that kind of vibe, it would have to be over my dead body.

'Feeling safe was the most important thing. Before that you'd had years and years of not feeling safe when you went out. It wouldn't intimidate me that much, but I knew other people that could get very intimidated. I wanted an environment where these people could go and not get bullied.

'But some people were so desperate to get in. I suppose I used to play sick games. Guys would turn up with their girlfriends and sometimes I'd say to the girl, "You can come in, but he can't." To be honest, the power went to my head in a way, but it kind of worked.

'I knew that it also made it more exciting for those who did get in. It made it hot. And I knew how to keep the crowd there and not let too many people walk away. Always have about fifty people out-side. If I saw a few people I knew twenty yards away, you'd get them through – "You, you and you" – and let some others loiter. I got really good at doing that, so they wouldn't know they were not coming in.'

One of Ollie's duties as host was looking out for the increasing number of guests that Dagger would send down to see the scene in all its glory.

'If there was someone important to look after, Steve didn't even have to tell me,' said Ollie. 'I'd look after them supremely. I'd show them a night they'd never had before. That must have happened to twenty or thirty record company people.

'Steve would get down the club early and give me a list, explain who everyone was – "Record company, A & R, journalists, photo-graphers . . ." When they came down, first of all I'd make sure they stood back. I'd make them see it was busy and very hard to get in. Make them wait a little while, then let 'em in – "You know Steve Dagger? Of course, of course, come in . . ." Completely change. Make a massive fuss over them like Steve Dagger was the most important man in the world. Ply them with drinks and try and introduce them to girls and people. Just make it my job to make sure they had a great time.'

I was a delighted beneficiary of Ollie's largesse.

'I remember when you first started coming to Le Beat Route you just seemed ecstatically happy,' said Ollie. I was. I grinned so much that I later learned from photographer Neil Matthews that my nick-name for those first few months (and possibly beyond) was Simple Simper.

In deference to that moniker, I did still manage to sometimes cock things up if Dagger or Graham weren't keeping an eye on me. Months later, Ollie assured me, with quiet incredulity, that I was always on the guest list after he discovered I'd been meekly handing over my cash to Fiona (who admittedly was quite fierce) ever since my first visit.

On another occasion, it was Graham who picked up the pieces at the end of the night. The only place to drink when Le Beat Route finally ejected everyone at 3 a.m. was a dingy little basement bar opposite called Jean Pierre's. Late one Friday, Graham had gone over and was doing a bit of polite catch-up with its owner.

'How's it going, Jean Pierre?' asked Graham.

'It's good,' replied the Frenchman. 'Except when we get *that*.'

Looking in the direction of Jean Pierre's disdain, Graham recognised the figure slumped on the floor. Getting me to my feet, he handed over the keys to his Westbourne Park flat. I awoke there the next morning to find myself sharing a cosy front room with Graham's flatmate, Beat Route DJ Steve Lewis, and Steve's girlfriend, neither of whom was aware of my presence on the opposite sofa until they were fully engaged in some Saturday morning loving. I'm not sure who was the more mortified, but I spent the next three hours feigning sleep whilst they made toast and tea and discussed the state of the world before finally leaving me be.

Graham was already up and out as Blue Rondo were around the corner in Queensway recording their first single, 'Me and Mr Sanchez', as Mr Branson looked to recoup some of the cash he'd splashed. I was briefly allowed to sit in on proceedings but as relations between the band and pop producer Pete Wingfield started to deteriorate, with Chris Sullivan muttering darkly in the corner what he intended to do to the not entirely simpatico knob twiddler, Graham smartly sent me off to while away a couple of hours watching Mel Brooks' *History of the World Pt I* at the Odeon Westbourne Grove (coincidentally Wingfield would write 'The Hitler Rap' with Brooks soon after) whilst the situation was defused.

From Dagger's, Graham's and even Ollie's point of view, it was of course great to have an enthusiastic young music press journo under their tutelage. As already mentioned, the traditional press was deeply suspicious of a scene that they had neither helped create nor been invited to. But as other bands started to sprout from it on an almost weekly basis – Blue Rondo, Animal Nightlife, Haysi Fantayzee, Culture Club, Wham!, Haircut 100 – like Gizmo fed after midnight, it was clear this wasn't going away any time soon.

The papers needed some absurdly dressed bugger to cover it and the scene needed some absurdly enthusiastic bugger to understand it. The tricky bit was managing the expectations of both.

4

SPANDAU VALET

'Can't you do something about Paul Simper? I realise that many companies employ a certain percentage of handicapped people. In fact, I generally applaud this as a humane and fair policy, but . . . mentally handicapped? Isn't it rather excessive to employ one as a "journalist"?'

Not every reader was delighted that I had somehow wheedled my way into the *Maker*. If *NME* was the playground of the more flashy, snarky writers (Paul Morley and Ian Penman madly deconstructing everything), *Melody Maker* was where the musos went for a more straightforward, informed appraisal of everything from rock to folk to jazz. It was not where you expected to find 3,000 words on a bunch of soul boys having a weekend beano in Bournemouth.

My first Spandau cover feature had not gone down well.

'When I read the article about Spandau Ballet in the 17 April [1982] issue, I decided that it must be a public relations exercise: the style of breathless, uncritical enthusiasm is not *MM*'s usual method of journalism,' wrote a furious Jane Orton from Poynders Gardens, London.

'Where is there any serious constructive criticism of their music? The whole thing reads like an article from *Jackie*. Are you aiming at a readership of pre-pubescent girls? You do not do this on other pages of your paper. Why do you allow this Simper to get away with it? Please relocate him to the *People's Friend* without delay.'

She had a point, did Jane. Whilst I was in thrall to this riotous new scene and immensely keen to share the love, what was of more interest to *Maker* readers when it came to Spandau (if they had much interest in them at all) was why the band now appeared to be sporting orienteering gear and whether any of them knew that 'Instinction' wasn't a real word?

In my defence, I had done a lengthy interview with Kemp Sr more along those lines that same week, picking over *Diamond*, their game-of-two-halves (side one, club funk; side two, arty farty experimental) second album. But that was for the cover of monthly pop culture and style mag *New Sounds New Styles* – *Smash Hits* and *The Face* publisher EMAP's latest attempt to burrow deeper inside this ever-expanding scene.

Finally, I'd got to do my first proper sit-down Spandau interview with Gary after my first unrecorded effort that unexpected Saturday night last November at Mel's. I wasn't fully aware of it at the time but I was catching Spandau's songwriter and chief manifesto maker (after Dagger) at an artistic crossroads.

It had been a tricky six months for the band. After the highs of the summer of 1981 when 'Chant No. 1' rattled up to Number 3 in the UK, they'd faltered. Its Gap Band-influenced follow-up 'Paint Me Down' trod water for four weeks at Number 30 before falling away – the first time they had not made it onto *Top of the Pops*. By the time I'd moved to London at the start of 1982, things had got worse. 'She Loved Like Diamond' – Gary's first go at a Bond-style ballad – juddered to a halt at 49. Now everything was riding on a

Trevor Horn 7-inch remix of 'Instinction' to stop things being cut a lot shorter than anticipated.

As we settled down in Gary's bedroom that March 1982 at his mum and dad's in north London just off the Essex Road, there was a sense that he was trying to put some distance between the club scene for which Spandau had (with Dagger's canny instruction) become standard bearers. With funky young pups like Haircut 100 and ABC now also occupying the dance floor it was time to (fingers crossed) look at new horizons.

'I don't think we've ever tried to do that,' said Gary, rejecting the standard-bearer tag. 'I wouldn't like to have that pressure. We change our music out of boredom, basically. We like to experiment with different sounds, which is why we chose to do what we did with the second side of the new LP. I never ever want to stick to a formula to be successful. I think we've established ourselves now as a group . . .'

He winced at the word.

'I don't want to say a group as that's a band of musicians. I mean a group of people with ideas. I'm not really worried about keeping ahead all the time. I don't think we're the kind of band that needs to survive on its last single. I think that's proven. Some other bands are only singles bands. I'd like to look on Spandau like, if this was 1972, then we'd probably be more like Roxy Music or David Bowie. While certain other bands that are around at the moment would be more like The Sweet – a lot of Top 5 records and maybe a couple of Number 1s but not so much sustained energy.

'I'm glad to say that we were one of the first bands to go on telly and put fashion back as a serious thing. Young kids were really excited again by what they saw on *TOTP* for the first time in ages.

Bands realised that if they were going to sell records at all they were going to have to look quite good. I think we influenced a certain kind of person to form a band. Bands like Depeche Mode and maybe Haircut 100 and Soft Cell even – I can't see those people before last year even wanting to be in a band.'

The road to Damascus moment when Dagger first stepped down into the thrilling new subterranean scene gestating in the tiny Soho basement bar of Billy's in the autumn of 1978 had had a similarly defining effect on Spandau. It was something that was never mentioned by the time I innocently strolled along, but while Spandau Ballet – the name, the look, the attitude, the music – had sprung directly from their embracing of this new scene, the five of them and Dagger shared a previous, slightly less on-message, musical history.

Gary, Steve, John and Tony (not Martin, he was up the road at another school) had begun in the music room of their local grammar as an R & B outfit called The Roots, doing high-speed versions of sixties favourites like Gary Pucket's 'Young Girl' and The Beatles' 'I Wanna Be Your Man'. After they'd left school they were briefly The Cut before, in 1977, becoming a bristling Rich Kids'-inspired power pop group called The Makers with three-minute songs written either by Gary Kemp or Steve Norman, including the great Spandau single-that-never-was, 'Confused'.

The Makers came tantalisingly close to making it but Dagger, who was now managing them, spotted something was still missing. Little brother Martin was then installed to smoulder on bass and they became The Gentry – same kind of music but with a more soul boy look with clothes from Warehouse in beige and brown.

And yet there was still something holding them back. What they lacked – and what Dagger identified after studiously dissecting the strategies of sixties pop managers like Brian Epstein with The Beatles, Andrew Loog Oldham with The Stones and Peter Meaden with The Who – was a relevance that would take them beyond a local partisan audience.

'The problem was, they still didn't mean anything special to anyone,' Dagger told me years later when such information could no longer mess up any grand plan. 'I thought: "Why are they different to a group in the mid-sixties? What is missing?" And that was it. They had an audience that was largely culled from Islington people who liked the band and were their friends. But it wasn't an influential crowd. It wasn't going anywhere. What was the sell? They were attractive, the songs were good – Gary and Steve Norman were both writing a lot of songs – we were selling out the Rock Garden . . . But what made the group different? What was the angle?

'As soon as I went down the steps in Billy's that first time I thought: "This is it." Billy's was sexy, new, modern dance music, which you couldn't find anywhere else in the world, being danced to by a load of people with a common purpose – music that was very doable by our group. I thought: "This is what's going to happen to pop culture in the immediate future."'

Flash forward four years and Spandau and their core club audience were a little less sure of each other. The funky first side of *Diamond* with 'Chant' and 'Paint' and another potential floor-filler, 'Coffee Club', had kept them in touch with Spandau's nightclubbing roots. But as groups like the aforementioned Haircut 100 started to leapfrog them in the charts, the question was where to take things next.

Whatever that change might be, the one thing that Gary was absolutely certain about was that it would not involve any form of rock music. As the younger brothers and sisters of punk, Spandau and the Blitz Kids were resolute about continuing to fight the good fight and reject and replace the flared denims and hippy values, as they saw it, of seventies rock. Whole record collections – save for the holy cows of Bowie and Roxy – had been culled. For Spandau (although certain Queen-, AC/DC- and Bad Company-loving band members may have kept their counsel on this one), rock was a dirty word.

Hence Gary's horror at the stray acoustic guitar that photographer Virginia Turbett's lens momentarily happened to focus on as we conducted our interview.

'I hate that acoustic guitar,' said Gary, glaring at it reproachfully. 'Can we move it? It's a bit rock and roll – you know what I mean? – having an acoustic guitar in the corner. When I was a kid I used to see interviews of bands at home and they always used to have acoustic guitars in the background. Of all the things to do!'

The offending artefact was banished to the corner, far from Gary's portable TV, telescope, globe and James Ramsey Ullman's hardback, *The Age of Mountaineering*.

Gary was also none too pleased when I informed him that there were some cheeky whelps in the *Melody Maker* office who were suggesting that Spandau were actually becoming a bit rock and roll themselves – what with their forthcoming tour ('It's not a tour,' Dagger had told me emphatically. 'It's a collection of dates') and the fact that there was an actual lyric sheet with the new album.

'The lyric sheet?!' spluttered Gary. 'Jesus, you get blamed for everything. That's just ridiculous. You know, we set the standards and then we get measured by 'em. We didn't release lyrics on the first album so everyone thinks: "Mustn't release lyrics. That's rock and roll." And then the second album we release them and they're like: "Aw, they're releasing lyrics."

'For *Journeys*, I just thought when you listen to music you should take it all in. The words and the pictures are all part of the song. You shouldn't separate them at all. But when I came to *Diamond*, I disagreed. I thought I'd like people to read the lyrics. People out there who like the lyrics are mostly young kids. Girls sitting at home singing along to records, and I don't want them missing out on it.'

Young girls sitting at home singing along to Spandau songs was a new concept. Whilst their arch rivals Duran had very easily settled into the *Smash Hits* market with singles like 'Girls on Film', 'Hungry Like the Wolf' and 'Rio', Spandau were still, in 1982, a few weeks – and a much-needed return to the Top 10 – away from experiencing their first full-on teen mania. At Liverpool Empire, on this 'tour that was not a tour' the screaming from a new, predominantly female, audience would make them sit up and take note.

But back to the dreaded rock and roll.

'We always hated anything to do with rock and roll,' said Gary firmly. 'We never liked it. We would never get into rock and roll because we changed that. We got rid of the words "rock and roll". We changed pop music. How many bands now don't tour conventionally? I think we've changed people's attitudes to music. I think we've also attracted a market that before wasn't interested in bands. They were only interested in club records. So when we play, we're playing to an audience that a year ago wouldn't have previously gone to see bands. And if they did they would only have gone to see an American band.' A pause. 'I'd much rather play in a soul band than a rock and roll band.'

Most of this rock and roll diatribe didn't make it into my final copy. Hindsight is a wonderful thing but at the time it didn't seem that significant. Who was to know that within a matter of months they would jettison their clubland Spandau Mk. 1 model completely and head off to the Bahamas to record their third album – initially called *The Pleasure Project* after the album's opening cut, 'Pleasure' – only to return in Mk. 2 as an international, chart-topping pop group who would later spend as much time hanging out with Def Leppard, Bruce Springsteen and Queen as with their club mates down Le Beat Route or the Wag?

One other footnote on our interview, again only funny in hindsight. We were talking about the 12-inch remixes of 'Chant' and 'Paint Me Down', which feature Grandmaster Flash-style, cut-ups. Did he think, I asked, that the rappers coming out of New York could move beyond the club scene and find a larger audience as Kraftwerk had done? ('The Model' had just gone to Number 1 three years after it was first played by Rusty in Billy's and Blitz).

'No, I don't, really,' said Gary. 'I don't think they're commercial. I don't think rap in itself is commercial.'

Yup, we've all done it.

Still, the good news for Spandau was that by the time their 'collection of dates' hit the south coast they were back in the Top 10. John Keeble celebrated by tying my shoe laces together at the end of a long night and I disembarked from the band's coach rather more spectacularly than expected. I also once again proved I had a way to go in the sartorial stakes when, much to the band's amusement, I left the same lace-ups in a Brighton bowling alley that we visited and kept the ones I'd hired instead.

One thing Gary had been totally on the money about in our *NSNS* interview was how much Spandau had been instrumental in giving a leg-up to others on the scene. Not just emerging London bands like Blue Rondo, Animal Nightlife and Haysi Fantayzee, but also to clothes designers Melissa Caplan, Willie Brown, Simon Withers and Stephen Linard, graphic artist and photographer Graham Smith, and writer Robert (Bob) Elms.

'It was a good little revolution in the Arts,' said Gary of the Blitz Kids days. 'The group was like a little pinnacle where everyone could get on with what they wanted to do and try to be successful.'

There was even room for a latecomer like me to squeak in. It was Graham Smith who, after our first chance meeting in Spandau's Mortimer Street Reformation office one Friday night, had directed me to Bob Elms, newly appointed features editor at *New Sounds New Styles*.

New Sounds, based in Soho, was the brainchild of Dutch-born but Birmingham-allied editor, Kasper de Graaf, and graphic designer Malcolm Garrett (record sleeve designer for Magazine, Simple Minds and Duran Duran). But for me it was Bob who would play the key role as another member of clubland's multimedia think tank.

Both former LSE students, Bob and Dagger were cut from the same cloth: savvy, working-class, with their eyes on the prize and the gift of the gab. If Dagger was the scene's media general (amongst other things), Bob was his able lieutenant.

It had been Dagger who first propelled Bob into a career in journalism by suggesting he review Spandau for the *NME* when they played the Scala Cinema back in March 1981. In fact, he did more than suggest it. In a break between lectures, Dagger walked Bob round to Steve's mum and dad's council flat in Holborn, handed him a notepad, and the piece was written there and then in the Dagger family living room.

Steve then accompanied Bob to the music paper's Carnaby Street offices where he waited downstairs on the pavement whilst Elms, now with the bit between his teeth, gave the first rendition of his 'Where were you lot when this started?' speech to Live editor Tony Stewart, who agreed to print it the following week. Nine months later, and Bob was writing all things pop cultural for a new lifestyle magazine more embracing of his talents on the other side of Carnaby Street – *The Face* – and easing into his broadcasting career by hosting Manchester-based BBC2 youth culture Friday nighter *The Oxford Road Show*, where he didn't entirely endear himself to the local populace by referring to them as 'northern scum'. He was also a key cog in *New Sounds New Styles*.

The great thing for me as far as *New Sounds* was concerned was that rather than feeling like some necessary evil, as I did at *MM*, here was somewhere I seemed to fit. Whilst *Melody Maker* was a sprawling open-plan mess of an office that looked more like a sullen-faced student common room, *NSNS* was a few neat little cubicles with editor's assistant Plaxy Exton (now Locatelli) – a cheery, super-cool waif who wouldn't have looked out of place in a Godard movie – as your point of entry. They were even indulging of my obsessions. 'You wanna write about James Bond, John Carpenter and Hammer Horror as well as ABC, Spandau and Dollar? Sure, get stuck in.' Like *The Face*, it was a refreshing alternative to the mainstream and the familiar.

In Bob, as with Dagger, I had another invaluable guide to the finer points of London living. One lunchtime he whisked me into Chinatown (walking with Bob was always done at breakneck speed

– it showed you knew where you were going) to Wong Kei – the four-storey cheapo Chinese restaurant famed for its fantastically rude staff who never let you sit downstairs – where he made sure I mastered the art of eating with chopsticks. On another day, it was off to the Eros sex cinema on Great Windmill Street (where *American Werewolf in London*'s undead David Naughton and Griffin Dunne famously watched faux porno flick *See You Next Wednesday*) to get a crash course in the raunchy hip auteur delights of Russ Myer with a double bill of *Vixen* and *SuperVixens*.

We even formed the Rebel Writers Club, a preposterously self-regarding quartet of myself, Bob, David Johnson and Graham K. Smith. Quite what we were rebelling against I can't remember but it was probably anyone else whose writing we didn't agree with, and Kasper's much frowned upon Birmingham allegiance to Duran Duran.

Graham K. was from Epsom School of Art, with its terrific fashion department. Another angular fresh face with floppy fringe writing about new clothes shop The Foundry and the return of sixties' pop queen Sandie Shaw. David Johnson, on the other hand, was from a previous generation of both clubbing and print journalism. Down from Yorkshire as a student in the Swinging Sixties David had frequented the Bag O'Nails and The Scotch of St James – 'affluent aristo celebrity bars' – and then done his seventies clubbing at Chaguaramas in Covent Garden, Sombrero's on Kensington High Street, Masquerade in Earls Court and Bang below the Astoria in the underground mixed and gay London scene which played the best black American dance music.

As editor of the *Evening Standard*'s London arts and lifestyle column 'On The Line', (everything from the new yoof club culture to the first liberating 'jukebox in your pocket' Sony Walkman) it was David that Dagger (and Steve Strange for that matter) had buttonholed at the start of the new decade to get the media ball rolling on both the band and all that came with it. David got it immediately and did the first Fleet Street scoop on Spandau after witnessing their first Scala gig with *Record Mirror* journo Barry Cain.

'We both turned to each other after thirty seconds and went: "They can play!"'

Never without his notebook and camera, David comprehensively diarised the nightly thrills and spills, capturing both the poses and the plotting, whilst also holding his own at the bar (a prerequisite with this crowd). As his shapersofthe80s.com website still demonstrates, he delighted in all aspects of the scene, but had a particular soft spot for The Firm, the huddle of young managers, scribes and scene-makers who were as fascinated by the whys as the wherefores.

Importantly, David was also the grown-up. He was the only one who would rein in Bob when his mythologising played too fast and loose with the facts. And he'd also cast a weather eye over my fledgling efforts. We first met at an early Blue Rondo gig at Sherry's in Brighton. David wasn't quite sure where I had sprung from and, being both a proper journalist and much earlier to the party, he was rightly suspicious. But he soon proved to be very funny and fiercely loyal. When I was the recipient of an early tongue-lashing from Boy George in some bar on Kensington High Street for having my foot firmly in the Spandau rather than Culture Club camp, it was David who indignantly came to my rescue.

Needless to say, the instant our illustrious band of rebel writers was formed *New Sounds New Styles* folded after thirteen brightly burning, glossy issues of the sub-cultural. Bob went off to write about Hard Times and ripped denim for *The Face*, Graham K. went to *Blitz* and on to a career in television – with an early feather in his cap being the researcher on Jonathan Ross' *The Last Resort* who booked Tom Jones to do Prince's 'Kiss' – and David continued to extend the horizons of his clubbing reportage across the length and breadth of Britain whilst holding down at least one day job.

I, on the other hand, was back to wondering quite where I fitted in. How much longer would the good readers – and indeed commissioners – at *Melody Maker* put up with Paul 'Flymo' Simper?

5

NOT MAD ABOUT THE GRILL

Remarkably, despite the protestations of some of its readership, I had managed to hold on to my freelance work at *Melody Maker*. Thanks to Colin Irwin's continued benevolence, my output had even increased.

Much of this was of course still shining a first light on clubland's precocious young things but, as luck would have it, I was also getting some of America's most notable dance acts sent my way. Kool & The Gang, The Gap Band, Patti Austin, Patrice Rushen and – the biggest thrill of all for a lad who was spending his Friday nights shuffling and spinning to 'Searching', 'A Lover's Holiday' and 'Never Too Much'– Luther Vandross.

Meeting the great man in his suite at the Montcalm in Marble Arch, resplendent in a fetching pink jumper, was a bit of a moment. His forthcoming two nights at the Dominion Theatre were already sold out – Groove Records, London's hippest vinyl import shop located slap bang opposite Le Beat Route, had even organised a raffle for a few precious tickets – and the shows were all that clubland was talking about: 'Going to Luther?' 'Got any tickets for Luther?'

The album he was promoting was his UK debut, a gorgeous blend of self-penned originals like 'She Loves Me Back' and the destined-to-be classic 'Never Too Much', alongside his seemingly effortless but utterly fantastical reimagining of Smokey's 'Since I Lost My Baby' and Bacharach and David's 'A House is Not a Home'.

He was far too gracious to dish any dirt on his holy trinity of divas – Dionne, Diana and Aretha – who he was in various stages of writing with and producing. But he did tell me that he'd been a bit peeved with Bette Midler the first time he met her when she bit his nipple, and he was extremely mad with Nile Rodgers for having recently beat him to the post as the producer of Bowie's yet-to-be released *Let's Dance* album.

'We were getting ready to call David,' he said with a shake of the head. 'I mean, I know where he *lives*. He's in the same block as Carlos.'

It was guitarist Carlos Alomar's wife who had brought Luther along to the *Young Americans* sessions in Philadelphia back in 1974. Luther suggested the title track could do with some fills – 'something like "All Night"' – and the next thing Bowie had hired him to handle all the album's vocal arrangements whilst himself rewriting Luther's own 'Funky Music (Is a Part of Me)' as 'Fascination'.

'He didn't want to be as presumptuous as to downright say "Funky Music",' said Luther. 'So he retitled it.'

It was not Luther Vandross, though, who was causing me sleepless nights. Four stars had battled for supremacy on my bedroom wall during my teens. Kate Bush, Debbie Harry, Bob Geldof and John Travolta. Now, unbelievably, thanks to the *Maker*, I was about to get my chance to interview three of them within a matter of months.

I was under no illusions as to which would be the toughest. Not only was Geldof the most garrulous, he was also the only one for whom I'd already (quite literally) laid my arse on the line.

Full disclosure here. Before heady New Romanticism swept me off my feet, Geldof had been my first pop rebel. I'd had a few to choose from staring moodily (or in Weller's case Mod-ily) out at my sixteen-year-old self from the weekly music press, but Weller was too angry, Johnny Rotten too scary, Elvis Costello too speccy and Sting too pretty.

Geldof, on the other hand, was unkempt, gobby and funny with a saucy, posh peroxide girlfriend, Paula Yates, who was prone to getting her kit off – important for a hormonal teenager. There was one other massive point in Bob's favour. Some girl at a party in the summer of 1978 had said I looked a bit like him.

Sold. I scruffed my hair, affected the scowl, had a crack (craic?) at the Dun Laoghaire accent and from thenceforth only answered to the name of The Burbage (village where I came from) Rat.

My arse-on-the-line moment for Geldof had come that autumn when I'd brilliantly landed myself in school detention on the very night that I was due to see the Boomtown Rats in Southampton – my first ever gig.

I was beside myself. I'd already pulled something of a fast one by going cap in hand to my school's owlish headmaster, Mr Macnaghten, pleading that I be allowed to attend a recitation by Robert Geldof, the popular Irish folk singer.

I suppose in pre-Internet, pre-Google days it was harder to run a rapid check on people and events outside one's immediate frame of reference and so, trusting soul that he was, he'd taken this in good faith.

Now that massive whopper would appear to have been for nothing. Thunderstruck at the stupidity of my actions, I racked my brain for a way out. What to do? Clearly I needed some sort of bargaining tool. It took a while but slowly from the recesses something stirred.

When you broke it down, all I'd been given was detention, normally a very ho-hum sort of punishment but one that on this occasion had me well and truly scuppered. So what else could trump that?

For a lad who'd been to boarding school since the age of seven, my experience of corporal punishment was surprisingly limited. I'd been thwacked after lights-out at prep school by overenthusiastic dormitory heads and caned by two subsequent housemasters for illicit trips into town to buy tuck and James Bond paperbacks.

By the late-seventies, however, things had mellowed since *Tomkinson's Schooldays* and being caned was now more of a big deal. So what if . . . ?

When I took the short walk across the courtyard from School House and knocked once again on the headmaster's study door to parlay a deal where my lowly detention might be up-graded to six of the best, I really have no idea what I was thinking. And I have even less idea why he agreed to it.

Still, the six red welts I took back with me to my study for forensic inspection by my study-mate told their own tale. The deal was done and off to the Rats I went – a veritable beacon of fanboy, tender-arsed devotion.

Touching story though this is, I think it's fair to say that I wouldn't have got within a country mile of interviewing my still eminently quotable Irish troubadour if the Rats' star hadn't been by now in the descendant. I still had tucked away the five-page cover interview Geldof had done with the *Maker* three Christmases before when the mag's assistant editor, Allan Jones, had visited him at his gaff in Clapham.

Back then, their last big hit, 'Banana Republic', was just about keeping them on *Top of the Pops* and *Tiswas* and within touching distance of their peers. But a quick glance at the eighties' biggest-selling singles artists in that same issue sees Madness, Blondie and UB40 in the top three slots while the Rats are looking like the pro-verbial drowned ones scrabbling around at 31 next to Barbra Streisand and Don McLean.

Only two years before, save for Boney M, they'd been the biggest-selling band in Britain. Now, instead, 1982's charts were teeming with the shiny, electro-pop of the Human League and Soft Cell and the Burundi glam of Adam and his Ants.

Anyway, I'd got the gig, and was under no illusions that this might stretch to another magnum opus. My only directive from a cheery Colin Irwin, was to 'Give him a good grilling.'

It's not the sort of thing a superfan – even one purporting to be a music journalist – really wants to hear. Still, putting aside such misgivings, off I toddled to Guildford one Sunday afternoon to catch the Rats on their *V Deep* tour ready to talk to my idol about his illustrious pop career (and how it was going down the toilet). What could possibly go wrong?

Listening back to that interview now, it's abundantly clear that I hadn't really considered how this was going to play out – a devoted fan attempting to go medieval on the ass of his hero. A famously argumentative hero at that.

We got off to a stuttering start. When you've spent literally years dreaming of all the things you're going to ask your pop idol – and even entered those music mag 'Complete in twenty words' competitions where you basically string together a list of your band's song titles as proof that you and only you should get to hang out with them for three crazy nights in New York – there are a lot of questions jostling to get out.

On reflection, 'Have the venues been pretty full, Bob?' may not have been quite the Frost/Nixon opening zinger I was hoping for. To his credit (and he later told me he could see how nervous I was), Geldof took it in his stride. He patiently informed me that Stoke was the worst – about 600 people – 'But surprisingly full is the way I'd put it for the rest.'

Groundwork approximately laid, I then cracked on with the more pressing business of pissing on his doorstep by suggesting that the Rats' recent hit, 'House on Fire', sounded (deep breath) 'a little bit dated'. In fact, I made so bold as to suggest it smelled a lot like a rip-off of The Special AKA's 'A Message to You, Rudy'.

'Isn't it time the group brought out something with nice poppy synthesisers on it?' I ventured.

Sportingly resisting the urge to knock me clean into next week, Geldof hummed the two songs' brass refrains, clearly unconvinced, then suggested that it wasn't his chart-topping band's sound that was redundant so much as my lousy question.

'If we wanted to do that, certainly we'd do it – have no illusions about that,' he said, directing a mid-strength thermonuclear glower in my general direction. 'Personally, I don't give a fuck what the fashion happens to be at the time. And if we wanted to do things with loads of drums and me wearing an Elastoplast over my nose, we'd do that as well.'

Might the Rats be better off doing a few select dates rather than a lengthy tour? I hazarded, thinking of Spandau's modus operandi, and also thinking that might mean fewer tickets to shift.

Geldof didn't agree with my point (there was a pattern developing here) but the mention of Spandau – a band almost as unloved as his by the music press – piqued his interest.

'I like them,' he said. 'I can't really see why everyone is down on them. They've had the bravery to try new things on this album [*Diamond*]. They're good players, they're nice guys. They enjoy style – what's wrong with that? English rock and roll cannot be divorced from style.'

All of this was music to my ears (although probably not the paper's) because leaving to one side my 'grilling' brief, the other elephant in the room I was trying to circumnavigate was the unfortunate truth that I was now rather more Team Spandau than Team Rats.

I did my best to keep the good ship afloat as we pressed on through perilous waters. He couldn't see why The Clash were taken seriously while the Rats were trashed – '*White Riot*'s not only sloganeering, it's dangerous and fascist'. He had no interest in being rent-a-gob on Parkinson's and Russell Harty's chat shows, although he was very good at it – 'I go on TV to counteract what people say about me in the press. Then they can decide for themselves whether I'm the cunt they say I am.' He was disgusted by a reviewer's personal attack on Altered Images' Clare Grogan – 'I found it astounding when one of the reviews called her "Scarface". The personal hurt that that involves is so awful.'

He said his outlook on life was summed up by the Rats' single 'Like Clockwork', that you're born in tears, die in pain and that's your lot.

'That's what I think,' he said.

His seismic emotional response to Michael Buerk's Ethiopian famine report was still a good two years off, but the final quote of our forty minutes before he went off round Guildford for a much more fun time with photographer Jude Calvert-Toulmin, was the most on the money.

'I wish I was doing things that were consequential,' he said, as his soon-to-be-bride Paula entered the room and settled silently on his lap. 'This is inconsequential. I've all these dreams lying there, waiting for me to wake and make a life of them. I don't know what that is. But it's something.'

Something of nothing as far as the *Maker* were concerned. The piece was spiked.

Bearing in mind how the Geldof encounter had gone, I have to admit to feeling a certain ambivalence when Colin Irwin casually plucked another pop icon from my bedroom wall and lobbed her over as my next assignment. That poster of Kate Bush – long dark tresses, a single dove earring and full, scarlet, pouting lips – had flanked Geldof with one of Debbie Harry wrapped in a bed sheet.

Unfortunately, at the time we were due to meet, Kate's career was also having a bit of a wobble. 'The Dreaming', the second single and title track of her fourth album, had not troubled the Top 40. So when better for us to settle down and have a lengthy chinwag about her career options? I was getting to know the drill.

Mercifully, whatever the portents, La Bush couldn't have been less filled with doom and gloom. When we got together that October evening in the Abbey Road Studios canteen, she was exceedingly chipper about it all, delighted with the new album – the first she'd produced herself – and really not that fussed whether she ever made it back onto *Top of the Pops* again.

'I've given up on the singles market, to be quite honest,' she told me cheerfully. 'I wasn't really disappointed at what happened with "The Dreaming". I had a sneaking suspicion it wouldn't get any-where, but if I had the choice of putting out a single at that time again, I would still go for that same one. Now I'm in the situation that I have to go for an obvious single ("There Goes a Tenner") because you can't keep putting stuff out which is totally uncom-mercial. But I don't really mind what happens to it. It'll either do something or it won't.'

It did the latter.

What rankled more with her was the notion that she might be currently residing in pop's last chance saloon after *two* perceived singles failures. The punchy Peter Gabriel-influenced 'Sat in Your Lap' (she contributed backing vocals to his previous album, *Peter Gabriel III*, before duetting with him on 'Don't Give Up') had actu-ally got to Number 11 earlier that year, which in the days when a Top 10 hit still sold hundreds of thousands, wasn't too shabby at all.

'Yes, everyone's suddenly decided that I've been away for two years and that's it,' she said. 'They've just made up their minds. I would say that "Sat in Your Lap" is one of the highest charted singles that I've had for a long time. Yet no one is taking that in. "Wow", only got to Number 16 [actually 14] and yet everybody remembers that. "Breathing" got to Number 16 and yet everyone said that was a flop. I thought that had a lot of potential as a single and I think the fact that it got to Number 16 shows it did. And yet so many people said: "It didn't do anything."

'It's interesting. It's not really how well it does but what's said about it. I'm sure if you asked the majority of people about "Sat in Your Lap" they'd say: "Pfft, it didn't do anything, did it?"'

She laughed. 'I don't know.'

All of which meant she was having to spend a lot more time than she honestly intended banging the drum for this new album and talking to chumps like me. Something, of course, which she was far too gracious to say bluntly.

'I think when you get to about three or four years through this business you just realise how tiring it is,' she said. 'You spend all your time fighting. Fighting off some rumour about having a third ear or something; fighting to make sure your art gets the right treatment; and fighting for the business side of things. You don't ever stop fighting. It's really the industry and media side of it that you have to keep fighting. But there's enough of a fight on the artistic side to wipe you out anyway. I think it's a very hard business.'

She'd started playing piano when she was eleven.

'I started with one finger, then moved to two and just over the years got something together.'

That something included writing the extraordinary 'The Man With the Child in his Eyes' at sixteen and then twirling into all our lives with her chart-topping debut 'Wuthering Heights' (her choice of first single, not EMI's) at nineteen.

'That was an incredible feeling,' she said. 'It really was a very big reward, it being such a success. But at the same time, it was really scary because along with that came a complete whirlwind of change to my life. I was nineteen and felt reasonably prepared but I still felt quite vulnerable. The fact was I wouldn't be left alone from then on.

'I think I'm still trying to get used to that – that most of my life is being interfered with and pestered with responsibilities. Then whenever I sit down and really think about it, I'm so lucky to have got the breaks so young and to be in this position and to be doing what I want to do. I'm so lucky that I could never complain.'

She felt nothing but sympathy for Musical Youth, a bunch of kids from Birmingham who were at Number 1 with what would prove to be a far more fleeting brush with pop success.

'Those kids are so beautiful,' she sighed. 'But already I've heard people on radio programmes saying: "Ooh, it's not an original song, you know." They're knocking the kids down and they've only just got there. It's almost because they're so beautiful and so pure that people can't understand that there is something truly positive about them. They've got to blow their lights out. It's really sad because I think those kids are far out. I just hope they don't get eaten alive.'

She had no qualms about pointing out that she'd stuck a couple of fillers on her last album, *Never For Ever*.

'*Never For Ever* was the album I'd got closest to feeling happy with except for "Egypt" and "Violin",' she said. 'The problem with "Egypt" was it was a song that had originally been conceived quite a while back and been used for the live show and I didn't have anything better to put on that album at that time. Both songs were really fillers. There were some nice ideas in there but compared to the other songs [including the momentous 'Breathing', 'Babooshka' and 'Army Dreamers'] they were very superficial. For me on this new album, although there are a couple of songs that I don't think are as deep, they all have a thought and a reason behind each one. I think it's why I feel much more satisfied with this album.'

I'm not sure I've interviewed a pop star before or since who admitted to sticking a couple of fillers on their precious album. Not only was Kate refreshingly honest, she was also immensely sweet.

She listened intently to me blethering on about a boy I'd shared a study with at public school, which had some tenuous thematic link to one of her songs, and was happy to debate at length the merits of the Alan Parker screen adaptation of Pink Floyd's *The Wall* (Dave Gilmour having exec produced 'The Man With the Child in his Eyes' and 'The Saxophone Song' on her first album), a movie which I deemed 'a little too obvious'.

'I think the film itself is an absolute masterpiece,' said Kate. 'As a piece of art I thought it was absolutely devastating. But I felt that it wasn't nearly real enough. The whole film was exaggerated on a completely negative level. Not once in Pink's life was there a moment of relief or happiness, which I know in any human's life happens. Even if you have the shittiest life there is always one little moment where you smile for a second or you feel in love or happy. For me that film was completely negative recall. It was a person who considered himself hard done by. Bullied and insecure, he completely retold his life in a negative, self-pitying way. He had no compassion and no objectivity at all. But I thought the film was absolutely brilliant.'

The one remaining question was when she'd be playing live again. Foolishly, I'd failed to get my arse in gear to see her previous Tour of Life with its seventeen costume changes and Kate being rolled around in a giant egg, which *Melody Maker* described fairly unequivocally as: 'The most magnificent spectacle ever encountered in the world of rock.'

Still, it didn't sound like we'd have that long to wait for the next one.

'I've wanted to do a show ever since the last one,' she said firmly. 'But I knew that it had to be really different. That first show was the first two albums and it was just the right amount of material [twenty-four songs] to make it a big and varied show. So the only way to do it is to have two other albums that are moving much more into the direction I want to go visually.

'Now that this album is finished, I've got the other two. So this is the first time I can actually think about doing a show again. I just have to get promotion out of the way first because that's very important having spent such a long time on this album. Then I want to sit down and really think about the show, but it's going to take me ages. It's going to take months.'

Three hundred and eighty-four months, or thirty-two years, to be exact. But who's counting? Her rapturously received 2014 residency at Hammersmith Apollo was something to behold, but I have to say a show based entirely around *Never For Ever* and *The Dreaming* still gets my fanboy heart beating.

When our time finally drew to a close – after seventy generous minutes of me doing far too much talking when I should have been listening – I could hardly have loved her more.

My now flatmate Graham Smith, who was doing the photos but wasn't that fussed about her music, had been more sceptical. The next evening, he spent an hour shooting her in one of Abbey Road's cavernous studios with all the lights out, her face simply lit by a candle. He returned home utterly entranced.

Blessedly, this time my piece wasn't spiked. It made it into print with the not overly positive headline of 'Dreamtime Is Over' and a schoolboy error on my behalf, calling 'Them Heavy People', 'Rolling the Ball'. Otherwise, no complaints.

The following day the phone rang in the first floor Maida Vale flat where I was now happily renting a room from Graham. I was faffing about in the bedroom when he knocked on my door. 'It's a Kate for you.'

I would love to relay to you every last syllable of the conversation that followed but sadly somewhere between realising: 'Ohmigod, it's Kate Bush calling me in my bedroom!' and gathering she wasn't doing this to tell me what a massive dickhead I'd been for getting one of her song titles wrong, it all becomes a bit of a heavenly blur. Bottom line, she was grateful. I, on the other hand, was several solar systems north of ecstatic.

No pop star before or since has ever tapped up their record company to get my home phone number. Although there was that filthy Valentine's Day call that I have a strong suspicion came from one of Dead or Alive.

6

CUP OF COLD SICK TO GO

There are many conundrums in the day to day life of a music hack. When to get out of bed? When to lug your bag of freebie vinyl to Record and Tape Exchange? When to call your favourite record company PRs for a booze-heavy expenses account lunch? But one choice no hack should ever have to make is: Debbie Harry or Kate Bush?

Yet there it was. I was getting to have a crack at both.

From that very first Blondie *Top of the Pops* appearance for 'Denis' back in 1978, Debbie in her red-and-white stripy one-piece, black jacket artfully draped to reveal one bare shoulder, and waggling a long, silver microphone had eclipsed all competition with one slow-mo flick of her peroxide blonde hair. *Parallel Lines* had been pop perfection, *Eat to the Beat* equally majestic. And if *AutoAmerican* had challenged the well-oiled hit machine with Europa soundscapes and a scattergun effect of jazz, blues and reggae influences, it still delivered 'Rapture' with its bonkers B-movie rap about men from Mars eating cars and bars.

So it was back to the leather furnishings of the Montcalm in Marble Arch where Debbie and Chris Stein were snuffling their way through a bout of flu. Still new to this game, I may have been slightly more trusting of this self-diagnosis of theirs than was strictly necessary, particularly considering that the book they were promoting, *Making Tracks: The Rise of Blondie*, was brimming with lurid tales of angel dust at CBGB and hard partying in the Bowery. I later learned this was also about the time that mysterious packages started arriving at their UK record company Chrysalis's offices containing illegal sustenance. The book's title should have told me something.

Still, they sniffled cheerily away with Chris answering most of the questions and Debbie, wearing a straight, long blonde wig, rather sweetly putting her hand up any time she wanted to add something. I can't remember whether I'd actually received a copy of the book, which is great and precisely the sort of book your record company would rather you didn't publish when you're the label's number one teen-friendly pop group. But if I had I'd have been much better off quizzing them on that than their latest album, *The Hunter*, which was a definite tapering off from Blondie's glory days.

All the same, Chris Stein had a bit to say about Joe Strummer, who had reportedly dissed them declaring: 'I'm ashamed to be white because I hear Blondie playing reggae.'

Meanwhile Debbie was following up her indie movie, *Union City*, with something that I mistakenly wrote down as *Video Drum* with Canadian director David Kronenberg [sic], in which she and Chris assured me that, despite tabloid reports, she was not 'naked, chained to the wall and being whipped by a guy with a hood'.

Almost right on cue, we heard a clattering from outside their third-floor balcony window and there, juggling cameras and balancing precariously on their fire escape, was a paparazzo. Neither Chris or Debbie seemed particularly bothered or even surprised. Once a pop legend always a pop legend.

The most notable aspect of my Blondie interview was that it

actually made it into print at all. Not for once because it was in danger of being spiked but because the long-hand version I'd so painstakingly written had found itself taken on an unexpectedly perilous journey, on one of those occasions where my day job and night-time activities collided more calamitously than usual.

One of the results of this thriving new swinging London club scene was that everyone wanted a part of it. New yoof magazine shows were starting to sprout – *The Oxford Road Show*, *Riverside*, *White Light* – and all needed the prerequisite trendy audience of goths, zootists, rockabillies and soul boys and girls. It was for this reason that TV producer Tony Wilson got onto Ollie O'Donnell to furnish him with Le Beat Route's Friday night rent-a-crowd to populate a telly special with Kid Creole and the Coconuts that he was making at Manchester's Granada Studios – home of *Corrie* – on Quay Street.

August Darnell had been the Latino godfather of the London club scene ever since a similarly zooted Chris Sullivan had met him with Bob Elms on an exploratory trip to New York in the summer of 1980. 'Cherchez La Femme' by his first outfit, Dr Buzzard's Original Savannah Band, was a Beat Route favourite as were Kid Creole's 'Latin Music' and 'Going Places'.

But it was with his latest album, *Tropical Gangsters*, that he finally broke into the charts proper. 'I'm A Wonderful Thing', 'Stool Pigeon' and 'Annie, I'm Not Your Daddy' were all zesty, floor-fillers that also sounded great on the radio and Darnell was sometimes to be seen propping up the Beat Route bar – the greatest endorsement the club could hope for.

So, the day after my Blondie interview, there was a coach leaving from Kentish Town bound for Manchester, packed with London clubland's finest. All sartorially turned-out in honour of their hero in box jackets, billowing high-waisted trousers, low slung keychains and two-tone shoes. Unfortunately, there were two things that had not been taken into consideration. Firstly, that this look, which had been de rigueur the previous summer (when it was all 'Chant No.1'), had since been replaced by ripped denims, studded belts and motorcycle boots from Lewis Leathers. Secondly – and I guess this is something that very few TV pop shows anticipate when selecting an audience – that someone had brought along a generous supply of acid to enliven the journey.

I didn't partake. At this stage, I was very much of the opinion that drugs were not for me. But as I travelled up sitting next to Graham Smith, it was clear I was in the minority. Halfway to Manchester when a bottle of poppers rolled the length of the coach and lodged itself under the brake pedal and the incensed driver threatened to drive us directly to the nearest cop shop, it looked like we might not get there at all.

Somehow, the parlous state of most of our crew when we finally arrived didn't cause undue alarm amongst the programme-makers. We were simply herded in and the show began. I'd already broken my *Top of the Pops* duck, having been invited to the famed White City studio by Dagger to witness Spandau's chart resurrection with 'Instinction', so I knew a little about the stop-start nature of telly-making. But not everyone was as patient, especially when the studio was emphatically alcohol-free.

Thirty minutes into the record, I looked around and noticed that of the forty-strong coach party there was now only me, Graham and another of the emerging pop managers, Lee Barrett, left.

Lee managed a band called Ariva (a bit of a Blue Rondo rip-off) who had just mutated into a more pared-back funk outfit called Pride fronted by one male and two female singers who would then jettison more members and end up with a rhythm section from Hull and a smoky-voiced chanteuse from Wood Green, via Clacton-on-Sea and Nigeria, called Sade.

Clearly the three of us were no longer where it was at so we took our cue to slip out of the back of the studio and head for the nearest pub. I can't remember its name, but just as we were about to step inside, one of our mob, a baby-faced be-quiffed lad called Jason Pollock, zipped past us with the words: 'There's been a bit of trouble.'

From what we could gather, some of our lot had been cutting out the middle man and helping themselves to drinks and this had not gone down well. There didn't seem any point in us further testing their good will so we just followed Jason to the second closest pub which was where everyone was now enjoying themselves.

And enjoying themselves they were. I had just managed to push my way to the front of the bar to get my first drink since the coach ride, when two police cars and a couple of police vans pulled up outside. In marched Manchester's constabulary and before I could get a round in, we were being frogmarched out. Having actually made it to the furthest side of the pub, this meant I was the last to emerge. I could see that things were hotting up. Ollie was already being hoisted into one police van and another officer had grabbed Lee round the neck. Lee is not someone to make a fuss but he looked to be in some discomfort so I protested and only managed to make matters worse.

The next thing we knew, all three of us had been bundled into the back of the van and were on our way to a night in the cells charged with drunk and disorderly; charges that were later dropped for reasons too tedious to go into here. Before that, though, the police van decided to do a little detour back to Granada Studios where our coach was still waiting, just to wind us southern twats up a bit more.

Now with their very own police guard of honour, everyone (minus us three) was counted back onto the coach before being strongly advised not to visit their fair city again. As I watched disconsolately from the back of the van, quietly fuming at the injustice of it all, I spotted Graham Smith settling into his seat then suddenly leaning forward. It was only the next day that I discovered he'd been sick into a convenient bag. The convenient bag containing my now extremely soggy Blondie cover piece.

Thankfully, neither Debbie Harry fans nor *Melody Maker* features editors needed to know of that article's painful journey into print, particularly as I already had someone else baying for my blood.

Relations between pop stars and the press have travelled a fair old way since the 1980s. In the twenty-first century, one of the most enabling aspects of social media if you're Lady GaGa or Lily Allen is the rapidity and directness of your ability to reply if someone – be they jumped-up journo or common or garden troll – starts slagging you off.

Back in the pre-Internet eighties, though, doing that was more of a faff. Of course, if you were a pro-active sort like Bob Geldof or John Lydon you could always do a little surprise visit – SAS style – to that person's place of work. Geldof was forever hoiking unsuspecting critics out of their seats. But mostly it was the job of the artist's much put-upon manager or publicist to lodge a phone complaint.

Hence the distressed tinkle I received one morning at *New Sounds New Styles* from a woman at Rocket Records, the label of Elton John.

'How could you?' she castigated me. 'How could you be so mean?!'

Sitting as I was at the time in another part of Soho wearing my *NSNS* hat, it took me a moment or two to grasp what she was on about. Then I remembered.

First, let me at least try to make some sort of case for the defence. In my early record-buying and radio-listening years, I was very much an Elton fan. 'Rocket Man', played over and over on my crappy little Grundig cassette player, had got me through a nasty bout of flu one winter. 'Crocodile Rock' had inspired me to throw caution to the wind and take to the dance floor (alone) for the first time at Belinda Gent's sixteenth birthday party. And 'Honky Cat' had shown me that it was perfectly acceptable to wear man-sized animal outfits when appearing on *Top of the Pops*.

But things had moved a little further up the yellow brick road since then. Now here I was, this opinionated twenty-year-old with a turntable, a typewriter and – as I fondly imagined it – my very own 60,000 strong readership. I may have overdone it a bit.

I'm not sure that even Elton John would claim that *Jump Up*, his twenty-third studio album, was up there with the best of them. This was a time just before he came rollicking back with songs like 'I'm Still Standing' and lavish pop videos in the South of France with choreographer (and later *Strictly Come Dancing* judge) Bruno Tonioli dressed as a bellboy. But *Jump Up* does have 'Blue Eyes' on it, which is rather lovely, and in no way deserving of the cup of cold sick that I chucked over it.

I really had got properly stuck in, mocking everything from the material – 'That sentimental, half-digested sludge in the stomach.' – to Elton's pre-hair transplant shiny pate – 'This heap of pap'n'roll flesh and bones is certified dead from the bald patch down.'

'Let's leave the poor sod now,' was my closing remark. 'If he didn't make me rather queasy, I might pity him.'

It's hardly up there with Burchill and Parsons (though having recently purchased their *The Boy Looked at Johnny*, an assassination of the Old Guard, I've no doubt that was exactly who I was aping). But if the aim was to piss off as many people as possible, it did the trick.

MM reader Phil Light from Lewes, for one, was not impressed.

'How about giving a review of Elton John's album instead of insulting a man who has written some of the best songs of the last decade?' said Phil. 'It does seem uncalled for. Who knows, Elton might come along and beat the fuck out of you. PS: If printed, please leave in the fuck.'

It would be crediting me with way too much sensitivity to say that I took much heed of this. Despite my fanboy roots, I was learning that pissing off pop stars was part of the music journalist's job description. Although I was a little taken aback when Pete Burns of Dead or Alive filed his 'Portrait of the Artist as a Consumer' in the *NME* and popped me on his Death List – Paul 'Flymo' Simper – along with 'Dowdy George' (Pete was apparently not in the Culture Club camp either).

Still, things change. Dear Pete Burns and I later became well enough acquainted for him to merrily pose for a picture next to my ball sack (a snap unfortunately later discovered by my mother after it had been made into an enormous Get Well card, which she pondered over for many years before telling me).

Meanwhile, Elton John and I would get to share a very special day, which we shall return to later.

Actually, the *Melody Maker* cutting from that period that now shocks me the most is one not of my doing, but instead the handiwork of some anonymous sub.

It's a 'Next Week' box for my first Steve Strange interview:

'Why is his current single poncing up the charts? Read all about it in a special Shirtlifters Edition of *MM*.'

In my heart of hearts, I felt there had to be a more suitable home for me than this.

7

ENJOY WHAT YOU DO

There's an episode of *The Phil Silvers Show*, 'Bilko's Perfect Day', where from the second Sergeant Bilko gets up, everything he wishes for comes true.

His lighter, which hasn't worked in six years, lights. The shower, which is freezing for the rest of the platoon, is for him hot and steamy. He gets crossword answers without hearing the clue. He picks seven racehorse winners without a second thought. He even tells Doberman the number of jelly beans in a jar in the window of MacGregor's hardware store to the very last bean. The only catch is that by the time he realises it's his perfect day, it's over.

There's a little of that about my days at *No.1* magazine – I had a dream job without really knowing it. On any given day one might be required to fly a reader to the other side of the world to hang out with Spandau Ballet, accompany Bananarama's Keren and Wham!'s George on a blind date, help Frankie Goes to Hollywood chuck assorted items of furniture out of TV studio windows in Rome, watch Boy George styling and flirting with Paul Weller in fake furs, or come up with a photo story which has you walking off into the sunset with some newbie called Madonna.

All of which seemed like exactly the sort of thing the twenty-year-old me should be doing when I wasn't too busy clubbing. In fact, it was principally down to two fellow Beat Route habitués that I got the job in the first place.

It was in October 1982 in a tiny first-floor office at the bottom of South Molton Street that I first met George Michael and Andrew Ridgeley. They had not yet had a hit but their second single, 'Young Guns', of which flatmate Graham had been sent an advanced white label DJ copy, was about to give them one. So off we went to the Hog in the Pound, a once popular, now long-gone, watering hole by Bond Street tube, to discuss rival bands, bad American dancing and a couple of surprising things that never made it into the *Melody Maker* piece but raise a smile now.

The pair of them had been going to Le Beat Route even longer than I had, though sometimes it was another schoolmate, David Austin, who accompanied George. George and David used to busk at Green Park station when they were sixteen or seventeen, covering Elton favourites (George particularly loved Elton's *Captain Fantastic and the Brown Dirt Cowboy* album).

'Only it was a bit useless our busking because you were moved on the whole time if you didn't actually have a pitch,' George told me later. 'There are certain places that the police leave you alone. If you get there early enough, you write your name down on a piece of paper for the time you're supposed to play. But we were never up early enough to do that so we just got moved on all day. We never really made any money. We'd make on average a fiver each on Friday afternoon. I'd bunk off school and then I'd go back to David's house to change before the club.'

Le Beat Route spoke to him as much as it had to me.

'I loved dancing at Le Beat Route,' said George. 'Nobody gave a fuck who I was so you could throw yourself around. If Shirlie was with me we'd do that pair dancing. It was cool. We'd always make a bit of space and really show off.'

There's footage from a BBC *Nationwide* report on the club which appears in Spandau's *Soul Boys of the Western World* movie showing a bearded, curly- haired George in an alarmingly orange suit slap bang in the middle of the dance floor from a time when he and Andrew were still in a ska band called The Executive with Andrew's brother, Paul Ridgeley, and David.

'Andrew and I were at Le Beat Route when Andrew started going "Wham! Bam! I am a man!" and doing this terrible rap,' said George. 'It was supposed to be funny. But that's where he had the idea.'

By that October club-wise we had all moved on. George and Andrew deemed Le Beat Route now 'too packed' and had started frequenting Ollie's new Saturday night with Chris Sullivan at the revamped Whisky-A-Go-Go on Wardour Street, the Wag. There was also talk of an even more chaotic club venture, Dirt Box – the work of Phil Gray and Rob Milton – which had recently opened above a chemist's in Earls Court, which took the new Hard Times ethos to the nth degree.

It'd be wrong to say that George did all the talking at our first encounter. Andy also had plenty to say but as they had helpfully pointed out when we were first ordering our grub, my microphone (attached to a massive, cumbersome boogie box) was not quite up to competing with the pub jukebox's lively selection of current club tunes like Evelyn King's 'Love Come Down' and such new Top 10 hits as Culture Club's 'Do You Really Want to Hurt Me' and Spandau's 'Lifeline'.

If Andrew is a bit muffled, George at any rate is loud, clear and competitive, especially on the merits of 'Lifeline'.

'I'm amazed this is Number 7,' he said with a shake of the head.

Sometimes the charts surprise us all. Martin Kemp told me that two years later George played him 'Wake Me Up Before You Go-Go' on George's mum and dad's stereo before anyone else had heard it. Being the gracious man that he is, Martin made all the right noises, but back in the car his verdict for wife Shirlie was a little more unvarnished.

'I thought it was awful, absolutely awful,' said Martin. 'I sat in the car with Shirlie and said, "They're over".'

Considering they were still a couple of jittery weeks from securing their first *Top of the Pops* ('Young Guns' wobbled dangerously until an independent plugger was hired by Innervision and George and Andrew's Chinese slippers and immaculate, camera-aware, pair-dancing delivered one of the show's most impressive debuts), Wham! weren't short of confidence.

'Once we have a hit we'll get more expensive budgets,' said George, like this was just a matter of time.

'This one is more of a compromise to make sure we get it onto the radio. Then "Wham Rap!" is going to be re-released so our sound could get harder again. It's hard to know which way it'll go. Every time we've planned something we've ended up coming up with something different that we're just as pleased with. But we don't want to be a cult thing. For a while "Wham Rap!" looked like it might just be a trendy record.'

They made no bones about also having their eyes on the prize in America; a prospect that was only that month starting to become a reality for this new generation of British pop groups. Led by Soft Cell's 'Tainted Love' and The Human League's 'Don't You Want Me', and buoyed by the rise of MTV and the music video, it was the first genuine British invasion of the Billboard singles chart since The Beatles and The Stones in the mid-sixties.

'We've got a few numbers that could apply to the American chart,' said George matter-of-factly. 'Very big. But we won't put them out till at least the middle of next year.'

'We don't mind having a totally different image for America and just releasing records that will sell in America,' Andrew concurred. 'We don't really care about America except for the cash.'

'That's what it's for,' said George. 'People over there have absolutely no taste anyway.'

He'd sensibly revise this opinion when Wham! went on to be the only pop group of their generation to have four successive US Number 1s.

This led us on to a recent trip they'd made to New York where they had hired one of the big-name dance record producers of that period, François Kevorkian, (responsible for the deconstruction of Sharon Redd's 'Can You Handle It' and the classic D Train 'You're the One for Me') to do a remix of 'Wham Rap!'. It hadn't worked out – Kevorkian had thrown out most of the hit components and gone off on his own tangent – so they'd got rid of him. But it had given them – well, George, as Andrew had bust his foot – a chance to check out the New York underground club scene.

'I was really pissed most of the time,' said George, who took in Danceteria, AM/PM and the Peppermint Lounge before arriving at the shocking conclusion that nobody he met over there could dance.

'It's incredible,' he said. 'They've had that black culture for so long. They must be so segregated not to have picked it up at all.'

It's at this point that I chimed in with a few club-going

suggestions of my own, based on my very first trip to New York a few weeks before them with another British band (more of this later), which had proved to be a bit of an eye-opener.

'You should have gone to the Anvil and the Hellfire Club,' I enthused. 'The Anvil is where they filmed *Cruising* [the Al Pacino leather movie where he goes undercover tracking a homophobic serial killer on Christopher Street and gets more than he bargained for]. The music is really good but it's disgusting because there's piss all down the stairs. Still, it's great. The Hellfire Club is even worse because there's people chained to the walls being whipped. And fat Mexicans saying: "Piss on me!"'

'Yes, we were told about those,' said George brightly. 'We saw *Cruising* last week, didn't we? I thought I was going to be horrified, but I wasn't.'

That part of our lunchtime chat didn't make it into the *Maker*. I'm not sure I thought it would be their sort of thing.

Thankfully, even without my mini-dissertation on the more colourful side of downtown Lower West Side, the piece was enough to catch the eye of former *NME* deputy editor Phil McNeill. Phil was now on the look-out for writers for a new weekly IPC publication, *No.1*, their answer to the half-a-million-selling fortnightly *Smash Hits*.

Or as Paul Morley put it when he reviewed us for C4 magazine show *Loose Talk* when we launched the following April: '*No.1* larked into life . . . packed with the inane poses that are the symbol of today's pop, [cut to leather-jacketed Wham! 'Bad Boys' pin-up back cover of our first issue] smeared with nice colour, advertised during *Crossroads* and boasting a vocabulary of twenty-seven words. That's three more than *Smash Hits* and two less than *NME*. *No.1* is the latest, richest attempt to smash into the terrific *Smash Hits* market.

'Accepting *Smash Hits*' crazy simplification of super pop life was the commercially correct decision. *No.1* won't disappear like *Trax* or *New Music News*. IPC Magazines, who *NME* live with or vice versa, are supporting it with the kind of money they only usually spend on *Woman's Own*. Enough money to hope that its arrival will lead to the very sad death of *NME*.

'The staff of *No.1* has been ripped from the rotting black-and-whites. Karen Swayne from the dirty *Sounds*; Mark Cooper [cut to 10 x 8 photo of me] from the deeply puzzling *Record Mirror*; Paul Simper [cut to 10 x 8 photo of the future all-powerful head of BBC music, most definitely not me] from the deeply crippled *Melody Maker*. Like me, editors Lynn Hanna and Phil McNeill leapt away from the *NME* just in time. That's a neat staff and they have a refreshing attitude.'

He was right about the attitude. No doubt about it, *No.1* was fun. Paul might also have mentioned another former *NME* colleague, Max Bell, who as writer of *No.1*'s weekly gossip column, 'Whispers', and later the voice of Snabber, the mag's canine, bushy-tailed letters ed, very much set the tone for all the piss-taking of pop stars and all the attendant nonsense that surrounded them.

Smash Hits had already led the way in advancing an acute sense of the ridiculous, which often was at its best when directed at the more po-faced artists – Jon Bon Jovi, Sting, Bono – who took themselves very seriously indeed. The *Hits*' reporting of bands' more rock-and-roll bad behaviour – of the sex and drugs variety – tended to be fairly oblique, ever mindful of the youngest end of the magazine's demographic. *No.1* – at least in the hands of Max and

'Whispers' main contributors – wasn't quite so fussed about that. If anything, our default objective was to try and smuggle through as much filth and depravity as possible, on the basis that that's what pop kids really wanted whether their parents and our publishers approved of it or not. There's an urban myth about the BBC children's pirate series *Captain Pugwash* that three of the subsidiary characters were named Seaman Staines, Roger the Cabin Boy and Master Bates. It's 100 per cent untrue but that's about the level of japery that appealed to us.

'As long as the work gets done,' was the mantra that we tried to foist on a succession of editors, Phil McNeill, Lynn Hanna and Maureen Rice, with varying degrees of success.

There were others at *No.1* that contributed just as much to the daily eccentricities of the mag and plucked from less likely sources than the music press. Anne Lambert and Debbi Voller had done their time on IPC photo love titles like *My Guy* before they made their way up to the twenty-sixth floor. Anne's job was principally song words, which meant many a long hour spent cross-legged next to the modest office record player checking just how many times Boy George sang 'karma-karma-karma chameleon' in the fade-out. Sitting in a fenced-off middle section of the office with just myself and Karen Swayne, Anne was also our den mother, often providing a comfy hiding spot on a pile of as-yet unopened records under her desk, where we could sleep off a bit of the night before. She would also do interviews, but with a more direct, no-nonsense approach than some of us. My favourite was her phoner with Meat Loaf. Quite rightly she thought it absurd to address him as either Meat or Mr Loaf so instead looked up his birth name.

'So, Marvin . . .' said Anne. The interview was terminated not long after.

Debbi Voller was our only *No.1* staff writer who'd already made it onto the telly as a reporter on BBC2's music/arts show *Riverside*, hosted by Steve Blacknell and Mike Andrews. The Vole, as she was dubbed by Max and thereafter forever known, had a soft spot for Steve Strange, Marilyn, Kate from Haysi Fantayzee and pretty much any pop star with hair that sprouted upwards, theatrically applied make-up (Peter Gabriel, Fish) or a general penchant for peacockery. When a fresh-faced young freelancer from Basingstoke with shrub-like hair modelled on The Cure's Robert Smith took up residence at an adjacent desk, it wasn't long before our office had produced its very own lovecats. The Vole and Paul Bursche have been together, perfectly, ever since.

Production editor Deanne Pearson didn't let having to deal with the tedious day-to-day slog of chasing writers' copy and 'putting through' pages deter her from getting involved with all the pop fun. It was Deanne who riled my old mucker Geldof at the time of Live Aid when he tried to force her to empty her pockets for the cause – 'Give me *all* your money!' – which she stoutly refused to do.

Deanne also had a keen eye for a trip, pouncing on the legendary once-a-year pop press beano, which involved spending a week with Eddy Grant at his massive house in Barbados (formerly owned by a sugar plantation slaver) and getting so stoned that she hallucinated she'd been hospitalised after a terrible traffic accident that never actually took place. In actual fact, the only people who did manage to write off one of Eddy's buggies – thankfully without doing themselves any damage – were Kate Bush's old pals Musical Youth who the 'Electric Avenue' star was producing.

Just as much of a lark, but not as appreciated by the editor, was the time the Pearson unofficially accompanied Max Bell on his first Frankie Goes to Hollywood interview in Liverpool only to phone in sick on press day the morning after. All would have been fine and dandy if she hadn't unfortunately been captured on film by photographer John Stoddart making merry the night before. Phil McNeill took a while to see the funny side of this, flinging various Stoddy snaps of her straddling an automobile with The Lads and snogging Holly (yes, Holly) on Deanne's desk – but he did eventually relent and let her keep one of the pix as a memento.

Andrew Panos was a later arrival on the writing front, but most welcome. Much to our delight Panny's claim to fame was that he was George Michael's cousin. But Andrew had much more to contribute to the cause than just this pleasing pop connection. When he wasn't out interviewing various soul acts or Rick Astley (who warmed to his easy-going manner), Andrew, along with Max, was the chief purveyor of *No.1*'s comedy memos, purportedly from the editors or assorted pop stars and PRs, which commented on our daily activities. I have two bulging folders-worth of these that suggest we could have published a whole sister magazine (albeit an entirely libellous one) pretty much every week.

It was Andrew who was once rumbled by Bryan Adams; serving as a handy reminder to us all of what can happen on those occasions when, for whatever reason, you decide to wing it with an interview. Panny was in Miami at the time with publicist Chris Poole, at the largesse of A&M, and after a few days of soaking up the sun had finally found himself confronted with a hopefully not too taxing half hour of chatting to said talent.

The fact that the Adams had rumbled that his interviewer might not be entirely conversant with his whole back catalogue became apparent when the Canadian rocker posed a question of his own.

'So, Andrew . . . tonight's gig – which three songs from my new album would you definitely play?'

There was a long, considered pause.

'Erm, well, "Run to You", obviously . . . ah, "Summer of '69" . . . aaaand, the title track?'

Well, it was a decent stab at it.

The other person to join *No.1* was my initially sceptical landlord and flatmate, Graham Smith.

If Dagger, Bob Elms, Graham Ball and David Johnson had initially given me my crash course in London living it was Graham who tutored me through my degree.

I have no doubt he thought he had a right wally on his hands when he first offered to let me his spare room one Beat Route Friday night, but needs must when you've got a £22,000 mortgage (younger readers, we feel your pain) to pay off.

Graham would take me off to the Chelsea Potter down the King's Road of a Saturday afternoon, where soul boys had usurped the punks, to get me fitted out in my first bespoke suit from Robot (my black-and-white dog-tooth pride and joy till someone slit it up the back one New Year's Eve) and pink winkle-pickers that would have your eye out.

I could see his satisfaction when I kind of got something right. Like the night we had friends over to Shirland Road and I'd been sent a review copy of ABC's *The Lexicon of Love* before either Graham Ball or Bob. But at the same time, he would despair of my love of the Bee Gees or much that he dismissed as 'disco shit' whilst he extolled the virtues of real soul singers or that Cajun 'Duelling Banjos' song from *Deliverance* by Arthur 'Guitar Boogie' Smith.

As a result, a magazine as pure pop as *No.1* was never going to be a perfect fit for Grazza. But as he moved away from designing for Spandau, there were bills to be paid and, anyway, as he and his new girlfriend (now, wife) from Manchester, Lorraine Davies, knew from hanging out with the *No.1* crew, there were good times to be had.

Talking of Spandau, one of the other key assets of the *No.1* team that Phil McNeill had pieced together was the fact that between us we appeared to be on speaking (or even better, drinking) terms with most of the current chart acts.

Or at least, we had been. In fact, my relationship with Spandau in the run up to *No.1*'s launch had gone just a tad awry. I blame it on Bournemouth. I possibly even blame it on Spandau. If my previous two bank holiday visits to the south coast had given me a taste of what merriment could be had, April 1983 was when I decided to properly get stuck in.

At least this time our accommodation was sorted. No more nights in freezing car parks. Myself and Bob Elms had secured a double room, which would also be housing Graham, Lorraine and anyone else who could bunk in through the first-floor balcony windows, which, from photographic evidence, looks like Lee Barrett, Spandau's fan club secretary Jacqui Quaife and a couple of her mates.

Steve Dagger loves his pop moments – those zeitgeist instances when a band locks perfectly into its time. Already Spandau had enjoyed two – 'To Cut a Long Story Short' and the Blitz Kids of 1980, then 'Chant No.1' and the sweaty, scorched summer of funk of 1981. Now as the charts became saturated with glossy pop, they notched their third with 'True', an unabashed, going-for-the-jugular ballad, fittingly knocking their very own returning hero David Bowie's 'Let's Dance' off the top of the singles charts.

In many ways, it should have been the ultimate bank holiday weekend. Spandau were in their pomp with two sold-out nights at the Pavilion and Animal Nightlife – the third trendy cab off the rank after Blue Rondo, and now, like Wham!, also signed to Innervision – were playing the Thursday. There was even a Saturday night Dirt Box party thrown in for good measure. But as I had garnered from sharing a flat with Graham, a parting of the ways was pretty much upon us.

Graham had been Spandau's record sleeve designer right from the start, through the neo-classicism (or neo-Nazi as *Melody Maker's* Lynden Barber would have it) of *Journeys to Glory* to the squirly Native American designs of 'Chant' and 'Paint Me Down'. But by the time of our first meeting, when Graham dropped off the artwork for 'She Loved Like Diamond' at the band's Reformation offices on Mortimer Street, his enthusiasm for what his pals were doing was waning.

Move another six months down the line, and the look of despair on his face as he played me a cassette of their latest single, 'Lifeline', with its radio friendly mop-top-flavoured 'ooh ooh oohs' said it all. Spandau were no longer making records for the cool kids.

Though I could see that was disappointing for the likes of Bob and Graham, I wasn't that fussed by this change of direction. Having the door opened for me on the funky Narnia that was Le Beat Route had been completely thrilling and life-changing but there was still plenty of lovely, unabashed pop music held close to my heart.

It had only taken a blast of Trevor Horn's turbo refit of 'Instinction' to fire me up again, and though I wasn't big on either 'Lifeline' or 'Communication' by the time they peeled the title track off as single Number 3 I was on board with this breathy new Jolley and Swain- (purveyors of Bananarama, Imagination and Alison Moyet) produced incarnation. Indeed, I felt moved (pissed) enough to mark their reaching Number 1 by drawing a little 'True' dove on a toilet seat in the recently opened Camden Palace with the phrase: 'This Much Is Poo' inscribed beneath it, with the help of their press officer Julia Marcus.

So, it's fair to say, I was gagging for some celebratory mayhem that Bournemouth weekend. Spandau, unfortunately, less so.

This would be down to the events of earlier on the Good Friday when we'd finally checked into the band's hotel, after a post-Nightlife Thursday night spent unsatisfactorily half covered by a couple of tea towels on someone's floor. Bags deposited, we got right back into the swing of things.

There was a well-established order of play for daytime drinking in Bournemouth, honed over the years by legions of dedicated soul boys and girls from Widnes to Wales. With Graham the comparative old hand, and Lol and me the new blood, we picked up where we'd left off the previous day with the traditional tour of key bars and pubs. First the Palace Vaults and the Queen's Vaults, just down from the Gaumont where I'd once queued anxiously in the rain, clock ticking, with brother Geoffrey to see *Live and Let Die* for the first time. Then on to the seafront and up the hill to the Intrepid Fox, which apart from snakebites (lager, cider and black) and a new concoction Lol and I had come up with called Snake in the Bath (lager, cider and vodka), boasted a jukebox fit to busting with Evelyn 'Champagne' King, Candi Staton, Luther and The O'Jays.

This took us to mid-afternoon, and with no time or day yet fixed for my Spandau chat, it was back to the hotel bar where we could greet the latest arrivals rolling in and generally make plans for the rest of the weekend.

One girl who I'd not met before was Chrysta Jones. Chrysta was Animal Nightlife's latest vocal addition who had taken the lead on their just-released second single, 'The Mighty Hands of Love'. Funny and gorgeous in equal measure with golden curls, feline peepers and a Monroe-esque bee-stung pout, we hit it off as the afternoon got better and better.

There comes a point, though, when, however much fun you're having, if you possess a hotel room, it's time to check it out. As people started to drift off, I judged that moment had come. Having in front of me more pints than I could carry, I carefully placed one of the spare ones behind a hotel curtain to return to later. Pleased with my foresight, I then headed up with Chrysta to spend some quality time in what I was now thinking might constitute a potential love nest.

The room itself was hardly the Ritz but two beds, a bathroom and a balcony with a seafront view more than sufficed. So, as Chrysta popped to the bathroom for a bit of a freshen up, I set our drinks down and began a quick bit of furniture rearranging to get the two single beds better acquainted.

The exact timing of the events that followed are a bit sketchy. All I remember is a key turning in the door just as I projectile vomited in a dark, frothy, blackcurrant-coloured arc across both beds and Bob Elms appeared, looking fairly nonplussed as he stood in the doorway.

Whether Chrysta caught any of this on her return from the bathroom I have no idea. The next I saw of her was about two hours later when I finally awoke from my booze-induced slumber. She was sitting in Graham and Lol's adjoining room watching the Nightlife vid being premiered on Switch. I would waste the next six months trailing after her like a lovesick pup, but in my heart of hearts I knew I had already spectacularly blown my big moment.

So how did all this come to bear on my intended chat with Spandau? Well, amongst her many attributes, Chrysta was also the little sister of John Keeble's girlfriend (now lovely wife), Flea. The disasters of our afternoon were, I imagine, too good a story to waste so by the time I was up and running again, an executive decision had been reached between Dagger, the band and Julia – who was not unsympathetic to my plight – that, at least for this Bournemouth, I was someone too pissed to talk to.

Overall it wasn't Spandau's best weekend for music press relations. The *NME*, in the shape of my former *MM* colleague Paolo Hewitt, was also due to speak to Gary with pictures by the illustrious Anton Corbijn. Paolo was hardly a dyed-in-the-wool Spandau fan ('I thought "True" was fucking terrible') but he'd dug 'Chant No.1' and knew them socially through playing footie in Regent's Park for El Classico – a north London team of pop stars, journos and others, including Keeble ('best goalkeeper I ever played with'), Tony, Martin and Steve, with Gary sometimes videoing proceedings from the touchline.

Unfortunately, when he wasn't busy dealing with me and his recently redecorated hotel room, Bob had been busy giving Paolo the once over on behalf of Dagger and Gary and found his Spandau party credentials wanting. The upshot of which was that Paolo and Anton made the long drive back to London empty-handed. Paolo then wrote a scathing piece titled 'To Cut a Long Story Very, Very

Short Indeed', which resulted in Bob thumping Paolo at the Camden Palace, a spot of litigation and an out-of-court settlement that provided Bob with the down payment on his first Bloomsbury flat.

'We've all kissed and made up since then,' says Paolo. 'It's quite funny now, but at the time it was deadly serious *Guns of Navarone* shit. Music to me was life and death then. When you're young it's all black and white. This is wrong, this is right, fuck you.'

In fact, my interview ban turned out not to be quite a decree absolute. Martin Kemp took pity on me on the final morning and gave me fifteen minutes, sitting in the bar somewhere close to where I'd left that last pint, talking 'StarWears'. In this new weekly slot in *No.1* he described the first two-tone mohair suit his dad, Frank, had bought him ('With a little buckle on the back and double vent'), dismissed the recent London clubbing trend for ripped jeans, mud clothes and potato sacks ('How can you really fancy a girl in a potato sack?') and explained how shoes 'dictate the way you walk'. Well, I knew what he meant.

By the time *No.1* launched, I was fully back on track with the Spands who I think, particularly in Dagger's case, were delighted that at least one person from their clubbing days would be accompanying them on this next leg of their journey. Until I boarded a plane to Manchester with them one Friday afternoon that May, I'd not properly encountered the phenomenon that was Spandaumania.

Of course, Dagger had been laying the groundwork for me in dispatches from his traditional spot at the far end of the Wag Club bar. The band themselves had first become aware of their new scream-worthy status one night in Liverpool on the previous year's tour-that's-not-a-tour when they'd been drowned out – Beatles' Shea Stadium style – from the first note, and further emphasised by a great David Johnson photo of an intrepid Spandette scaling a drainpipe to their second-floor dressing room afterwards.

Now in 1983, Dagger was reporting back that Glasgow had proved particularly lively. According to Steve, the band's coach had been chased all the way up Sauchiehall Street before their Holiday Inn was spectacularly stormed in a scene he described as akin to the siege in *Zulu*.

That first evening in Manchester, Gary Kemp went to do a phone-in at Piccadilly Radio and had his car chased all the way back to the Britannia. With the band enjoying their third week at Number 1 it was escalating by the day.

The next morning, they were booked to perform three songs on BBC1's *Get Set for Summer*, a Saturday morning kids' show in the *Multi-Coloured Swap Shop* slot. A hundred or so lucky fans had actually been granted access to the studio and the mounting hysteria after each song was palpable.

A BBC floor manager told Dagger they had some roses for the band – 'If you want to use them for anything, we've put one in a vase on the piano' – so after the second number, Gary started chucking them out to the assembled throng. The fans, though, were intent on bagging themselves a bit more than a red rose and as Gary continued to make like a florist, they stormed him, the band and the stage.

Slightly shaken, they regrouped in the dressing room as their recently appointed head of security, Alf Weaver, an old hand from the days of shepherding Sinatra, warned them this was just an aperitif. He wasn't wrong. Before the band had even reached the end of

'True', the whole lot went hell for leather at them again. All except Steve Norman, who had to be dragged clear by the road crew, managed to dive through a hole in the back of the set.

The whole notion of teens and pre-teens going completely ape at their chart idols was nothing new. But this was the first time for a decade that it had happened across the board with Duran, Culture Cub and now Spandau (with the Wham! boys already snapping at their heels) setting off this feeding frenzy with chart-topping singles.

'When we played the Royal Albert Hall, the limo we were in got kicked in,' Tony told me delightedly on the flight up. 'They ripped the wing mirrors and the aerial off.'

Back in their dressing room, it was clear that the telly folk were as new to all this as the band. *Get Set*'s presenter, Mark Curry, and his wacky red spex came back all of a-fluster asking if it would be all right if two particularly hysterical fans who were absolutely beside themselves in the corridor could just pop in and say hi 'to calm them down'. A quick survey of the incredulous faces of the five sweaty, semi-naked objects of their desires told him this really wasn't going to help.

It was both thrilling and funny to watch this whole new story playing out. Where once it had been long, earnest talks with Gary about club culture, now it was Tony on fans' mums knitting him jumpers and the burning question of what he liked for breakfast.

'We were doing *TV-am* the other day,' said Tony, having successfully run the gauntlet from the studio and onto the flight back. 'Some kid popped up and said: "Tone, what do you like for breakfast?" I said: "I don't actually eat breakfast but I do like a cup of tea with chocolate chip cookies." Since then we've been getting cuddly toys, bangles and bloody chocolate chip cookies. No word of a lie, there's been chocolate chip cookies thrown onstage. We had one beautifully wrapped box with a big bow on top and when we opened it, it was just filled with chocolate chip cookies. Three or four girls had put all their pocket money together and bought twenty or thirty packets.'

For the Wham! boys it took a little longer for them to experience this sea change first-hand. They'd played Capital Radio's Junior Best Disco in Town, hosted by Gary Crowley, in the early part of 1983, but it wasn't till the autumn with their shuttlecocks-down-their-shorts *Fantastic* tour that the real fun began.

The first night of that tour in Aberdeen there were delirious screams even at home videos of them as kids.

George told me the next day he'd had a tiny preview of what was coming at the end of the summer when David Austin, now Wham!'s guitarist, had dragged him along to their local Kingsbury funfair (they'd been pupils at Kingsbury High) against his better judgement.

'David was going: "Come on Yog, just put your sunglasses on. If we get too much hassle, we'll come away." I used to go to Kingsbury funfair every year when I was a kid. So we went down there and got on the waltzer. By the end of the first ride, we were surrounded – people all round the edges of the ride peering at me and telling the guys who spun the cars round to get my autograph.

'You know what blokes at fairs are like, right? They're going: "Oi, mate. You something special?" I'm like: "No, I don't know what they're on about." The next ride, I'm not joking, we had four guys round our car. They were all whacking it round about three times the speed it's supposed to go. This went on for nearly a quarter of an hour. This guy was shouting: "There's no way you're fucking pulling tonight, mate!" They were so determined to make me throw up. It was so funny. I was really enjoying it cos I love the waltzer.

'The ride finished and we trotted off merrily, but in all the other cars all these girls were throwing up. Still, at least it cost those bastards four rides-worth of fares to do that to us. But after that we had to leave straightaway. That's when we realised we couldn't just go out and do things like that any more.'

If Wham! and Spandau were my first ports of call for *No.1* there was another gang of chart regulars I was about to get better acquainted with who would prove to be the most entertaining bunch yet.

8

NANA HI HI

Considering how it went the first time I interviewed Bananarama, it's remarkable they ever spoke to me again. I could not have been more patronising.

I'd like to attribute this to the fact that I was still wearing my rather more world-weary *Melody Maker* hat but doubtless many of *MM*'s readers and most of its staff would testify that that hadn't exactly held me back in the past.

I'd already interviewed their arch rivals, The Belle Stars, three months earlier. After the early promise of their rambunctious 2 Tone hit, 'Let's Do Rocksteady' as The Bodysnatchers, lead singer Rhoda Dakar had headed off to work with Jerry Dammers on 'The Boiler' and in her place was north London signing Jennie McKeown. Now called The Belle Stars and signed to Stiff Records, they initially failed to make any real impact with their own material. So after three successive flops, they had a rethink and went down the covers route, first with The Dixie Cups' 'Iko Iko' then with Shirley Ellis' 'The Clapping Song', which at least secured them a foothold in the Top 40.

Still, 1983 had started a lot more promisingly for them. Their self-penned Spector-flavoured 'Sign of the Times' single with its spoken intro by flame-haired, guitar-wielding siren Stella Barker rocking a black polo neck and sheriff's badge (I had a bit of a crush) had given them their first Top 5 hit.

Meanwhile the Nanas were navigating through their own choppy waters.

At first welcomed as a breath of fresh air with their just-hopped-on-the-dance-floor-making-it-up-as-we-go-along approach to being a girl group, their lack of polish had now been turned against them. Their early sequence of hits, 'It Ain't What You Do' (with the Fun Boy Three), 'Really Saying Something' and 'Shy Boy' had been broken by the winsome ballad 'Cheers Then' (best remembered for their video recreation of *The Sound of Music*) and a so-so cover of Shocking Blue's 'Na Na Hey Hey Kiss Him Goodbye', which had got them back in the charts but not the critics' hearts.

Now it was time for me to swing by on behalf of the *Maker* with a few lofty opinions of my own.

My piece kicked off with what I declared to be a commonly held view: Bananarama could not write, could not sing, could not dance *and* they looked a bit of a state. I then zeroed in on three shock discoveries that particularly alarmed me.

Firstly, they all smoked; secondly, none of them wore high heels (why on earth did I expect this?); and thirdly, all three of them were shockingly a good six months older than me (Keren and Sarah clocking in at twenty-one and Siobhan a truly ancient twenty-three. Oh the shame!).

Granted smoking was a bit of a bugbear of mine. I'd sampled my only cigarette at Le Beat Route from the very stylish vintage silver case of a lad called Richard, one of the cool, Zooted-up faces on the scene, but when I held it inelegantly betwixt my fingers, I was surprised by how light it was. Only having previously sampled Joe 90 sweet cigarettes (my schoolboy brand of choice) I was used to a heavier stick and as my hand floated uncertainly skyward I decided there and then that smoking wasn't for me.

Anyway, back to my appalling piece. Having damned the Nanas as a bunch of shoddily heeled, ancient fag ash Lils, I then moved swiftly through the gears, blithely dismissing them as three fairly naïve girlies (says the farmer's son from Wiltshire) with few original thoughts in their heads before airily casting myself in the role of head tutor as I delivered a damning end-of-term report on the trio. Quite how much of this I said to their faces and how much was written up afterwards from the safety of my bedroom is hard to say. But understandably they offered up some pretty terse responses whilst unenthusiastically batting their chicken escalopes around their plates and resisting the urge to stab me with their forks.

They patiently pointed out that, whatever I might imagine, they didn't actually spend any time plotting what would best appeal to the mums and dads – which along with the pre-teens I'd delineated as their target audience – and were very much involved in every aspect of the group, thank you very much. The interview concluded with Sarah explaining that they weren't really gushing people as she fixed me with what I would soon discover to be a trademark non-gushing Bananarama look.

Thankfully, by the time the article came out, my not entirely simpatico relationship with the *Maker* had ended and I was settled instead on the twenty-sixth floor of King's Reach Tower, IPC's stronghold on the South Bank, working for *No.1*, which had gone some way to loosening the pole up my arse. Not only that, but by the next time we sat down for a work chat, I'd already met Siobhan again, thanks to a new mutual friend.

Pete Barrett, like Graham Smith another graphic designer,

worked with Bananarama, Dexys Midnight Runners and The Blue-bells. Whilst Graham's sleeves for Spandau, Blue Rondo and Animal Nightlife tended to the classically stylish, Pete's had a more playful DIY approach, which reflected his punk roots from days following The Clash and the Pistols around with his pal and fellow designer Nic(k) Egan. The pair of them used to create their own piss-taking punk fanzines which they would slip onto the shelves of Virgin Megastore and Our Price, feigning outrage as they drew them to the attention of the very bands they were mocking (my beloved Geldof and his Boomtown Rats being one of them).

Pete was a massive wind-up merchant but immensely likeable with it. We'd initially met at a Haysi Fantayzee loft party, but really bonded later that night when the pair of us headed back to Julia Marcus' family flat off the Edgware Road for a VHS Sergeant Bilko marathon. Not long after, Pete suggested I pop up to his office in WEA Records on Broadwick Street in Soho (where he worked in-house for Clive Banks) for lunch. And as luck would have it Siobhan was there too.

The two of them had been mates since their college days in Harpenden when Pete had dated Siobhan's sister Maire (who he immortalised as 'Eileen' on Dexys' 'Come on Eileen' record sleeve and vid). Back then, Pete and Shuv had even cobbled some sort of home-based band together – Siobhan on harmonies, backing vocals and drums (wearing a tea cosy on her head) and Nic(k) and Adrian Thrills strumming away on guitars, while Pete generally bossed them about and drove them to distraction.

Now his latest idea for the Nanas was to kit them out in dunga-rees and have them swigging beers and shoving a bunch of burly truckers around, all for their latest single, 'Cruel Summer'. After the lameness of 'Na Na Hey Hey' this had been met with wholehearted approval by the girls who had even come up with their own trucking handles, Shamrock Lady (Siobhan), Daisy Roots (Keren) and Delaney's Donkey (Sarah) and were now getting ready to fly out to New York for the video, which promised to be a truckin' fest with more than a cowboy hat doffed in the general direction of Kris Kristofferson's *Convoy* movie and current hit TV series *The Dukes of Hazard*.

Before that they had time for a sit down with *No.1* over a cappuccino outside London Records' Hanover Square offices, thankfully with none of the battle-lines-drawn antagonism of our first encounter. Instead what I got was a sarky, breezy and exceedingly camp forty minutes in which we covered fan encounters, disastrous TV appearances and some hair-raising home living experiences that had started with a dodgy Soho squat, which had now been elevated to the three-bedroom council flat they shared in Holborn. Some of this made it into *No.1*. We'll go with the bits that didn't.

All three of them were still buzzing about a PA they'd done the previous weekend at Sheffield's local Top Rank.

'That was great,' enthused Keren. 'You always panic with PAs that when you go out there there's going to be no reaction but they were really surging forward. They were all singing "Na Na Hey Hey" and "Get your tits out!" Then they didn't even bother with the "Na Na Hey Heys."'

All three burst into a rousing chorus of 'Get Your Tits Out' to the tune of 'Na Na Hey Hey'.

Keren, being the only single one at this time, received the most attention.

'Someone said: "You haven't got a boyfriend, have you?"' she said. 'So they were all like: "Phwoarr!" When we went out the back afterwards they were all pretending it was their birthday so they could get a kiss.'

The high point of the evening was a dance contest that the Nanas had been elected to judge before heading onto the dance floor for a bit of a boogie themselves.

'I had the DJ trying to do The Bump with me,' said Keren with a roll of the eyes. 'I was so embarrassed. He put on "Ain't No Mountain High Enough" but he was awful. He kept missing all the beats. I had to just boogie backwards.

'But everyone was so excited about the night. They kept saying: "There's never any trouble here." Then they all got beat up. The manager and the area manager came back and one of them had a closed eye and the other had a bloody nose and a split lip. Apparently the same happened when The Bluebells played there. They said the same thing to them: "There's never any trouble here."'

The Bluebells and the Nanas had become good pals. Siobhan started dating songwriter/guitarist Robert Hodgens aka Bobby Bluebell soon after and their chart-topping 'Young at Heart' first appears on Bananarama's debut album.

After my interview, the girls were off to do a new Friday night music show, *Switch*, co-hosted by another pal of theirs – Capital Radio DJ Gary Crowley (Gary used to be the office boy at Decca Records when Siobhan was the receptionist). Talk of which got them thinking back to one of their earliest and most disastrous TV appearances on the late-night adult version of *Tiswas*, *OTT* (tragically not available on YouTube).

'My God, what was that like?' said Keren. 'Did you ever see it?

We've got it round the flat. It is so out of tune. We're jumping up and down. We were paralytic.'

'It was our second ever TV show,' said Siobhan. 'We just got stuck into the vodka. It was so embarrassing. That was in the days when we didn't have two halfpennies to rub together. We didn't have any clothes at all to do it in.'

'Apart from our spotted catsuits!' howled Keren. 'Polka dots. They were horrible.'

Financially they were still hardly rolling in it. The dream was to one day buy a flat each (the following year they all bought houses next to each other in Kentish Town like The Beatles), but at this point they'd have happily settled for a washing machine.

'We tried to nick one out of the laundry the other day!' said Keren.

They were at least off the dole. For all this, relations with their record company, London Records, sounded better than might have been expected.

'We got no advances,' said Keren. 'But they just let us get on with it. They've never suggested anything about what we wear. They just try to advise us on the records.'

'They've actually always been quite good about us,' agreed Siobhan. 'I think they didn't expect much. We signed up without an advance. They thought of us as just a throwaway thing but then something happened and since then they've been eating their words.'

Initially the group had been managed by the Boomtown Rats' manager Fachtna O'Kelly and then by the immensely patient Hillary Shaw (who would later take on the many entities of Girls Aloud), but at this point they were going it alone. Whoever was nominally 'in charge' of them, they were still very much marching to the beat of their own drum, even if that meant the odd altercation along the way.

'*Razzamatazz* [ITV's one afternoon pop show] won't have us on,' said Siobhan.

'I bet it was because we didn't crawl around the producers,' reckoned Keren. 'Siobhan jumped on my back in the middle of the recording and we had to do it again. She went careering across the stage.'

They revealed there was talk of them doing a pilot for their own TV show very much in the spirit of The Sour Grapes – the bunch of sixties' chicks on Hanna-Barbera's *The Banana Splits* who would freak out the four Splits (Fleegle, Bingo, Drooper and Snorky) with their cool shimmies.

'I'm sure if we did a show as ourselves no one would understand what we were laughing at,' said Keren. 'We come out with things that absolutely crack us up and no one else knows what we're on about. They all think we're laughing at them.'

Funnily enough this was one aspect of Bananarama that made me love them the most. Their tuts, eye rolls and bone dry asides set them apart – often to the point of exclusion – from most of their contemporaries. Find a green room or bar backstage at any pop TV show and chances are Bananarama would be housed in one corner with a bottle of vodka, taking the piss.

Partly it was their defence mechanism against a male-dominated industry, but there was also a healthy dose of dyed-in-the-wool punk ethic that had rubbed off on them from their time hanging out with the Sex Pistols – in particular Steve Jones and Paul Cook –

whose rehearsal room on Denmark Street had been Sarah and Keren's (and sometimes Siobhan's) previous abode.

Tales of their rat-infested squat are legion.

'There was a big pit outside our front door,' recalled Keren. 'One night it started moving. We had all these old polystyrene relics from *The Great Rock 'n' Roll Swindle* and they kept squeaking. I absolutely shit myself. It was so spooky there. It was pitch black and nobody else lived round there. We got some tourists to barge the door open and there were all these bloody skinheads hiding in the yard. One of them had got stuck in the pit.

'The pit was next to the outside toilet that didn't flush. We used to run round to the tube station [at Tottenham Court Road] to go to the toilet. At Denmark Street we didn't even have cold water when we first moved in. We had to go down and put a bucket under a dripping tap. We'd go down the Oasis [swimming baths on High Holborn, next to the *Melody Maker* offices] because they had hot baths down there. In between that we had to hang up a towel in our room and wash in a bowl on the floor. I don't think I better go into any more details. It was horrible. It was so wet. I used to get up for work in the morning [Keren was working in pensions at the BBC] and my clothes would be sopping wet. No wonder I had a bad back.'

The move to Babington Court (a council block adjacent to the one Spandau manager Steve Dagger shared with his mum and dad) was definitely a step up. But it was still not quite the pop palace you might have expected for chart regulars. The lift to the eleventh floor, when it was actually working, permanently smelled of wee. Heating in the flat was provided by a modest bar grill electric fire in the front room and phone calls were taken on a mounted pay phone in the hallway.

Their neighbours were also less than thrilled at the prospect of future *Guinness Book of Records* holders (as the UK's most successful girl group) living amongst them. Something that Keren discovered when she received a visit at four in the morning soon after they moved in.

'Siobhan and her boyfriend Jim (Reilly, Stiff Little Fingers drummer) had been having one of their many arguments,' said Keren, 'so Sarah and Mel had turned the music up loud to drown them out. Then I heard this knocking on the door so I asked who it was.

"It's Bill from downstairs!" The others hid so I got up innocently to answer the door.

"'Hello?"

"'Don't you hello me!"

"'Sorry, what do you mean?"

"'Don't give me that. You're joking, aren't you? That fucking music blaring! My wife has to get up five o'clock every morning. I knew you were going to be trouble the minute you fucking got in 'ere!"

"'Sorry, I don't know what you mean."

"'Don't fucking lie to me." He was waving his fists at me.

"'I'm the fucking chairman of the tenants' association. If you don't shut up you're out of 'ere. Petitions. The lot.'"

The lot did indeed include petitions. Jim Reilly had a shotgun stuck in his face and there was also an ongoing plan to burn down their front door (nothing to do with the tenants' association).

'It's lucky they didn't burn the door down,' said Keren, mistress of understatement. 'There was no escape on the eleventh floor.

What were we gonna do? Jump out the window? I was next to the washroom so I could have kicked the washroom window in and climbed round. What really worries me, though, is that I'm opposite the gas boiler. There was a huge explosion in the flats next door one morning. It was massive. I was stood by the window and I could feel it. The pressure from the explosion almost sucked me into it. But if that went it'd just blow me straight out the window.'

I got pretty well acquainted with Babington Court over the next year. Not long after, I started going out with Mel, who was every bit as caustic and funny and up for a night out as the other three. Actually, I say night out but although the Nanas prowess at drinking anyone under the table (even bands like Def Leppard) was legendary, in truth they were just as happy sitting in front of the telly watching *Blind Date*, *That's Life* or *Brookside* (they were big fans of the scraps between Sheila Grant and Marie Jackson and scallies Barry Grant and Terry Sullivan), picking fault with whoever was on, punctuated by riotous snorts of laughter.

Their favourite local was the Rugby, a tatty old corner pub where they would take board games like Monopoly and Frustration to while away the hours listening to Tom Jones on the jukebox or occasionally being furnished with the odd bit of hooky gear for the flat.

As our 'Cruel Summer' interview came to an end, Keren, in true Del Boy style, sweetly turned to me and offered to sort me out a new cut-price, no-questions-asked TV or video recorder.

'I'm not sure you should put that in the piece,' she said. 'But if there's anything you want, let us know!'

I say this was our second official Nanas' chat. Actually, I'd had a Friday lunchtime assignation back in April with Keren when we

kicked off another regular slot in *No.1* magazine – our 'Pop stars'
Blind Dates' feature.

The idea was to get two pop stars who had never met before and
– with the help of a bit of subterfuge by their record company PRs
– introduce them and see what happened. One pairing was Paul
Young and Paul Weller's Solid Bond signing Tracie Young (no re-
lation but a massive Paul Young fan since his Q Tips days), another
was Dee Snider of heavy metal band Twisted Sister and bee-hived
sixties throwback Mari Wilson.

First up, though, was the hot combo of Keren and George
Michael. Wham! were already doing well in the pop star on pop star
dating stakes – Shirlie Holliman was stepping out with Spandau's
Martin Kemp and Dee C. Lee was seeing Haysi Fantayzee's Jeremy
Healy. So how about someone for George? Surely there must be
some nice girl he fancied? I posited in the mag.

It had not got off to the best of starts. The night before, Spandau
had played the Albert Hall and after following those celebrations
with a trip to Steve Strange and Rusty Egan's massive new clubbing
emporium, Camden Palace, I'd got home to find some answerphone
messages from London Records press officer and all-round stand-up
gent Eugene Manzi, checking that everything was OK for the following day and to let him know if it wasn't.

Being by now slightly larupped, I may have misheard this last
directive. At three o'clock in the morning, I decided this was a
matter of some urgency so I better just let Keren know that everything was absolutely fine. As with Bill Downstairs, it was a weary
Keren who was the only one inclined to leave her bed to answer the
ringing phone and the next day, as we travelled down in the lift at

King's Reach Tower, Eugene explained to me that this was not the way to behave with the talent.

That settled, Keren, Eugene and I grabbed our table at the South of the Border restaurant (pretty much the only restaurant on the South Bank at that time and not a very good one at that) and ordered a round of vodka and oranges whilst we waited for her mystery date to reveal himself.

Keren was convinced it was one of Spandau. An hour later, when there was still no sign of anyone remotely famous entering the establishment, she looked like she might settle for a Belle Star. Thankfully just as we were giving up all hope, in breezed George with a pair of Walkman headphones round his neck and a suitably contrite expression on his face. The cab from his mum and dad's in Radlett had got stuck in traffic.

Considering that neither were exactly strangers to the Wag or the VIP top bar of the Palace, it was a surprise that they'd never met before. Keren had met Andrew Ridgely but admitted that the first time she'd had a hangover and the second time she'd been paralytic.

There was talk of fans. Wham! had one that sent Andrew angry letters about him dating Shirlie (pre-Martin Kemp) telling him that when she had found out he was seeing Shirlie she'd smoked twenty fags in a row – 'But just because I smoke don't think I'm common and easy!' Sadly there are no records of how she reacted when Andrew actually moved on to Keren a decade later.

Both groups had had their fair share of TV show run-ins over matters of quality control and general naffness. Wham! had binned a load of dancers on *American Bandstand* because the girls were wearing boob tubes and the blokes had white flared trousers, and the Nanas had got thoroughly trashed after a Munich TV show gave them girl dancers in little gold knickers and ponchos resulting in their record swiftly plummeting afterwards.

All too soon the liquid lunch (white wine for George) was over. Keren was off to do a satellite TV show with the other girls for David Frost, so there was just time to do some snaps in the restaurant's beer garden – George and Keren dressed down in jeans, me ridiculously overdressed in a black bolero hat. George then popped up to the *No.1* offices to give us a quick play of 'Bassline' (later 'A Ray of Sunshine'), a funky little offering from their forthcoming debut album, *Fantastic*. George sticking his cassette into our prehistoric hi-fi system trilling out through tinny little speakers while everyone else tried to 'get on with their work' is an enduring image of a less polished time in pop.

It would be remiss not to recall one other unexpected Bananarama encounter from this period concerning one of the tracks from their long-time coming second album and eventual Top Five single, 'Robert De Niro's Waiting'.

All three Nanas were equal parts De Niro and Al Pacino fans. The small stack of VHSs in their front room included *Dog Day Afternoon*, both *Godfather* movies, *Mean Streets* and *Serpico*. Before *Scarface* opened I'd even managed to wangle them into a press screening in a tiny viewing theatre on Wardour Street where the sight of Al's Tony Montana disco dancing had so amused Sarah and Keren that they'd collapsed the chairs they were sitting on. When Pacino appeared onstage in David Mamet's *American Buffalo* we of course bought tickets.

What was not expected, though, was that they would ever get to actually meet either of their movie star crushes. 'Cruel Summer' had given them a big US hit, thanks to its inclusion in *The Karate Kid*, so it wasn't beyond the realms of possibility that they were on their radar. Best case scenario, they reckoned, was maybe a signed photo might at some stage come their way.

Instead of which, Robert De Niro took Bananarama to Kettner's for pizza.

Amongst the many tragedies of the erosion of old Soho is the loss of Kettner's – a collection of four Georgian town houses (now absorbed by Soho House) that dated back to the nineteenth century and had seen everyone from Oscar Wilde, Lillie Langtry and Edward VII pass through its portals. Upstairs in the Grade II listed building were private rooms for sumptuous parties, whilst to your left as you entered was the champagne bar – exceedingly popular with *No.1's* writers of a Friday night – and to the right the brasserie where reasonably-priced pizzas (with a £1 levy on the Veneziana to the Venice in Peril fund) came with an accompanying pianist.

Mel's boyfriend I might have been, but that hardly qualified me (nor sadly Mel) for a place at the table. Even the girls' fellas – massive Travis Bickle, Vito Corleone and Johnny Boy fans one and all – had to eat on the other side of the room. Naturally the Nanas, being in a state of high excitement, hit the bevvies and by the time they decided to move on to the Zanzibar wine bar in Covent Garden, they were completely lashed. The evening ended with a hammered Sarah throwing up outside the bar whilst big Bob swooped for a hasty and unfortunately timed smooch.

Despite the distinct lack of romance, this didn't entirely dampen his ardour. Hence, a few Saturdays later when the pay phone rang in Babington Court and for once it was neither a pissed me nor an angry neighbour, but Robert Ruddy De Niro wanting to speak to Sarah.

I would love to say I had the presence of mind to switch on my trusty tape recorder to at least capture for posterity Sarah's end of what turned out to be a fairly lengthy conversation, but it was late on a Saturday night and it is possible we'd all had a couple of ales. Instead, Mel and I amused ourselves with a spot of how's your father in Keren's bedroom, a picture of Al from *Serpico* above her bed and De Niro (well, his disembodied voice at least) chuntering down the line outside her door.

So that's the closest I get to involving Robert De Niro in my pop memoirs.

9

IF WE TOOK A HOLIDAY

No.1's 'Blind Dates' had been the magazine's first attempt to make the new pop idols more accessible to our readers, but the features idea that really swung it was Phil McNeill's 'Journey to the Stars'. 'Meet your favourite artists on the holiday of a lifetime' we proclaimed, and with three carefully clipped coupons and a cheeky photo caption you too could be sunning yourself with the pop star of your choice.

Twenty-one-year-old Debbie Jones from Brighton spent three days in the South of France hanging out with Wham! while they recorded their second album, *Make It Big*, at Chateau Miraval. The fact that the recording studio was in the middle of a vineyard may account for the amount of time Andrew Ridgeley spent hungover in bed while George did most of the heavy lifting. Still, that didn't stop Debbie slotting in a photo shoot with the Butch and Sundance of pop in the hay barn immortalised on the sleeve of 'Everything She Wants'. She also copped an exclusive earful of their next single 'Freedom' and a surprise working men's club rendition of 'Careless Whisper', and landed the hot scoop that Wham! were planning a fifteen-minute mini-movie for their forthcoming Christmas single. She even got a taste of Mr Ridgeley's vaunting Formula 1 ambitions when he whisked her and George off on a seat-of-your-pants drive at breakneck speed through the pouring rain to Brignole. An adventure which ended safely but on a slight downer when their favourite restaurant proved to be fully-booked, despite their very best pop star protestations.

Not every young winner was so bowled over by these once-in-a-lifetime prizes. Fifteen-year-old Martin Hansford from Camberley got his golden ticket to meet the Thompson Twins in New York, but his first question on meeting his *No.1* chaperone, Karen Swayne, at the airport was not about Tom, Alannah or Joe, but whether they would be flying Concorde or not? Clearly his part-time job in a local newsagent's was better paid than one might have expected.

Fifteen-year-old Mary Gee from Stockport was thankfully more appreciative of her chance to fly to Milan with our Debbi Voller to meet Howard Jones. The new addition to the eighties pop firmament was throwing off his (and mime sidekick, Jed's) mental chains and performing at a star-studded festival on Lake Garda where the likes of Tina Turner and Billy Idol could also be seen strolling by, adding extra wattage to Mary's trip. She did admit to Debbi that she didn't actually fancy Howard, she just thought he looked a bit friendlier than most of the current crop. HoJo duly confirmed his amiability factor by buying her a pastel pink jumper from Benetton, but the photos of the pair of them feeding ducks, standing in a piazza, and holding a shrub did look a bit like they could have been snapped in his native High Wycombe.

Angie White, a Twining's computer data operator from Andover, got to hang out with Paul Young in Milan. Another, Joanne Harland, made it all the way to Japan with Frankie Goes to Hollywood.

Simon Le Bon spared us a health and safety nightmare by mercifully not taking any competition winners as crew on his ill-fated Whitbread Round the World Yacht Race (the boat sank).

Instead he treated Sian Wood and Tracy James from Bethnal Green to lunch in a mock-up restaurant (with non-mock-up food and champers) at *No.1* photographer Mike Prior's studio in sunny Wandsworth where the Duran frontman proudly revealed to the two Duranies that he'd recently made his first ever political statement by demanding the VAT be removed from Band Aid's single *and* bought then fiancé Claire Stansfield (Yasmin Parvaneh was just around the corner) *The Good Housekeeping Guide to Shepherd's Pie* for Christmas, thereby feeding both the world and his potential wife.

Of course, no such competition would have been complete without a spot of shameless globetrotting with the Spands. After the international success of 'True' – their first US Top 10 hit – their next album, *Parade*, saw them setting their sights on more extensive world domination.

The album's cover shoot, inspired by Gary Kemp's interest in the Diaghilev ballet with a nod to Peter Blake's *Sergeant Pepper* cover, featured a parade of characters. Carmen Miranda, American majorettes, harlequins, a New Orleans jazz band, a Chinese dragon and a posse of banner-carrying Trade Union leaders – a cast made up of old friends and family like Chris Sullivan, fan club secretary Jacqui Quaife and the Spandau dads, alongside current pop pin-ups Samantha Fox, Patsy Kensit and *Blue Peter*'s Sarah Greene and a certain *No.1* journalist whose left ear is about the only thing visible on the album cover apart from an Uncle Sam top hat and a massive drum.

For some reason, when it came to Spandau's 'Journeys to the Stars' I was the only writer Phil deemed in need of a substantial pep talk with a quietly concerned dep. ed Lynn Hanna by his side, before I could be trusted to leave British soil with one of our precious readers. Just to make doubly sure that I didn't lose them in Duty Free or palm them off the night before with a couple of beers down the Wag, I also had Julia Marcus along in her new triple capacity as record company press officer, minder of competition winner and *No.1* hack.

As it happened, it was nearly twenty-four hours before we lost Manchester's nineteen-year-old Julie Siddall in Lisbon. Thankfully, we found her doing exactly what any sensible girl would do after breakfast if she'd won a competition to meet Spandau in the Med. She was sunbathing by the pool with Martin Kemp.

Other than that, our three days in Portugal went off pretty much without a hitch. The band proved to be a gracious bunch when it came to their younger fans. Apart from her poolside chilling with Martin, Julie hit the dance floor with them at two of Lisbon's top nightspots – the Dela Rosa and the Juke Box – received a comprehensive dissertation from Gary Kemp on his current read – Phillip Norman's biography of The Rolling Stones – over a glass or two of fizz, rode co-pilot in the cockpit with Tony Hadley on the flight home, and was treated to a non-stop barrage of cartoon impressions – from Tom and Jerry to Wile E. Coyote falling off a cliff – by her eventual favourite Steve Norman.

While Julie filled her boots, I caught up with Dagger, who was amused by the fact that every foreign city they now visited always included a scene where the local promoter would take them to the trendiest nightclub and solemnly introduce its host as 'The Steve Strange of Lisbon/Paris/Barcelona' (delete where applicable). His boys might have left their kilts, bandanas and tea cloths far behind, but in Europe New Romanticism was still alive and kicking.

Fun though Lisbon was, an ever-competitive Dagger reckoned

Spandau could top it and any other prize their rivals might offer for that matter. So, to the great delight of fifteen-year-old Janine Brindle from Bolton and twenty-two-year-old P. Simper from Burbage, they did.

The one country where Spandau had enjoyed great early and continued success as far back as 1981 without actually visiting was Australia. Luckily for them, in this new video age, their pop promos and a lot of 'Hi, this is Spandau' TV links had so far done the job for them. But by the time of *Parade* the demand Down Under was fit to burst.

Shirlie Holliman, soon-to-be Kemp, had been reporting back to Martin just how pop-starved and thoroughly up for it the Aussies were after Wham!'s recent tour there, and now with the Spands having kicked things off in Sydney, I was being regaled by a well-tanned and white T-shirted Dagger at Christos Tolera and Simon Withers' Friday night Soho watering hole, Chez les Anges, on the extent of the fun to be had. The whole tour was being run by top Aussie promoter Paul Dainty, a softly spoken maverick originally from the UK, who had made his name bringing what he described as 'Event entertainment' acts like The Rolling Stones, Fleetwood Mac, ABBA and Yes to Oz in the seventies, and was now working the same principle with Wham!, Spandau, Bowie and others in the eighties.

This event entertainment aspect stretched impressively far beyond the shows themselves, as Spandau were discovering. Each night after they'd waved goodbye to the screaming thousands, a top-floor suite had been sorted in the band's hotel with a large bin filled to the brim with champagne on ice standing in one corner and a lot of very thirsty people comprising the band, girlfriends, friends and family, and a selection of models from the top local agencies in the other.

This, of course, was not quite the place for a fifteen-year-old to be spending her nights (however much she might have wanted to) so after a couple of glasses of fizz (well, she was on her holidays), Janine would be escorted back to her room by Donna from Festival Records (the group's Aussie label) before the fun was taken up a notch or two. In retrospect, it wasn't only Janine who was being shielded from some of the wilder partying. Although I had spent the last three years frequenting the same clubs as Spandau, my socialising was still predominantly with Dagger rather than the band – or 'my boys' as he used to call them – and so although there were powders a-plenty being snuffled up in various adjacent hotel suites, the most I got a whiff of anything irregular was a Gary Kemp 'special' cigarette.

Not that I was complaining. Between the champagne bin and the friendly natives, there was more than enough for an impressionable lad to be going on with. To make things even sweeter, Dagger and the boys had decided to double the length of mine and Janine's stay – out of their own pockets since they were in the middle of an increasingly bitter dispute with Chrysalis over their lack of any subsequent success in America after 'True'.

It was a tough ten days at the Melbourne Hilton. In the hours when everyone wasn't still recovering from the night before, Janine accompanied her pop stars to the zoo (where a less appreciative eucalyptus-leaf-deprived koala nipped Gary and peed on Normsk), enjoyed a private screening of *Beverly Hills Cop* (plus *Tom and Jerry* cartoons with Steve Norman overdubs) and took in a Springsteen *Born in the USA* four-hour marathon, along with 40,000 others, at the

MCG. Sadly, neither Janine nor myself was privy to the subsequent Spandau/Springsteen summit up in The Boss' hotel suite, which left the Spands pretty giddy and compelled to go off shooting .44 Magnums and pump-action shotguns for an afternoon (as you do).

Despite my confident assertion in the mag that Spandau were now developing into 'a fine pop/rock band', the new rock poses that accompanied their regulation mid-eighties pop star Yohji Yamamoto wardrobe were an unexpected gear change considering all the anti-rock assertions of their past (no hidden acoustic guitars here!). But Australia was certainly the place to give vent to it. *Beverly Hills Cop*'s soft rock and soul soundtrack of Glen Frey and the Pointer Sisters and Don Henley's 'The Boys of Summer' was everywhere and the after-show party playlist was as much Led Zep, The Who and the Steve Miller Band as it was Rufus and Chaka Khan with 'Ain't Nobody'.

The final night continued all the way through to breakfast with a spectacular food fight – leaving the top-floor suite with an interesting new club sandwich layer of carpeting – before we bundled onto the flight home with possibly over-optimistic plans to hook up with everyone else for the rest of the Easter bank holiday in Bournemouth as soon as we landed.

I had tried in vain to share my good fortune with Graham and Lol, and one particular night, I was enjoying a plate of oysters and a bottle of bubbly with an Aussie lass at about the time I imagined they were settling into their less salubrious seaside B & B. But international dialling codes, the Hilton's phone system and my general inability to see straight had defeated me. In the end ten days of indelible memories – and for Janine a *No.1* cover and four-page feature – was probably enough.

Not that getting up close and personal with pop stars always went to plan. A London-based hook-up with Madness where the Nutty Boys gave a guided tour of their beloved Camden Town to one lucky recipient appeared to have worked a treat until our winner let slip to Karen Swayne at the end of their fun-packed day that she hadn't actually entered this competition at all. She explained that she entered so many comps that when she got the phone call from *No.1*, she just assumed it was one she'd forgotten about. Unfortunately, in an unusual burst of efficiency, Karen had also written to the correct competition winner to notify her, and she was soon on the phone demanding to know when her day out with North London's Nuttiest was happening. Hats off to Madness and Stiff's equally accommodating press officer Jamie Spencer that they repeated the whole treat again with her and a pal.

On other occasions, it was not the momentous competition prize that didn't go quite to plan – it was the supposedly common or garden interview.

Which brings us to Madonna. Along with all the 'Blind Dates' and 'Journeys to the Stars' came another idea of how to mix and match pop's big new names for the amusement of our readers. With the mag residing initially in the same building – King's Reach Tower on London's South Bank – as such pre-teen IPC titles as *Oh Boy!* and *My Guy* it seemed fitting to do some mock-up photo love tales of our own. Two of *No.1*'s staff writers, Debbi Voller and Anne Lambert (nee Annie Wood), had of course started out on those mags so knew the drill. Debbi had even appeared in a genuine photo love story with a likely looking pair of young male models by the names of David Austin and George Michael.

So it was tasked to me to come up with a suitable story involving

Shalamar's Jeffrey Daniel and some new WEA girl vocalist whose black-and-white picture had landed on my desk along with a not particularly inspiring double A side 'Burning Up' and 'Physical Attraction' – the follow-up to 'Everybody', her hit-free debut. Sporting a pork-pie hat and copping plenty of attitude to camera as she leaned back sunning herself in the tall grass, Madonna looked like any number of would-be pop stars bubbling around the bottom of the charts that weren't Kim Wilde. Two singles in and quite possibly destined for obscurity (the fact that WEA supremo Seymour Stein had personally signed her and she was already making a lot of noise on the New York club scene had somehow escaped me), she did at least seem perfect in the short term to play the love interest in a piss-taking *No.1* spread.

The story I'd come up with was pretty straightforward: American chick on her first night out in London goes for dinner at ornate, medium-priced Soho pizza joint Kettner's and happens across some geek with a pair of tickets to see Jeffrey Daniel at the Lyceum. Pizzas consumed, she ditches the geek and is all over Daniel until his incessant moon-walking and body-popping whilst drinking at the bar gets on her tits. A little wiser, she heads off into the night with her new-found geeky guy. The End.

With the thumbs up from their record companies, a date was set for Friday, 14 October 1983, when Jeffrey Daniels was indeed doing a PA at the Lyceum and Madonna was over having made her UK live debut the previous night with a three-song PA of 'Everybody', 'Burning Up' and 'Holiday' at the Camden Palace, complete with backing dancers, crucifix and crop top.

So where did it all go wrong?

My big mistake, I think, was turning up to meet Madonna

The ecstasy and agony of 1970s schoolboy pop life.

And then twenty-two weeks of mournful silence . . .

Photo by Bridget Campbell

The last of the Geldof jumpers as NCTJ rookie Jane Moore mee the Wiltshire Massive aka Amanda 'Mond Saunders, Alex Tofield, Ant Wa and Bridget Campbell.

50p New Romantics and fledgling *Melody Maker* and *Record Mirror* stringers, with Gary Hurr.

No clown outfit but headbands and blusher make it to Burbage to 'dazzle' Guilietta Edwards, Teresa and Marietta Harrow.

Mr Smith teaches his new flatmate the art of the Shirland Road Pose.

New Sounds, New Styles rebel writers Elms, Johnson and Smith frown at the very thought of Duran, 1982.

Shillelagh hairdo menaced by
Boz and Phil Polecat.

Shillelagh's sea-front rescue
of Jacqs.

Old hand Graham and new
blood Lol preserve the well
established order of
Bournemouth daytime
drinking.

The only recorded evidence of Pride, under the arches at Heaven for Oxford Road Show promo.

Next stop, Radio City Music Hall . . .

In '82 downtown New York you could always count on meeting a man with a duck.

Photo by Fraser Gray

A DREAM JOB WITHOUT REALLY KNOW

Tea at Mrs Simper's.

Spot the knitted frog . . .

Matchmaker and match-mated, Patsy Peapod and Beatrice.

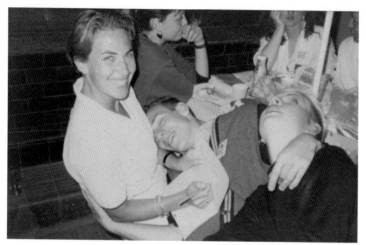

'Bit of a crush' Stella 'Belle Star' Barker klaxon.

Robert 'Bobby Bluebell' Hodgens takes delivery of the 22nd birthday boy at The Columbia.

Julie Siddall journeys to the stars, then dances with them (once Simper gets out of the way).

Pep talk, schmep talk.

Eucalyptus deprived koala assesses targets.

Ye Olde Laughing Stock.

A lesser spotted McCall,
captured by Jacqs.

Woh, oh, Joe Batty!
Ruthers and Joe
in Blackpool.

Everybody wigs good
Neighbours. Time to leave,
Mr Dennis, December 1988.

'See you at the premiere!'
Patsy welcomes various
Laughing Stock to the
Absolute Beginners party.

Belle Star Miranda Joyce
and (Tits 'n') Bum Star
Samantha Fox.

'If I see one more Red Devil . . .' *Faith* party at The Savoy, 1987.

Below left: First I play it, then I dance to it.

Below right: Madame Cyn and Emily Lloyd storm Brown's.

Incog. carolling. George and David, 1986.

Trying hard not to stare at George and Mrs S at Maximus, December 1993.

To cut a long story short, Tone made it backstage.

Hair by Sam McKnight.

Left: Slippry Feet Theme video shoot.

Below: Our fabulous dancers, Emma, Siobhan, Jody and Bayo.

Sue Tilley and Louise Ramsey collar Les Dennis at Jongleurs.

Mrs S picnics with Lucy and Alice Temple.

Put on your Slippry Feet . . .

already dressed as the geek. My later incarnation as freak boy rubbish magician Master Gerald in Lenny Beige's Regency Rooms revue was still a decade or more away, but for those of you who are familiar with that, this look was basically a cross between Gerald and *Grease*'s prom school geek Eugene with a bit of Charles Hawtrey thrown in for good measure. All matted down hair, NHS glasses and tweed jacket.

When WEA's head of press, the formidable Barbara Charone, gave me the once-over before taking me backstage to meet Madonna, she kindly kept her counsel. But as Madge herself clocked the fool in front of her and offered the most non-committal of greetings, I think it's fair to say my chances of walking off into the sunset with the Queen of Pop to 'Holiday, Celebrate', or anything else plummeted pretty much to zero.

To her credit, BC did her best to keep the whole thing afloat, calmly walking me to the stage door and suggesting we try again the following day in Paris, where Madonna was due to play the Fiorucci party and I was covering Gary Kemp's birthday.

In a packed Parisian nightclub, I once again got to see Madge and her lithesome lads gyrating away and turning the heads of even the most uber-cool fashionista. But as I looked down from the balcony in my now geek-free clobber, I realised my photo-love opportunity was gone. The next time I saw her, there were about 50,000 of us in Wembley stadium. Unless you count those photo strips with Naomi Campbell and Vanilla Ice in her *Sex* book, I don't think she's done anything approaching a photo-love story since.

10

MOTHER'S PRIDE

Bananarama weren't the first eighties pop folk to venture down to my mum and dad's.

Two years previous, a former St Martin's student now giving it a go as a singer in a seven-piece north-London funk band, had driven down in her dilapidated old Wolsey after a hard night's Soho clubbing. With her style commentator boyfriend crashed out on the back seat and me riding shotgun as she nursed, cajoled and threatened her trusty chariot down the M4, we'd arrived just in time to catch a startled Mrs S, still in her nightie and slippers, bringing in the milk from the back porch.

Save for a holiday to Durban in the early seventies, I don't think Mrs Simper had ever come face to face with anyone as exotic as Nigerian-born, Clacton-on-Sea and West-Bergholt-raised, Helen Folasade Adu.

Not that Mother rolled out the red carpet for her. Sade was still a long way off being rubber-stamped with her first *Top of the Pops* appearance. Mrs S had no inkling that one of the most iconic stars of the decade was kipping in her spare room and smoking a fag or three out back with my dad. She was just a girl in a band (called Pride) that nobody had heard of.

When we were invited up the road by Mum and Dad's farming pals for Sunday lunch drinks, people took a polite interest in 'this music thing' that myself and Bob Elms (Sade wasn't one for blowing her own trumpet) were talking up. But their looks suggested this was all a bit pie-in-the-sky and the chances that they'd be hearing any more about it seemed unlikely.

If afternoon tea with the comedy tea pot was the potential flashpoint for the Nanas' visit, it was Sunday lunch that proved to be high noon where Bob, Sade and Mrs Simper were concerned. Card-carrying Labour Party member that he was, Bob did not see eye to eye with true blue, Maggie and Enoch supporter Mrs S on pretty much anything.

Whether it's quite the 'done thing' to engage in a forthright exchange of political views with your hostess whilst tucking into her Sunday roast is debatable, but Mrs S's dogmatic views on the unions ('Lock 'em up!') and Britain's 3 million unemployed ('On their bikes!') would in fairness have tested the patience of a saint. Considerate lass that she is, Sade did her best to prevent World War III breaking out before the summer pudding arrived.

At least on this occasion there was no painful pub stare-a-thon. Instead, on the Saturday night we'd headed, with a few of my country pals, in convoy to Salisbury for what the *Wiltshire Gazette and Herald* had billed rather thrillingly as a 'Videotheque Disco'. The reality was more your usual bog standard disco but with a tiny mounted telly on the wall and a smattering of Duran Duran and Ultravox videos on heavy rotation whenever someone remembered to rewind the tape.

Still, it can't have been too terrible a weekend. The last time I saw Sade, the first thing she asked was how my mum was. Much the same, was the answer.

I owed her and Bob plenty. When I first moved to London I

couldn't have been more grateful for the existence of their north London home tucked away in multi-cultural Wood Green on the Noel Park Estate.

Their old sofa didn't exclusively have my name on it – fresh-down-from-Hull saxophonist Stuart Matthewman was pretty much clothed, housed and fed by them over the same period – but on the occasions I was invited back, I took some shifting. Sade reckoned that a pair of my old socks stuck around even longer than me until she ceremonially buried them, like high-grade plutonium, in the back garden.

I was never so bold as to turn up unannounced, but if Bob suggested a home viewing of an under-the-counter video of *Texas Chainsaw Massacre* or *The Hills Have Eyes* that he'd got his mitts on in Soho (I'd discovered in my early days in London there was a black market for everything), then I was more than up for it.

From 1982 to 1984, Graham Smith was both my landlord and, with Lorraine, my principal partner-in-crime. For my very first month in London, though, I'd been kindly taken in by two Beat Route regulars, Maureen Walsh and Lesley Walker – a social worker and nurse from Manchester and Leeds respectively – who lived in New Cross Gate and were also mates of Lol's. Not only did they put a roof over my head during one of the country's most sub-zero snow-bound Januarys, but they also polished me up to a presentable standard on the dance floor.

Not everyone on the club scene danced – pop management were more likely to huddle than hit the floor – but for someone still finding his way, it was an exuberant shortcut to making friends and meeting girls. One of Sade's early songs, 'Maureen', nails the value of some nifty moves succinctly – 'He looks good/Let's hope he can dance.'

Maureen and Lesley drilled me in the club jive that the Wham! boys and girls honed on that same Beat Route dance floor. Then, job done, they gave me the gentlest of pushes in the direction of Earls Court and a bedsit on Penywern Road. It was tiny with a shower at one end and a single bed. Just wide enough to fit a record player, but not a telly. As a result, my TV viewing, till I moved into Graham's five months later, was mostly round Bob and Sade's at 64 Hewitt Avenue. And that wasn't the only social interaction I got there.

Despite Maureen and Lesley's kind tutelage, fancy footwork or no fancy footwork, my success rate with girls in those early days in London had been a resounding zilch. I'd developed a bit of a crush on Maureen, who would let me snuggle up in her bed when it was particularly cold. But despite me trying to win her heart by writing to the *NME* to offer my services as a male feminist writer and buying Rhoda's 'The Boiler' and listening to it a lot (it really was quite a crush), I'd got nowhere.

All this changed one Thursday night out clubbing when I found myself being snogged by a stunning, fiery-eyed lass called Georgia. I guess if you hung around with Sade for long enough, things were eventually going to improve. Before I knew it, it was all back to Wood Green for more bootleg vids and a makeshift love nest on their living room floor. If the earth moved for Georgia it would have only been because she happened to cough in that fleeting instant. Whatever my shortcomings, by the time an amused Sade brought me a mug of celebratory tea the following morning, I was walking a little taller.

*

Neither my sex life nor my telly viewing habits were of primary importance to the residents at no. 64 by the spring of 1982, though, when Bob and Lee Barrett started talking up this new band that 'Shard' was in called Pride. Stuart Matthewman was also involved, as were fellow Hull lads drummer Paul Cooke and bass player Paul Denman.

Back in Hull, Stuart had been in The Odds, a pop/mod band similar to The Piranhas that had started out doing speeded-up punk versions of sixties hits like The Dave Clark Five's 'Glad All Over'. He then played sax in a ten-piece Elvis impersonator show called *Ravin' Rupert*, which covered the whole spectrum of The King's career from rockabilly to Vegas delivered by a front man sporting a quiff and wearing Rupert-the-Bear checked trousers. A tad cooler was Paul Cooke and Paul Denman's prog rock band, The Posers, which Stuart credits as being the only band in Hull trying to do something new at that time.

As for Sade, her singing career had only begun a few months previous when she sang onstage for the first time as part of another London band, Ariva. Considering Ariva were viewed as a bit of a Blue Rondo rip-off, ironically it was on the way to a Rondo gig on Barry Island that Lee first clocked Sade singing along to the radio and asked her if she could sing. She thought she probably could so said yes.

That wasn't quite the done deal. Some of the more sceptical members of Ariva needed two auditions before they were convinced, whilst Sade herself was contemplating other career options (since leaving St Martin's School of Art she'd already designed menswear for Axiom and modelled – 'The worst job known to man').

Now she was thinking of giving *Fear of Flying*'s Erica Jong a run for her money in the racy novel stakes.

'I'd just bought a couple of her books and I thought I could do it,' she said pragmatically.

Erotic fiction's loss was music's gain as she settled in next to Ariva's two other singers, Barbara Robinson and Nick Moxsom, who, like Lee, hailed from Barnet. Barbara's vocals were more Streisand smooth than Sade's smokey soul husk, while Nick's rough-and-ready rasp leaned towards the more strident end of funk. But it didn't take any of them long to realise that it was time for a change.

Nineteen eight-one's crazed summer of zooted-up Latin sounds had been replaced by harder street funk and rap like The Valentine Brothers' 'Money's Too Tight to Mention' and Grandmaster Flash's 'The Message'. So Ariva became Pride with new songs like 'Man-handled' and 'Ecstasy' written with the one other key player to jump ship from Ariva, their principal songwriter and guitarist, Mile End boy Ray St John.

But following the well-trodden path of Spandau, Visage, Blue Rondo, Haysi Fantayzee, Animal Nightlife and Culture Club as the next London clubland band wasn't looking like quite the walk in the park it had been. Neither Blue Rondo nor Animal Nightlife had set the charts alight, Haysi's follow-up to 'John Wayne Is Big Leggy' – 'Holy Joe' – had flopped, Visage's follow-up to their debut album had underperformed, Spandau themselves were pinning their future on a Trevor Horn remix, and Culture Club had reached 114 and 100 respectively in the UK with their first two singles 'White Boy' and 'I'm Afraid of Me' with 'Do You Really Want to Hurt Me' still a distant six months away.

Would the record companies go for another trendy London band? In fact, would London itself go for another trendy London band?

'There's definitely room for our group,' said Sade in one of our first taped interviews from that time. 'I don't think there's an awful lot of, er, exciting happenings coming from British bands. The most interesting thing, considering the way the charts have been going, is Dexys returning [their second album *Too-Rye-Ay* was out] and Grandmaster Flash with that single. But London audiences don't like to be told what to like.'

The decision was made to keep things under the radar with low-key gigs in St Albans, West Hampstead, Windsor, Southall and Barnet. But Lee, like Steve Dagger, loved the challenge of coming at things differently. If Spandau had done battleships and botanical gardens and Blue Rondo Latin American festivals and bank holiday Bournemouths, Pride would perversely take things to the other end of the spectrum with the most unsexy West End venue imaginable. Lee booked them into the Marquee.

'Playing the Marquee was a statement that we could play any-where,' said Lee in the same interview. 'We were being accused left, right and centre of being another group with this master plan to play select venues, only allowing your friends to come along and becoming extremely overhyped.'

And so, London's latest hip and happening thing followed in the unlikely footsteps of UK Subs, Hanoi Rocks, Marillion, Spider and The Truth, and did the Marquee. There were some hilariously grumpy club folk chuntering away about the pissy beer served in plastic cups in a venue few had visited (unless they'd been to see The Polecats) since punk days. Still, it got people talking. As did the night Pride rolled up outside Le Beat Route on the back of a lorry at two in the morning playing a couple of numbers and holding up the traffic as people hurried up onto the street to see what all the fuss was about.

My favourite Lee-style thinking outside the box was when Pride played Ronnie Scott's. He judiciously scattered likely looking paper wraps all around Camden Palace. Anyone picking one up might have been disappointed by the lack of powders inside but it got their attention.

There were some aspects of the Spandau blueprint, though, that Lee wasn't about to throw out the window, particularly the opportunity to place Pride in a more international setting. Hence their trip, in September 1982, to New York.

Sade, Bob and Lee had all been before. In fact, it was where Bob and Sade had first got together when Spandau's and London's scene-making gang of twenty-one (in age and number) had taken Manhattan the previous year with a gig and fashion show at the Underground. Sade was designing for Axiom, the fashion collective run by Jon 'Mole' Baker – another Blitz Kid making his name.

As usual, Lee had his own slightly perverse spin on it.

'We want to have as little association with England as possible,' he said. 'I've always hated the way that English bands have gone over there with a really big hype and rammed it down New Yorkers' throats. I've always thought New Yorkers have resented this. We want people to just come along, hopefully enjoy it and make up their own minds. I feel that could stand us in good stead and be a good foundation for making friends.'

'Making friends' turned out to be more of a key phrase than I'd imagined. No Simper family member had ever ventured to New

York before so my mum in particular was keen to know where I might be staying in this city that never slept.

Bob had managed to wangle himself, Sade and Ollie O'Donnell rooms at The Excelsior overlooking Central Park, courtesy of Island Records boss Chris Blackwell. Chris had been an early Spandau convert when he'd showed up by the mixing desk of their first ever Blitz gig and offered Dagger a deal after only three numbers. Ollie was getting married on 42nd Street to Michelle Young, a gal with a steepling quiff every bit as impressive as his own.

For myself and the rest of the band, the accommodation options were a little more freewheeling. 'Meet people,' Lee told us. So we did. A wedding reception at Danceteria proved ideal for getting to know the exceedingly friendly native New Yorkers. Within a matter of hours, they had taken us to their bosom, squirreling us away like so many acorns across the length and breadth of Manhattan in various states of undress and delight.

I discovered that New York girls were a lot more forthright than their British counterparts.

'New York girls give the best blow jobs in the world,' my hostess for the evening informed me at the end of a very long first night.

I learned a lot that week, much of it unprintable, but as an introduction to what remains for me the most thrilling city on earth, I couldn't have done better than to have shared it with Lee, Bob, Sade and Pride. Living on 99c slices of pizza and brown-paper-bagged liquor store beer by day, embraced by all manner of attentive folk by night, we covered as much ground as was humanly possible. From the previously noted 'delights' of the Anvil and the Hell Fire Club (as mentioned to the Wham! boys) in the Lower West Side's meatpacking district, through two well-received nights of Pride at

Danceteria and Joe Bowie's Defunkt at the Peppermint Lounge to breakdancing and Double Dutch crews at the Roxy.

Our Hard Times gear with the obligatory leathers, Levi's and biker boots caused some cultural confusion. Whilst drinking in a bar across from the Roxy, myself and Stuart Matthewman were propositioned by a couple of gargantuan leather-clad bears who towered over us, licking their lips as they enquired, 'Wanna go to the Eagle's Nest?' Who, what or where this eagle was nesting we were too dumbstruck to ask.

To help fund the trip, I had managed to set up a couple of interviews. Still in *Maker*-mode, I was momentarily able to escape from the heat in air-conditioned record company offices with founding Kool & the Gang member Robert Bell, and then downtown on Lexington at the Gramercy Park Hotel with avant garde jazz saxophonist James White, who Bob had been raving about since Ze Records had released 'Contort Yourself'. Breezing down the street with my trusty boogie box blasting out a freebie cassette of Kool's latest single, 'Let's Go Dancin' (Ooh La La La)', I could not have felt more at one with the world.

After a few early forays, most of Pride had ended up in Mole's loft down on Pitt Street and Lafayette in Alphabet City. Some precious floor space up on 14th that had been kindly offered to myself, Bob and Barbara by a local photographer, Bob Curithers, hadn't gone down so well with Babs – when a few residing cockroaches scurried out to greet her there was an ear-splitting shriek and Barnet's finest was off.

A photo session was arranged out and about around Pitt Street. Surrounded by the rubble of one half-decimated block of tenements, the band posed against a conveniently upended and abandoned Chevy, capturing the Hard Times trend possibly a little too realistically. Every so often some poor soul would emerge from one of the burned-out buildings, traipsing across the bricks and broken bottles looking for sustenance of one kind or another. Standing amongst the debris with a fawn tassel jacket slung over her shoulder, I'm not sure it occurred to Sade that three years from now she'd be returning to this city triumphant with her own sell-out show at Radio City Music Hall.

Once back in London, the advancement of Pride continued. I'd already done an introductory two-pager in the last-gasp June issue of *New Sounds New Styles* (where they pitched Gary Kemp as a suitable producer, citing 'Chant No.1' as an influence) and a *Maker* review of the West Hampstead Moonlight gig ('Away from the hullaballoo a new sound is growing'). Now post-New York, I got together with Sade and Lee at Hewitt Avenue for the latest updates.

That it was Lee and Sade doing the talking, rather than frontman Nick or songwriters Ray and Stuart (Sade was already writing lyrics), was a fair indication of where Pride was coming from. Despite its high Hull quotient, this was a London club band – a north London club band – with Sade the tastemaker and Lee, like Dagger with Spandau, the one making sure they remained allied to the current scene.

Sadly, much further down the line Lee and Sade would end up in years of litigation with a final settlement decreeing that neither can now talk about the other. But at this stage they were very much a united force, even if Lee did insist on jumping in to answer some of the more delicate, deal-related points, much to Sade's amusement ('Just in case I say the wrong thing!').

There was much work still to be done. A pre-New York show at

The Fridge in Brixton, beset by sound problems, had not been their big London moment. And although there had been some record company interest, there was a feeling that people were being a bit slow to bite.

'Presumably what we did in New York has given the record companies a bit of a kick up the backside,' said Sade. 'But the sad thing is that record companies don't always see talent. In fact, they probably very rarely recognise talent. There is an awful lot that gets washed away and ignored simply because the record companies don't have enough foresight.'

Ironically, one of Pride's biggest problems was their abundance of riches. Running alongside the seven-piece, both Barbara and Sade were developing their own sets, which made them a triple threat but also an expensive proposition.

The way Pride worked live was more like a soul revue show. The full outfit would kick things off with their sax-propelled street funk before a change of pace mid-set when Barbara would do a Ray St John ballad, 'Sweet Love & Music', and Sade another Ray song that had started out as 'Maximum Joy' (to which she'd added a spoken intro) and which was now known as 'Diamond Life'.

The only recorded evidence of the band's live sound is a video they made for BBC2's *Oxford Road Show* of the track 'Pride', one of three numbers they'd put down at BBC studios. Filmed under the Charing Cross arches at Heaven, the video relies on such classic eighties pop promo moves as walking coolly past a tracking camera – which Sade naturally aces – and then, er, doing it again. The rhythm section is driven by Paul 'Dink Dank' Denman's distinctive thumbed bass and there's some forceful blowing from Stuart snaking round the melody. Vocally, there's little chance for Sade to shine, straining at the top end of her range on backing vocals with Barbara.

Sade had been taking singing lessons but, strapped for cash, she'd recently knocked them on the head.

'I've had four with a man from Maida Vale,' she said, lighting another vocal-enhancing fag. 'But at the moment, I can't afford to carry on so I'll have to remember what he told me. I don't want to end up croaky like Siouxsie!'

The voice may have been a work in progress but she'd already got one ace in her back pocket. From first hearing, 'Diamond Life' sounded like a hit. The question was whether it sat best in Pride or as part of what was being referred to as The Other Set, a sparser, jazzier four-piece consisting of Sade, the two Pauls and Stuart.

This other set included 'Diamond Life', an early arrangement of 'Cherry Pie', covers of Timmy Thomas' 'Why Can't We Live Together', William DeVaughan's 'Be Thankful for What You've Got' and Julie London's 'Cry Me a River' (the latter annoying Animal Nightlife who did another London cover 'C'mon-A My House' with Leah Seresin on lead), 'Love Affair with Life' (another Ray co-write that would end up as a B-side) and 'Throw Me A Lifeline' – a name Sade wasn't happy about (possibly due to the echoes of Spandau's latest hit), but at that stage couldn't think of anything better to title it.

Lee credited Sade with the idea for this spin-off group. She was less fussed where it had originated but she knew what she wanted it to achieve.

'I don't want the new set to be considered just an extension to Pride,' said Sade. 'I want it to be a separate entity. That's how I feel about it. I can be more indulgent. So can Stuart, Paul and Paul because there're less people to consider. Obviously, they're from Pride so you can't completely isolate it but I think it's more of an offspring than an extension of it. It's Mother's Pride. Sorry, I had to say that before someone else did!'

It didn't take long for record companies to cotton on that this might be an easier sell, particularly when a Pride Ronnie Scott's gig in the upstairs bar was followed up with two Sade shows in the main venue that December of 1982 and the following February. To his credit, Lee tried to push the idea of a three-part deal right up to the last minute, but in the end, no major record company was prepared to take on Pride, Sade and Barbara as a complete package and the clock was definitely ticking.

By October 1983 – a whole year since New York – it was clear that Sade and her boys were the one that companies were most interested in. While half of London (*No.1* included) was out in Paris enjoying that same Gary Kemp birthday party, Lee was busy engineering a last-minute switch from Virgin Records (who were already celebrating, thinking they had it in the bag) to CBS Records, a label with considerably more international clout.

It was tough on Nick and Barbara, and particularly Paul Cooke who at the last minute was deemed the weakest link in the four-piece. Ray did at least have the consolation of a songwriting credit on 'Smooth Operator' (as 'Diamond Life' had become), which as a single and album track would end up selling millions. But where Sade really went to bat for her team was when it came to the rest of her band.

Stuart Matthewman and Paul Denman had now been joined by Brighton boy Andrew Hale on keyboards. The only problem was that as far as CBS were concerned, the first thing they wanted to do was ditch the band and stick Sade in the studio with a bunch of session musicians of their choice. She was having none of it. It was either her and her boys or they could all go and lump it.

They didn't go down without a fight, but in the end CBS knew when they were beat. After over a year of negotiations and frustrations, things rapidly changed gear. 'Smooth Operator' had looked the obvious first single but then Lee handed me a cassette of something called 'Your Love is King', which they'd knocked up in the studio that January in 1984. A month later, Sade was doing her first *TOTP* (even if the chart rundown billed her as 'Slade'), taking them all the way to Number 6 and even Mrs Simper's pals in Wiltshire were aware that something had come of that little musical venture.

In the pages of *No.1*, she was her usual self. She talked openly to Deanne Pearson (I was having to learn I couldn't keep her *all* to myself!) about her mum's split from her dad, her own later father/ daughter reunion and her impressive five half-grandmothers. By the time we next caught up in a work capacity – at a dress rehearsal for a *Wogan* performance of 'The Sweetest Taboo' – she already had two more hits and an internationally successful album under her belt.

Talk was of her old Saturday jobs – a meat round, baker's assistant and paper round she'd taken on all at once to pay for the upkeep of a beloved, but prohibitively expensive, horse – her love for Hollywood outsider Robert Mitchum, poor Ray St John being referred to in European publications as 'Racing John', and the time she called up the head of Tyne Tees sales department to plead with them (unsuccessfully) not to sell the distribution rights to an under-rehearsed performance of 'Cherry Pie' that had gone out on *The Tube*. She was never one for leaving someone else to do something if she could do it herself.

By now she'd got Graham Smith on board to do her record sleeves. It was his pix and posters that had advertised her early Ronnie Scott's gigs. An early photo shoot was done in our front room with Sade elegantly stretched out over the black-and-white floor tiles. 'Your Love is King' had happened too quickly for Graham to get involved but since then she'd loved his Blue Note/Reid Miles-influenced designs. Even if the record company had reservations.

'They were never too impressed with the black-and-white photographs and wanted something airbrushed, high fashion, more OTT glam,' said Graham. 'There were a few rows over that to start with but she always had her way. She was really adamant as to what she wanted and she had the final say every time.'

All the same, *Diamond Life*'s iconic album sleeve almost went for a burton.

'The most annoying thing about her without a doubt is that she will leave everything to the last minute,' said Graham. 'The night before the artwork was due to go to the printers, she hadn't even done the album photo session. Eventually she dropped it off at four in the morning, then the printers scratched the transparency – it was this new Polaroid film that was just on the market – and because in those days there were no duplicates, she had to do the whole session again!'

Away from work, she kept in touch. A particular tradition of hers was sending New Year rather than Christmas cards. The one to us at Shirland Road was addressed to 'Our favourite gay couple'.

In our *Wogan* chat, she'd been as good company as ever. But despite all the success, 1985 hadn't been the best of years. *Promise*, the follow-up album, had taken longer than expected to record, and just before she was set to tour, her father had died in Nigeria. She'd returned home for the funeral service and then gone straight into the madness of a seven-month global tour – her biggest to date.

Certainly the adulation had grown. Her dressing room in Hull took her by surprise with 'flowers everywhere' and a lavish four-foot high bouquet spelling out 'Sade' in pink carnations from a mystery admirer ('very odd'). A male fan ran on stage in Philadelphia with a handmade scarf for her. Then a female fan managed to get to her to give her a toreador hat to wear for the song 'Fear', a gesture of devotion only slightly spoiled by the devotee then coming backstage to ask for her hat back at the end of the show, much to Sade's amusement.

And so to Radio City Music Hall. Three years on from our downtown Pride adventure, this was now Times Square and all the glitz of a Broadway first night. Little old London, though, was still most definitely represented. Bob was there, but no longer as her boyfriend, that was instead another clubland face, Smile hairdresser Spike Denton. I flew out with CBS press officer Jon Futrell. The after-show party in a flash Japanese restaurant saw the likes of Siobhan Fahey and Phil Dirtbox, Virgin A & R man Mick Clark (who held no grudges from that last-minute gazumping), Spike's partner in clubland Neville 'Mad for It' Hyde, and former Blitz Kids Jo Strettell, Bic Owen and Melissa Caplan, who was now in charge of wardrobe.

The press scrum outside the restaurant had caught her a bit on the hop.

'Did you see those photographers?' she asked incredulously a few days later. 'There must have been twenty of them all bundling into the restaurant with flash guns and knocking people over. It was terrible. It was as if I'd just gunned down the president!'

The only Americans who might possibly have viewed her as public enemy number one were her US record company and some of the home-grown media. A stickler for getting things right, she'd been getting frustrated by various communication breakdowns with both and was not really playing ball with either.

'There's nothing more irritating than being interviewed by someone who literally hasn't got a clue what you're talking about,' she said as we sat in her hotel room at The Roosevelt.

'You're just wasting your time because whatever happens, the end result is going to be wrong. It's not going to be representative of you or anything you stand for. But there's nothing you can do about it. You can't correct someone when they look at things completely differently.'

She grinned. 'Unless they go back and start their entire life again!'

The record company battles had tested her more. She'd hit the roof when CBS had printed her name phonetically – Sharday – on the first album without consulting anyone and there were constant running battles – 'I won't bore you with them' – over what were clearly very different value systems.

Now she was trying to keep a handle on the publicity whilst CBS tried to capitalise on her unexpectedly huge success.

'CBS think my attitude is a bit peculiar,' she said, laughing. 'I'm trying to do as few interviews as possible. To talk solidly without taking a breather is not very sensible when you're about to go onstage. It's very difficult, though. Here, if you get any attention the record company gets you over, you stay here and you ignore the rest of the world. I don't want to seem entirely uncooperative and stubborn so I'm trying to be reasonable and do a few. But the most important thing on tour is the tour itself, not the seven TVs and sixty interviews in the same day. If you allow anything to jeopardise that, you're being a fool.

'It's obvious people want to know a little bit about you but I don't think it's good to do too many interviews. Then you just basically belong to the press.'

Sade – or Auntie Sade as she dubbed herself – was far more concerned with looking after her boys. Whatever extra pressures had come her way with this sudden upturn in her fortunes, it hadn't affected the tight-knit band of brothers she had in Stuart, Andrew and Paul. She'd told me at *Wogan* that there had been moments when she'd debated whether she wanted to carry on – this after just one album – but when it came down to it she had a responsibility to the three of them as well as herself. And she thought leaving them in the lurch was ludicrous.

As for looking after herself, there was a heat log to protect her voice from the dreaded hotel air conditioning and plenty of vitamin C that she confessed she never actually took but found reassuring to have around. The tour photographer, Toshi Yajima, had introduced everyone to the delights of backstage sushi but there was the odd fast food lapse.

'I do feel physically ill after I've had something like a hamburger,' she said. 'But they're really nice to eat – I love things like that. I do make a conscious effort to *try* not to eat too many hot dogs. But I'm not paranoid about it. I'll eat anything if I'm hungry enough and it's the only thing available.'

Going global hadn't dimmed her love of England.

'I wouldn't consider myself at home anywhere else but England,' she said. 'I want to get somewhere in Spain. Maybe. But I don't know how happy I'd be away from England. You're better at home because you know all the games and you know how to play the game best.'

Typically, old friends and family were paramount. No famous faces were allowed backstage unless there was room for the band's friends and family as well. Although she and Bob were no longer together, he was very much there, chiding her to get some sleep while we were doing our chat.

In my case, she had sweetly stalled our interview for as long as possible so I could enjoy a few extra days in New York. This was just as well because in the enjoyment stakes, my life had just gone into orbit.

11

SHAKING YOUR EYES

The cab ride from Radio City Music Hall to Sade's after-party had started off simply enough. With the show over and the venue emptied, I'd nipped backstage with Jon Futrell to get the party's address and hopefully cadge a lift. That was all fine and dandy, but what I hadn't expected was the little red capsule that some kind soul popped in my mouth just as we all departed.

You may recall that in my early days in London I'd had no truck with drugs. Like Mrs Slocombe, I had remained unanimous in that until the moment at a Spandau after-party – this one more humbly set above a chip shop called the Midnight Express in Bournemouth – where someone had beckoned me into a cupboard, produced a little twizzled piece of white tissue paper and said: 'Here, you'll like this.'

They were not wrong. Within the twinkling of an eye that tatty little upstairs bar had been transformed into the South coast's very own Studio 54 as I spun around with Beat Route girl Jill Humphry, like *Saturday Night Fever*'s Tony Manero and Stephanie Mangano, to Chaka Khan, Change and Evelyn 'Champagne' King as the effects of what my benefactor would later reveal to be a heady mix of MDA and mescaline kicked in. If this was drugs, absolutely, yes please, I was in.

Being very much a party-don't-stop kind of person and working with a limited budget my stimulant of choice for the next few years tended to be speed. Speed was not only good for non-stop dancing, but a little dab every now and then could also keep you wide awake through all-night movie binges or indeed army-based US TV sitcoms.

The only cheap alternative of any interest was acid. If a wrap of sulphate set you back twenty quid, a tab of acid was even more of a snip at a fiver or less. For eight or nine hours of variable mind trickery that seemed like the bargain of the century.

Of course, I'd also heard of the perils of LSD. People mistakenly believing they could fly or being marauded by imaginary swarms of bees. No one wants a bad trip. I was exceedingly grateful that nothing had come my way on that Kid Creole jaunt.

Instead, my first acid adventure was kind of down to Mrs Simper.

A lover of antiques, my mother had for a while worked part-time in Charnham House Antiques in Hungerford. Here she would do her best to extract generous sums of money from the many dedicated browsers and occasional famous face like Maggie Smith (no sale), Johnny Morris (no sale but a cracking impression of a parakeet) and Princess Margaret that came her way. But what her customers didn't know was that concealed in the room above her were the drug squad. This was part of a top priority stake-out called Operation Julie, a two-and-a-half-year investigation involving eleven police forces across the country that ended up seizing a reported 6.5 million tabs of acid. With Mrs S as their front, it had all the makings of a classic Ealing comedy, though possibly one directed by Dennis Hopper.

My mother's secret life as a member of the DEA had rather

passed me by back in 1977. My interests were more cricket-related (England regaining the Ashes, Boycott notching his 100th hundred). But fast forward six years to the long hot summer of 1983 (correctly predicted by the Style Council) and much had changed. Somehow, a number of those impounded tabs had found their way back onto the open market and were now burning a hole in my wallet as a few game individuals headed down to Wiltshire to open the portals of our minds. Whether it would be quite up there with William Hurt in *Altered States* nobody was too sure but we were prepared to give it a go.

First things first, we had to see off Mrs S. For the life of her, my mother couldn't understand why we were all so desperate to spend an afternoon back at Harepath Farm, my childhood home, which the family had moved from the previous year when Dad had retired.

'No, Mother, we're just going to hang out here for a while. Yes, I know it's where we no longer live. My London friends are just really keen to see where we kept the chickens.'

Then we handed out the little blotters and waited.

It was quite a wait. There was an age spent standing hopefully in the driveway. I'm not quite sure what I was expecting. But something dramatic. A few years before an oak tree had almost flattened me on a windy day in the same spot, so something a little less lethal than that but with plenty of bells and whistles. A little bit *Wonka*, a little bit *Fantasia*, a little bit *Wizard of Oz*. Instead, all I was feeling was a bit of a headache at all the squinting.

The first sign that 'it' had taken some sort of grip on any of us was the floaty sound of peals of laughter from the other side of the barn. No one knew what had triggered it but once started it was a tap that proved impossible to turn off. The next three hours were spent in uncontrollable hysterics. Over nothing. Then, just to mix it up a bit, we decided to create our own cut-price Wiltshire version of the Wag Club using Dad's old empty garage – the sole point of the game being not to let anyone in. At which point I turned into a Hitachi camera salesman.

Phase two posed trickier problems. As dusk fell, it suddenly dawned on me that all I was capable of doing with my dad's car (our only means of transport down the three-mile road to home) was hugging the steering wheel. Hours were then spent concocting an elaborate and extremely wearisome lie revolving around a fictional village pub crawl of places that I very rarely frequented but which had on this occasion, somehow – gasp – put us *over the limit*.

In those days, the concept of drink driving being in any way 'wrong' was one that my parents and their country friends were still having trouble coming to terms with. If some poor sod got knocked into the hedge by a slightly over-refreshed motorist, then so be it. Those were country ways. Therefore, the notion that we should need to abandon our car and trudge home on foot – all because of a few pints – was pretty flimsy.

Once we finally all agreed that this was the most plausible excuse – and, man, try making any decision by committee on acid – it turned out that the walk in the dark was probably the best bit. Yes, there was the odd freak-out about keeping in exact single file every time we saw some headlights in the distance, but the smiley cartoon faces of the flowers in the hedgerows were proper Disney and when we all simultaneously spotted a tree whose branches were the exact same shape as the silhouetted heads of the Fun Boy Three it felt like our work was done.

The final, again more tedious phase, had me holding everyone hostage in my parents' kitchen waiting for the last remnants of the LSD to wear off whilst forbidding them to do anything 'weird' like lie on the floor or eat a bowl of cereal because Mum and Dad might come down (it was all of ten o'clock) and then of course *they'd know*.

As fate would have it, the following year we really did have a night on acid where we couldn't get into the Wag. Winston, the benevolent doorman, who always called me Pete and Pete Paul, would allow in any combination of two but only two of the three of us. You can imagine how many hours that took to resolve.

Off the back of another Bournemouth bank holiday marathon, that trip ended with me waking the next morning not able to move the right-hand side of my body, having gone down with pneumonia. Two months of enforced convalescence at my mum and dad's later, I decided that acid and I might not be such great bedfellows after all.

So it had been all quiet on the pharmaceutical front . . . until this crosstown cab ride.

It had all come in a rush. A whoosh of MDMA warmth, saturated colour, tingling and light. Like Sade, I remember the bedlam of the flashing cameras as we dismounted, but whilst she was shocked and appalled (and drug-free having to cope with being the actual eye of this storm) I was just utterly absorbed by it all. Suddenly everything was intensely interesting. The pushing, the shouting, the drama. Much is made of the euphoria that comes – or came, it's been a long time – with ecstasy, but what got me just as much was this curious sense of a fourth wall, like you were watching the telly. Confronted by all this bedlam, I felt like pulling up a seat.

The rest of the party was a blur. A lot of going up and down staircases, an unexpected appearance by Shuv Fahey with then boyfriend Phil Dirtbox, and some indignation and incredulity from Mr Futrell that there was no tequila at a Sade party – 'Sade only drinks tequila!'

The next I knew, it was dawn, raining, and I was curled up in a small concrete tunnel in a kids' adventure playground being called 'Paul Simper' a lot by a DJ called Fat Tony. How we ended up there and who the other people were in this remarkably cosy hidey-hole I had not the foggiest. Nor where my hotel was. Nor when I was meant to be doing my Sade interview.

What I did know – and I would confirm this many, many times over the next twelve months – was that I felt wonderful. More wonderful than I had ever felt before. I had a warm Ready Brek glow about me, emanating from my belly and stretching all the way out to the top of my head and the tips of my fingers and toes.

Thankfully, I did eventually reconnect with my hotel room and luggage at some point later that day. I'd only visited it briefly before Radio City Music Hall but something had most definitely happened in the interim. Now the bed was more springy, the towels more fluffy and the taps a whole new crispy cold. It was a lot more thrilling than the usual complimentary mint.

As for my Sade interview, that, it seems, would have to wait. All sorts of reasons were given as to why it couldn't happen within my allotted two-day time frame. But as two became three, became four, became five days, the main reason was clear. She could see we were all having the time of our lives and was happy to let that continue.

If that cupboard assignation in Bournemouth three years before had set me on the yellow brick road where hallucinogenics were concerned, New York 1985 was where I finally hit the Emerald City. It was as if the whole island of Manhattan had been redesigned as some sort of sensory heightening theme park. Ecstasy (MDMA) had only been criminalised as a Schedule 1 controlled substance in the US that July and its influence on club culture was everywhere.

Clubs like the palatial Palladium, on East 14th and 3rd, which had been recently converted from a concert hall and opened by Studio 54's Ian Schrager and Steve Rubell. Here in one cavernous room you could clamber up onto a giant mantelpiece and spend whole evenings observing all the comings and goings down below. In the Hall of Colours, a psychedelic room playing hurdy gurdy early Bowie, handles dangled from the ceiling like you were on the subway. Quite why you should want to ride a subway train that took you nowhere mattered not a jot. You just had to get involved. Some went as far as Piccadilly Circus. A couple of our lot reckoned they'd got on at Finsbury Park.

On 157 Houston Street was Area, a nightclub-cum-art-installation with its own secret bouncy spot where you crossed the walkway into one of the rooms. Whether this amazing springy step had been specially designed for those of a chemical persuasion nobody knew for sure (Area was totally transformed by a host of carpenters and artists every six weeks), but the general feeling was that everything had been laid on for our benefit and we could not have been more grateful. I tried that step again and again, surprising myself afresh each time, whilst Sharon Brown's 'I Specialise in Love' affirmed our general condition.

And if you weren't on a mantelpiece, a make-believe tube train or a random bouncy floor part, you were squished inside a giant egg. The egg chair at the Milk Bar is where I would still be now if someone hadn't hauled me free. This chair (suspended from the ceiling?) with its obvious womb-like attributes was the go-to destination. Like an incredibly benign car crash, you could squash four well-trollied individuals like marshmallows inside its shell. Although which body part belonged to whom was anyone's guess in this mass cuddle-fest. The only guarantee was that whenever any of your gang went missing, this was where they would be. It was like an E lost property office.

I didn't appreciate it at the time, but once again I'd lucked out timing-wise. The mid-eighties were to be New York's last great hurrah. The end of a decade of hedonism launched in the mid-seventies at Studio 54.

It wasn't just the clubs, though, that appeared to be serving up bespoke E-nhanced E-ntertainment. Convenience stores were now shimmering, gleaming treasure troves, filled to bursting with extraordinary produce. We would gawp and gasp in awe, like the little *Toy Story* aliens, at the magnificence of these well-stocked shops.

But gawping wasn't always great. One night an argument started inside one such store as we were passing. The next thing a guy walked out and smashed a bottle in the face of a resting bum who, unsurprisingly, went completely ape. An audio recording of the incident as the bum screams: 'You motherfucker! Are you insane? Are you insane?!' sounds like the slow-mo finale of *Taxi Driver* when Travis shoots the pimp's fingers off and continues up the staircase. As we stood there passively watching it all unfurl (me with my portable tape recorder) like it was Saturday afternoon *World of Sport* wrestling, someone shouted: 'That's not fun. I don't want to watch that.' It wasn't. But I kind of did.

On the third night, we did actually lure Sade out, but unlike the rest of us, she was keeping a clear head. She watched amused as we did our little daily diary Star-date audio updates and we got her as far as Area.

'For half an hour,' she said. 'I want to dance. I just want to dance.'

Once my record company hotel ran out, I was welcomed into the bosom of my new-found friends. Confusingly, they all appeared to live in the same midtown block so I was never sure whose place I was in. Music wafted from one apartment to the next fusing everything together. Vangelis's *Blade Runner* score, Love Unlimited's 'It May Be Winter Outside', Barbra Streisand's 'Somewhere' and, seemingly on permanent loop, The Art of Noise's 'Moments in Love' wrapped around you as you attended to such pressing business of the day as caressing someone's cashmere coat or playing dress-up with what appeared to be an inexhaustible supply of costumes, masks and wigs.

I'd never known a drug that involved so much dressing up. The initial waves of MDMA proper knocked you off your socks but once you'd ridden the ecstatic bit – the jibbidy eyes and the little e-vom – there were hours more of communal entertainment to participate in. The props and music were a big part of it – as were the paper baths (thousands of shreds of newspaper dropped on you, like snow, in the dark) and cut-and-paste scrapbooks. If the DEA had busted down the door they would have found what looked like a highly motivated playgroup beavering away with paints and scissors and crayons, albeit not always with any clothes on.

There was a touch of Nic Roeg's *Performance* about it, but the overall atmosphere was probably best summed up by a then recently released cartoon short from the Canadian Film Board that had become a sort of touchstone for everyone. *The Big Snit*, written and directed by animator Richard Condie, was the story of a married couple trying to play a game of Scrabble that is forever being interrupted – much to the husband's mounting irritation – by eye shaking, accordion playing, unwarranted hoovering and Armageddon, when husband and wife finally find peace as angels and resolve to finish that game of Scrabble after all.

Funny, quirky and surreal it scored big with all manner of detail that seemed to speak directly to us. The wife shaking her eyes (she actually takes them off like a pair of glasses) was key – the self-same jibbidy effect that the California Red Es had on your vision. And if that wasn't enough, the husband's stack of seven letters, which was driving him so nuts, was all Es. It was as if they *knew*.

When the five days finally did come to an end, I glided back to London feeling indecently refreshed and altogether new. Clearly word had come through in advance that my arrival would need a little extra something as the travellator at Heathrow was 100 per cent more springy than it had been on the journey out.

In no need of sleep I headed straight to the office, wrote up Sade and waited expectantly to see what was next.

12

THE WELL STOCKED POP

There was certainly something evangelical about the way that ecstasy made you feel. As its smiley-faced explosion across Britain two years later would testify, it was a euphoria and sense of well-being that you wanted to share on a massive scale. Friendships were accelerated at a ridiculous rate. You felt you'd be friends for life with people you'd cuddled for an hour.

On the flip side of that, because you felt so fantastic there was not a moment to be wasted on anyone who might kill your buzz. Passing the time of day propping up the bar at the Wag was out, making a secret ankle-level hideaway under one of the sofas with your new nearest and dearest was the way to go.

In fact, sofas and paper baths and not going out at all were even better. In this new super-sped-up social whirl it had taken all of a week back in London to find some like-minded souls. Nineteen eighty-six was seen in with an ever-expanding number of loved-up lads and lasses and two supremely strokeable glove puppets from Hamley's – Sammy Squirrel and Harry Hedgehog.

Whether old school London clubland was ready for this was a moot point. Whilst Leigh Bowery had launched Taboo – the most hedonistic eighties club of all – in Leicester Square, the sight of what was now a thirty-strong crew of chemically enhanced mischief-makers brazenly rolling around any nightclub or party that took our fancy, alarmed some.

One night at the Wag, another new club band, Habit's, manager, Oliver Peyton, had a word with one of our gang. 'You're the laughing stock of London,' he said. It was a title too good to waste. By the autumn, the Laughing Stock of London was throwing its own party at Limelight.

What was taking a little longer to quantify was the effect that this was all having on pop. The appearance of one Cindy Ecstasy in Soft Cell's ranks, Marc Almond later revealed, was more down to her procuring skills than any musical qualifications. And in clubland, the subject matter of Pride's encore, 'Ecstasy', was fairly unequivocal – but that wasn't a song that had travelled into Sade's set.

Before people started disappearing down a rabbit hole in SE1 in late 1987 at Danny and Jenny Rampling's Shoom, the most significant effect that it had on the pop scene of 1986 was that it made some people decide that there was something even more fun they could be doing than being full time pop stars.

Paul Rutherford had been my favourite Frankie since they'd first ram raided the charts in 1984. Holly may have had the soaring pipes and the wicked turn of phrase and The Lads a propensity for causing uncomplicated, unvarnished mayhem, but it was Paul who could still pull focus with his dips and spins – a gay matinee idol who could really dance.

The Bluebells' Robert Hodgens was always winding me up that I had a crush on Paul, particularly when I went down to *Top of the Pops* when The Bluebells did 'Young at Heart' and 'Two Tribes' was into its seventh week at Number 1. In fact, it wasn't until that August bank holiday when we properly met. Lorraine now had a job as an accountant at ZTT so along with Graham and layout artist and occasional bongos player Tim Parker from *No.1*, we blagged a spot on the roof of Sarm Studios for an afternoon of speed, beers and bar-b.

Paul showed up with Miranda Belle Star and his fella Joe Batty. Despite the odd bit of posed photographic evidence to the contrary, I was mostly too star-struck to talk to Paul and instead had a very funny chat with Joe about wanking in the bath leaving you with a scum line round your neck when you got out.

By the time our paths converged again in early 1986, things had changed. An advised but unhappy tax exile in 1985 (the band had a terrible deal with ZTT which would later be rectified in court) had meant Paul had spent most of the past year either recording in Dublin (where they spent as much time racing cars and getting stoned and hammered with the equally frustrated Spands) or Amsterdam (a place Paul declared as deadly dull as Milton Keynes).

'I just felt really lonely,' said Paul. 'Still, when I got to go to places on my own and had a *say* in it, I liked that!'

One of those places was New York where Paul had run into the same gang as me with an equally transformative effect. The recording of the long-awaited Frankie follow-up album to *Welcome to the Pleasuredome* was still ongoing as a lot of my early 1986 desk diary entries of the 'Ruthers back' variety would testify. Mostly Paul was mucking about with us.

He and Joe had bought a spacious loft in Telford's Yard, a recently converted block in Wapping which looked out not only over the Thames but also the *Sun's* new printing plant. A location which turned into a full-on battleground when 6,000 News International employees went on strike in January 1986 over the move away from Fleet Street. Surreally, our Saturday nights would often be spent being ushered by the police through the gathering protestors, our pockets bulging with illegal goodies, before cosying down with our blissed-out balcony view of the running battles that raged through the rest of the year.

Whole weekends would be spent on Paul and Joe's two huge sofas, listening to Jam & Lewis, Anita Baker, The Carpenters and Luther and indulging in more wigs and dressing up. It soon became apparent that the day (or days) after were just as much fun as the night before with everyone still up for trouble. In the wilderness of Wapping, there was one booze warehouse where cases of beers could be decimated in five minutes flat if you played shotguns (puncturing a small hole in the bottom of a can then pulling back the ring-top it would be propelled down in one giddy gulp).

While Paul would be the one to entertain us with his bountiful dressing-up box, Joe was the oasis of calm. A gentle, proud man hailing from Bradford, Joe kept his job in a hairdressing salon in Fulham even when he could probably have just ridden on Paul's success. Whatever the mayhem of the night before, Joe would be up for work on the Saturday morning and then be back to see us all later – often bearing treats from the outside world – when all we'd managed to do was watch a BBC2 Cary Grant double bill, play Janet Jackson's 'Let's Wait a While' and 'Funny How Time Flies' ad infinitum and suck a bottle of Liquid Gold through a cigarette.

It wasn't until August 1986 that Paul and I got to speak in an official capacity for *No.1* with Frankie finally releasing their first new single in eighteen months, 'Rage Hard'. They'd already had a few days of press stuff and it's fair to say that Paul was now quite ambivalent about it all. Back in 1984 they'd had the fun of duking it out with the big four of Duran, Wham!, Spandau and Culture Club.

Since then Duran had split into the two fairly fractious factions of Arcadia (Simon and Nick) and The Power Station (John and Andy); Spandau had changed record companies (from Chrysalis to CBS) and only just released their fifth album, *Through the Barricades*; Culture Club were in disarray after George's heroin addiction; and Wham! were no more after bowing out with a perfectly judged farewell at Wembley Stadium.

In terms of pop pin-ups only a-ha had really stepped into the breach while for chart outrage Sigue Sigue Sputnik had been giving it a go but as Frankie bass player Mark O'Toole pointed out: 'They had good hype but they didn't have the goods to back it up.'

'It's all dull again,' said Paul. 'And I don't know whether we're just going to add to the dullness. We only done it for one year. It wasn't that big. It didn't change much. It's not like The Beatles. They're the only true band ever really. They were the ones to do it before anybody.'

Paul wanted to be Ringo.

'He always looked really happy. He looked like he was riding it for the reason that it should be ridden. Played his drums, did his films, got paid for it and had a great time.'

Holly was less bothered about the lack of competition in their absence.

'Who wants fucking competition!' He laughed. 'I'm pleased it was quiet while we were away. Frankie was this huge stroke of luck for everyone involved. Then the hard work began. The more elevated you become in people's eyes the harder it gets. We could have worked on this mythological second album for five years.'

The legendary Lads pad in Maida Vale that was the staple of so many Max Bell *No.1* 'Whispers' columns was no more. Mark was now living in Hampstead with his Latino Miami-raised fiancée, Laura.

'She's a bit of a maddy as well,' said Mark, not wanting to let the side down. 'And she's a good cook. She cooks that Spanish stuff. You know, the stuff that makes you shit a lot.'

Most exciting news to report from Casa O'Toole was the discovery of a groundbreaking new fast food delivery service, Cable Nosh. 'You order it off the telly then they come to the door and you say: "Nosh?"'

The novelty of having their picture taken and being asked their thoughts on the price of fish had worn off. A pop mag interview Paul had done earlier in the week had properly wound him up.

'I don't think anyone really wants to know whether I had an Action Man when I was a kid.' He frowned. 'I told him I made it fuck Barbie. The journalist asked: "Didn't he mind?" I said: "He was mine, right. He had no fucking say in the matter." He must have thought I was nuts. I know it's for a kids' paper but you might as well just go dribble, dribble, dribble. So I just lied.'

Keeping the old gang together is possibly the hardest thing any band has to do. Paul said they'd all been talking earlier in the week and realised none of them had picked up the phone to each other in their time off.

'When we were apart we never rang each other up,' he said. 'It's very strange when we were so close but I'm much more relaxed about it now. We're not a matching tea set any more.

'I'm definitely more carefree since . . .' He mimed swallowing a pill. 'But I think the freedom to be myself again has taught me that. I used to get really uptight about going out and being drunk. It's so stupid. You can go anywhere. You can do what you want. I don't think there are any rules. People just adopt them along with their new job, along with their new title.'

Lovely though it was to mostly have Paul to ourselves, as a Frankie fan I still wanted them to come back as thrillingly as before. They'd given 'Rage Hard' and 'Warriors of the Wasteland' an airing at the Montreux Pop Festival and caused a bit of havoc smashing up their equipment, which seemed to have worked as a bit of a team-bonding exercise, getting the old juices going again.

'Frankie Goes to Pieces!' was the tabloid headline, claiming they'd gone on a £100,000 rampage. Best was the fantastically literal photo caption – 'Paul: Drink and laugh' – which accompanied a photo of Paul drinking and laughing.

'Montreux was a really good laugh,' said Paul. 'Too many people when we arrived were playing their little pop star games – being cool in the bar, all dressed up and posing. We went: "This is horrible. This is not fun. This is not what it's supposed to be about." It didn't feel like anyone was enjoying it. We just thought: "Sorry, boys, we're gonna blow youse off." That's the thing we can still do.'

For all that, 'Rage Hard' didn't take them back to the top of the charts, peaking at Number 4, and their follow-up, 'Warriors', only just squeaked into the Top 20. For *No.1* mag there were four lively days in Rome for some Italian TV show where I got to stand in for Nash on camera rehearsals. Things went up a notch when having been confined to their dressing rooms for too long, someone decided to hoik a rather large hatstand out the window. Luckily there was no one lurking in the narrow alleyway below but the arrival soon after of a fairly fucked off squad of armed police suggested we'd best not hang around for any post-show nibbles.

As for Frankie's middling chart return, was there anything else the band could have done the second time round apart from come up with another 'Relax' or 'Two Tribes'? Holly said he was keen not to repeat himself and the last-minute switch of album title from the fantastical but pointed *From the Diamond Mine to the Factory* to the more homey and sentimental *Liverpool* was symptomatic of that, but not in a good way.

Getting DJ Mike Read all hot under the collar first time round when he'd called for 'Relax' to be banned and unwittingly lit the touchpaper had been a stroke of luck. This time the only thing that got banned was the Christmas singles column The Lads did with me for *No.1*.

I think I was more outraged on their behalf than they were when it got spiked by our new ed Alan Lewis, but on reflection you can see it wasn't quite the thing for a teen pop magazine: Aled Jones ('He should have been drowned at birth'). Rolf Harris ('Stupid Aussie twat'). Elaine Paige ('Shite'). Mike Batt ('Deserves a bat shoved up his arse'). Wendy Richard ('She's got tits on her knees'). The Barron Knights ('The Barron Shites').

The only acts to get the thumbs up for their Christmas efforts were Slade, Frank Sidebottom and Shakin' Stevens. Although Mark did have one caveat about Shaky.

'I asked him for his autograph once at *Top of the Pops* and he fucked me off,' said Mark. 'Well his manager did – but then Shaky did it for me after all.'

Good man, Shaky.

Our gang went up to Manchester a month later to see Frankie fill the G-Mex and the party afterwards provided the unexpected photo op for Pete Burns, wife Lynne and my willy. But relations within the band were clearly not great. When a few days later Mark belted Holly backstage just before they went on it seemed like a good time for Paul to start exploring his new-found freedom a bit more.

One young soul who was still trying this whole pop star lark on for size was Patsy Kensit. I'd known Patsy since she was fifteen. In the days when she and her best mate and dancing partner Beatrice Venturini used to tear up the floor at Gary Crowley's fantastic Tuesday night club in Harrow, Bogart's. Patsy did a bit of matchmaking and set me up on a date with Beatrice, which was very lovely of her, except for the fact that Beatrice was already going out with Gary.

'Why don't you just pop round?' said Patsy when she phoned me out of the blue one evening at Shirland Road. 'I'm sure she's not busy.' Beatrice lived with her mum in an apartment building up on the Edgware Road, about a ten-minute walk away. So pop round I did.

All went swimmingly until our goodbye smooch on the front steps, at which point who should come looming out of the darkness but GC the Busy Bee, now looking quite an angry bee.

'I should knock your block off,' said Gary when we went to sort this out over a cappuccino in Soho the following day. Being the gracious gent that he is, he didn't. He didn't even bar us from Bogart's.

One thing Patsy neglected to mention through all this, when she wasn't dancing to Club Tropicana or chasing after Nick Heyward, was that she was a veteran screen actress with a CV that ranged remarkably from Birds' Eye frozen pea ads where she stuck her finger in her mouth and went 'pop' (earning her the moniker Patsy Peapod) to playing opposite Hollywood royalty like Liz Taylor (*The Blue Bird*) and Robert Redford (*The Great Gatsby*).

By 1986 she had also decided that she wanted to be a pop star. She'd joined her big brother Jamie's band, Spice, around the time we were first hanging out. This then became Eighth Wonder when keyboard player Alex Godson came on board, after handing the chance to play with Sade to his mate Andy Hale. Initially managed by Graham Ball, then Dagger, Eighth Wonder had signed to CBS where Patsy was now being billed as the missing link between Brigitte Bardot and Debbie Harry, something the girl herself was doing little to discourage with a lot of pouting and squealing and some very short dresses.

To make things even more interesting, Patsy had now been cast as Crepe Suzette, the sex kittenish lead in *The Great Rock 'n' Roll Swindle* director Julien Temple's very eighties take on Colin MacInnes's *Absolute Beginners*. All of which you might think left her little time for partying. Far from it. Patsy was determined to have as much fun as the rest of us.

When we did a cover shoot with her and John Taylor for *No.1*'s Valentine's Day issue she was a good enough sport to recreate the same pose very late one Saturday night purely for our entertainment with Phil Polecat doubling as the Duran bass player, aided by a fairly alarming plump-cheeked face mask and wig.

Whether John and Patsy ever got it on after their photo shoot date I know not. They did go for dinner, but considering his then fiancée, Danish supermodel Renée Simonsen, even helped John answer my Valentine's questions I'm thinking the window of opportunity may have been minimal.

Patsy was an hour late for the photo shoot as her beloved cat was giving birth, which didn't overly impress JT but she did win her favourite Durannie round by being such a lurch klutz on arrival – knocking over a hatstand – that he couldn't stay mad at her for long.

My abiding memory of playtime with Patsy, though, was the Sunday morning press show of *Absolute Beginners*. It was the culmination of what had been a fairly fraught movie-making process. Whilst coach-loads of clubland extras (cherry picked by Chris Sullivan) had been bussed out to Elstree on a regular basis to spend a lot of time hanging about drinking snakebites in their fifties gear, the shoot for Patsy and her co-star – newcomer Eddie O'Connell – and director Julien Temple had been pretty hairy with no time for rehearsal and the whole production ultimately hijacked by the money men.

'A lot of things could have been done differently,' reflected Patsy a few months later. 'We weren't given a lot of help. We were really thrown in at the deep end. I was totally aware of it at the time but there's nothing you can do about it when you're filming. You've just got to get on with it. For Eddie, it was his first film but even though I'd been working for years I was still panicking. We just didn't get any direction. Everyone was pushed for time and money and had a million and one things to think about. And in the edit, things got taken out.'

By the time everyone was done, Temple had been removed and the producers, in their infinite wisdom, had taken the results off to edit in three separate completely uncommunicative suites. The British film industry – seemingly on its last legs after the big budget failure of Hugh Hudson's costumed Al Pacino (and Sid 'Rickaay' Owen from *EastEnders*) epic *Revolution* – waited with bated breath. Could one great David Bowie song and a just-turned eighteen blonde who squeaked a lot save the day?

Bearing all this in mind, we should probably have encouraged Patsy to get a good night's kip before her big screening. Instead, she got no sleep whatsoever. So, on the morning of the screening, off we tootled down the Edgware Road along with Miranda (formerly Belle Star) Joyce and others to the Odeon Marble Arch. I can only remember one other instance where the driver of a car I've been riding in has decided to do so with her right leg stuck out the window – and that was after another messy day in Ibiza – but this was certainly the only time the driver was also the star of the movie we were about to see.

Fair play to Patsy, she got us there in one piece. We even made it to our seats without too much kerfuffle in time to see David Bowie roll out that majestic title tune of his. How much the row behind us saw after that I can only hazard a guess. The tell-tale waft of a bottle of poppers was the first indication that things were going somewhat awry. The two large feet plonked either side of Pats' head as she tried to focus on her first big starring moment and the low sustained rumble of snoring that accompanied the next two hours were another. God love her, she made it to the end, bid us all a cheery farewell as we headed for more trouble at Speaker's Corner and looked forward to seeing us at the Leicester Square premiere, which she duly did.

Whether it was her hectic social schedule or busy double life as actress and singer that slowed the progress of Eighth Wonder is open to debate. Suffice to say their second single, 'Will You

Remember?', which was due to be released on Boxing Day, 1985, finally emerged January 1, 1987. Soon after *Absolute Beginners* – which did at least top the UK box office for a month despite its manifest faults – Dagger steered Patsy away from the Laughing Stock. This may have been less fun for some of us but no doubt helped her land a raunchy Christophe Lambert movie, *Priceless Beauty*, ('The way it's written it's very steamy with quite a lot of sex but not like knobbing') and *Lethal Weapon 2*, by which time she could command a tidy £400,000 per Hollywood movie.

By the time we caught up again over a bag of crisps at the start of 1987 as she continued to search for her first UK hit with the Mike 'Blondie' Chapman produced 'Will You Remember?' she was busy putting some daylight between her and other recent pop blondes like Sam Fox and Mandy Smith who had also entered the fray.

'It's all a bit Stringfellows and Page Three,' said Patsy. 'I don't associate myself with those girls. I've got a band.'

She was still good company but possibly struggling quite how to pitch things in a world that suddenly had the threat of AIDS breathing down its neck. She had just recorded a show *Sex with Paula* with Paula Yates, which involved her copping off with both Gary and Martin Kemp but with George Michael's 'I Want Your Sex' already banned from daytime radio simply for having the word 'sex' in its title, it didn't look like it would be airing any time soon.

'Gary and I get to snog, which I really enjoyed,' she said. 'Then in the story, a year's passed and he's really preoccupied with other things and ignoring me so Martin comes along as this big hunk and *he* starts snogging me. So I had to snog them both, which was a rather nice day's work.'

She wasn't sure how much on-screen snogging she'd get to do

for the next Eighth Wonder video which had model James Le Bon as her love interest.

'How far do you go? It's really taboo at the moment,' she said, no pun intended.

She was at least relieved to have finally shaken off the virgin tag, which rather ickily had become something of a press focal point when she'd just turned sixteen.

'At the time I first said it, it was true,' she said. 'Then about three days later it wasn't any more. But then it all got blown out of proportion. It was really embarrassing because people were saying to me: 'You what? Didn't I see you with so and so?' It just started wearing a bit thin. You've got to realise your mum and dad are reading all that and when you're seventeen – sixteen even – it doesn't sound good.'

So would she continue to flash her knickers in this cautious new world?

'I'll always flash my knickers,' she grinned. 'But I actually don't wear any.'

13

IT'LL BE ALL POLITE ON THE NIGHT

Knowing when and how to say goodbye in pop music is never easy. All too often groups fall out, get too thin on top or simply lose the plot. Sometimes that's down to extraneous girlfriends, boyfriends or hangers-on sticking their nebs in. Other times it's a spin-off vanity project. Fairly frequently, it's just a rush of royalties and a big bag of drugs.

Blessedly, in the summer of 1986 Wham! deftly sidestepped all the above, heeded their own mantra (Wham!tra?) of doing it right and headed off into the sunset on top of the charts and at the top of their game with their friendship still admirably intact.

As a fan from 'Young Guns' days, for me, there had only been one wobble. Four hits in, George and Andrew had been forced to take a twelve-month sabbatical whilst their lawyers extracted them from a deal with their original Innervision label. For us poor fans the only sustenance had been a poxy *Stars on 45*-style *Club Fantastic Megamix* released against the duo's wishes. By May 1984 we were gagging for them to return.

Then one Friday evening, Gary Crowley premiered Wham!'s new single on his TV show, *Ear Say*, and it was evident there had been some changes. A decidedly creaky archive clip of couples jiving and jitterbugging was the accompaniment to an extremely lightweight (though super catchy) song about putting the boom-

boom into your heart. I was baffled. Where was the cheeky, chunky funk of 'Young Guns' and 'Wham Rap'? Or the sinewy grooves of 'Club Tropicana' and 'A Ray of Sunshine'? Or such gorgeous soul boy laments as 'Blue' and 'Nothing Looks the Same in the Light'? In a year already being bossed by Frankie's meaty 'Relax', 'Wake Me Up Before You Go-Go' was distinctly lacking in welly.

In due course, that initial dodgy video was replaced by the DayGlo-drenched camp fest of Andrew tootling on his horn and George stroking himself coquettishly with his fingerless gloves. But as we progressed into the even more Frankie-fied summer of 'Two Tribes' and 'Welcome to the Pleasuredome' I continued to feel a disappointing disconnect from the Motown-lite 'Freedom' and even (heresy, here) the plaintive 'Careless Whisper'. The fact that all three singles shot to Number 1 on both sides of the Atlantic and sand-wiched – or Whamwiched, if you will – Frankie's first two behemoth Number 1s (both sets of fans rejoicing in their 'Frankie Says' or 'Choose Life' Katharine Hamnett T-shirts) would indicate that I was in something of a minority.

Still, Beat Route boy that he was, George was mindful of not entirely forsaking that original soul boy section of Wham!'s audi-ence. To this end, nestling on side one of *Make It Big* was a track that would make it all better again. If I'd not been quite so lost in the world of Frankie, I might have discovered it a little earlier than Christmas 1984. As it was, it took till Boxing Day. Someone at Radio One flipped the twinkly 'Last Christmas' and I heard for the first time the hypnotic, synth-driven strut that is 'Everything She Wants'. I was back in.

A couple of nights later, I bumped into George at the Wag, just as with perfect timing Fat Tony stuck on the new 12-inch with its soaring extended middle eight of romantic recriminations. George had given it to Tony to test out the dance floor and grinned delightedly at my reaction. He'd delivered Wham!'s club classic to its target audience.

From then on, Wham! didn't put a foot wrong. I joined them for *No.1* in Los Angeles the following summer where they were now so exalted that home-bred soul stars like The Pointer Sisters, Sister Sledge and Chaka Khan opened for them. There was no time set aside for an actual interview. I was meant to be on an A&M three-city beano talking to Squeeze in Philadelphia, Sting in Denver and Bryan Adams in Vancouver, but obliging press officer Chris Poole didn't see why we couldn't pop over to LA – just to be sociable – and a shout of 'Simper!' from Pepsi and Shirlie on the sun loungers right next to us at the Mondrian took care of the feature.

These were the shows when they first premiered 'The Edge of Heaven' though it would be another new song, 'I'm Your Man', that leapfrogged it to become their next Number 1 that winter. A management fall out with Simon Napier-Bell and Jazz Summers – who had masterminded Wham!'s American success by coming up with the global headline-grabbing, groundbreaking shows in China – propelled them into making their final curtain call just eighteen months later when possibly they'd have liked a little longer.

Come the week of 23 June 1986, though, all their ducks were immaculately in line. On the Monday, they played the first of two sweaty, first come, first served nights at the Brixton Academy for Help A London Child. Tuesday, *The Edge of Heaven* – their four track EP with nods to the past in a remixed 'Wham Rap!' and the future in the stripped back Prince-like 'Battlestations' – went straight to Number 1. Wednesday, George celebrated his twenty-third birthday.

Thursday, they performed their final *Top of the Pops*, complete with leather tassel jackets and fantastically improbable Andrew guitar solo. Friday, *The Tube* special – 'Wham! Wrap' – gliding up and down the Seine with Paula Yates in full flirt mode. Then Saturday, well, that'd be bidding farewell on a blazing hot summer day in front of 72,000 devoted fans at Wembley Stadium.

Whambley was just one of those days. The previous year's Live Aid might have provided 'the greatest jukebox on earth', as Geldof put it, but as with all jukeboxes you couldn't always rely on some-one sticking on the right record. Wham! made no such mistakes. From the opening long, lingering tease of 'Everything She Wants' eight-and-a-half minute intro, with George in black leather flanked by two male dancers and Andrew in long coat accompanied by a mini-skirted Pepsi and Shirlie, through every hit and guest appear-ances by Elton John (dressed as Ronald McDonald) and Simon Le Bon (dressed as Simon Le Bon), to the last gasp of 'I'm Your Man', Wham! nailed it.

There were plenty of thank-yous from both of them throughout the night but it was Andrew's final: 'And thank you, George,' as the pair shared a massive bear hug in front of us that was the loveliest.

There was a lot of love and hugs about. I travelled up on the tube with my Wham! buddy June Montana and her sisters Sandrae and Sharon. Whilst I was always pleased to bump into George out and about, he and June were properly good mates. Pretty much every Wham! or George Michael-shaped treat that came my way was thanks to either June or George's fantastically considerate and endlessly patient PA, Siobhan 'Shiv' Bailey. It was June who made sure I got an invite round to George's for a bit of Sunday night dinner and Pop Trivial Pursuit (where, much to our delight, we beat him). And for birthdays and celebrations it was again June who gave him a prod, be it for my twenty-fifth upstairs at Il Siciliano, Aldo Zilli's first Soho eaterie that became the setting for many an extended Chianti Classico-soaked night, or the Laughing Stock of London party at Limelight, or even carol singing round High Street Kensington where George was currently residing. Meanwhile, Shiv would be the one who graciously sorted all the ticket requests and made sure we didn't miss out on all the fun.

Naturally, for such a momentous day as Whambley, I'd packed provisions and carefully studied the itinerary. To provide value for money the bill had been packed with extra entertainment – some, with the benefit of hindsight, more appropriate than others. Gary Glitter as the opening act is perhaps one reason the event has never made it to DVD. Nick Heyward's supremely sunny set of 'Love Plus One', 'Fantastic Day', 'Favourite Shirts', 'Take That Situation' and others that followed was more on the money.

Neither act, though, seemed quite the moment to pop a pill. Thankfully there followed the premiere of Lindsay Anderson's *Foreign Skies* documentary of Wham! in China. In the middle of that was one of my all-time favourites – 'Blue (Armed with Love)', the sparse, soulful B-side to 'Club Tropicana' that had first caught me by surprise when they performed it live on the end credits of Russell Harty's chat show. From there we were off and running.

There was plenty of incident to supplement the already not inconsiderable rush of witnessing your favourite pop group bidding you a joyous farewell. At one point June returned to her seat calmly announcing that she'd just put out a fire in the Ladies toilets. Mid-show, Steve Strange came to the rescue of Yasmin Le Bon when security threatened to call the police and eject her for obstructing the gangway. Miles down in front of us, on the other side of the fencing on the Wembley turf, we spotted two of our mob, Swiggy and Ana, waving frantically. I don't know quite what they said to security but somehow they managed to crawl under the fence and up over row after row until they miraculously squeezed in next to us.

The after-party at the Hippodrome had its own excitements. Having already distributed my party tickets to various deserving folk, I suddenly realised that I was in danger of not getting in myself, which wouldn't have been great since burning the midnight oil back in the *No.1* office was Deanne Pearson waiting for my 'Whispers' party report.

Not that June was about to let that happen. With a glint in her eye, she marched purposefully back through the pleading throngs to see who might have a spare. The first person she saw was Nick Heyward. 'Who's it for?' he asked. 'Paul Simper,' she replied. 'No,' said Nick emphatically. I'm not sure quite what I'd done to irk the Heyward but no doubt he had his reasons. Undeterred, June magicked a ticket from someone else. Mercifully, it wasn't Gary Glitter.

Inside, all Wham-related themes were covered. There was a snow blizzard for 'Last Christmas' in the entrance, pink fountains as camp as 'Go-Go' throughout and giant beach balls (and drinks that were free) for 'Tropicana'. The highlight was the netball court that had been set up over the dance floor where the beach balls were being batted back and forth with gay abandon. It was when some of our lot spotted the twenty-foot high inflatable animals dotted around the room, which could also be brought into play if you mounted them on your backs, that the action got a bit wiggy.

If Whambley was the perfect fan farewell, running it a not too shabby second that same year was the chance to do a bit of Christmas carolling with His Nibs. This had apparently become a bit of a tradition with George and David Austin essentially revisiting their busking days with a bunch of pissed-up friends, a box of wigs (I brought my own just to be on the safe side) and no pressing need to make any money. Still, David made sure there was at least some reward as he taxed each and every pub for a free bevy.

Everyone was in good spirits despite Wham! being no more. Since the summer, Pepsi and Shirlie had scored their own hit with 'Heartache' and George had just finished the video for 'I Knew You Were Waiting', his Aretha duet, which he gave me a little preview of whilst we waited for everyone else to assemble.

Perfectionist that he was, George wasn't about to let us loose on Kensington High Street without a rehearsal. So, wigs in place, we gathered in his kitchen and went through 'The Holly and The Ivy' and the rest until he was satisfied we could pass muster. Whether the bus conductor we surprised with a rendition of 'Ding Dong Merrily' on the Number 27, just as he clocked George in his flowing hippy locks, appreciated our vocal drilling it's hard to say. But he let out a high-pitched yelp and no fares were taken.

Post-Wham!, George was clearly enjoying himself. When he wasn't in America with much publicised new girlfriend – make-up artist Kathy Jeung – he was down the Wag or Il Siciliano or the latest addition to London's nightclub scene, Brown's – an upmarket den of iniquity run by Jake and Angelo Panayiotou on the site of the old Blitz Club. For really late nights there was somewhere called Fidenzi's, a subterranean half-empty affair off Regent Street, which did at least have a DJ to pester with requests for 'Battlestations' and

'Everything She Wants' if you were one of the very few people –
mostly me, George and June – who made it onto its minuscule
dance floor. George never had any problem dancing to his own
records – which is as it should be. If you won't even dance to your
own tunes, why should anyone else?

It was one such Fidenzi's late-nighter where we first christened
George 'It'll Be All Polite on the Night'. Being some time between
three and five in the morning whenever we ended up there, there
was a good chance that whoever decided to have a bit of a chinwag
with him was either hammered or off their nuts. God bless him,
whatever the frothing nonsense being spouted, (sometimes quite
possibly by me) he always greeted it with a nod and a cheery grin.

By the next time we got together for *No.1* readers' benefit it was
May 1987 and the first fruits proper of solo George were upon us.
Of the two new tracks the official B-side 'Hard Day' was the sounder,
funkier option but it was the three-parter 'I Want Your Sex' that
deliberately pushed buttons and made headlines in a climate now
increasingly dominated by fears of HIV and AIDS. What he hadn't
anticipated was quite how conservative broadcasters had become.
At the very mention of the word 'sex' Radio One refused to give the
single any daytime airplay and when it made it only as far as
Number 3 in the UK it was very chastely billed on the *Top of the Pops*
chart rundown as 'I Want'.

Thankfully none of this deterred him from getting stuck into
plenty of sex chat over two bumper spreads for our benefit. The
question mark over his own sexuality was already being bandied
around. If it wasn't Fleet Street, it was Fat Tony from the Wag's DJ
booth cheerily changing the words of 'Last Christmas' to: 'I gave it
to someone *male*.'

George's posse was close to belting FT that night but he was a lot more sanguine about any trial by Fleet Street.

'I've got very philosophical about my life in general compared to how I felt last year,' he said. 'I can't allow myself to believe that building a relationship with the public over the past six years, and working at it as hard as I've worked, is not stronger than a story in the *Sun*.'

My gaydar has always been rubbish so when friends or work colleagues asked me about George at that time I had neither a clue nor frankly much interest either way. In 2008, George told *Gay Times* that he came out to Andrew and Shirlie as bisexual when he was nineteen. But nine years before the LA arrest that outed him and inspired his glorious unabashed, disco toilets riposte, 'Outside', he clearly wasn't about to share such information with me over a croissant at Blake's Hotel in sunny west London.

'As long as the people around me don't believe that,' he said, as I asked about 'the gay angle'. 'If not then maybe I'll have to recover from it but I'm sure it won't take long. I knew I was setting myself up by doing this single. I've never really talked about sex, except for early on when I was just spouting shit that I knew the papers wanted to hear. But you can't run your career in fear of the press. And I refuse to. Whatever will be will be.'

I asked him if these days he was happier singing about sex than getting involved? (Although as the video was him and Kathy writh-ing around naked under a sheet, you'd assume he was getting some action.)

'All I know is I don't intend to go back to a series of affairs,' he said. 'Given the right circumstances I think most people are totally capable of monogamy. I think it's the only way, at the moment, that you can possibly control things. You cannot pretend that young kids are not aware of what's going on in terms of AIDS. They know that there's something very strange and very dangerous going on. It's making sex all so unpalatable. It's going to be very frightening for them because at the age of thirteen/fourteen sex is something that is constantly on your mind. And right now it's something that you're supposed to think is dangerous or dirty or threatening you in some way. I don't know what generation of people that's gonna breed.

'I have got very kind of monogamous ideas anyway. I think that everybody's ready for it again. It's nothing to do with morality; it's to do with nature. You can't expect to turn nature around the way we've turned it around in the last thirty years with the advent of effective contraception. I honestly believe men are more highly charged sexually anyway and want more sex than women do.'

He contested my snort at this last observation.

'It's true. I'm not blaming them. Men have a history of getting women pregnant and running away, which was always possible. Women could never run away from the fact that they were pregnant. In the last thirty years they've had the opportunity to say: "Right, I do want a sexual relationship with you but I don't want to get pregnant. So I'll try it and if I don't like it I'll go off with someone else." It was basically in their hands, which gave men the opportunity to be even more promiscuous. But now everything has got to turn around because nature has decided it doesn't like how we've reacted. It's nothing to do with morality, we've just fucked about with nature so much. The natural thing now is to turn the clock back again. I think it's what most people want.'

The single was featured on the *Beverly Hills Cop II* soundtrack but as with the new Bond movie, *The Living Daylights*, where the usually rampant 007 risked only the mildest of on-screen encounters with an exceedingly prim and proper cellist, there was no romantic involvement for Eddie Murphy's Axel Foley whatsoever.

'There's no sex apart from two points in the movie,' said George. 'One is in a striptease bar and the other is at Hugh Hefner's house and there are all these Playgirls there. I think that's the wrong way round to do it. That's exactly what shouldn't be happening. It's sectioning sex into promiscuous areas and sleaze. I really can't see that that's the way to go. The attention needs to be on re-emphasising where sex should come from – in other words the idea of relationships rather than strangers. That's the exact opposite to what's being done. And of course, "I Want Your Sex" is used in the scene with a striptease. But I had no say in that.'

Paul Rutherford noted after Whambley that he thought George was more camp as a performer now than he'd ever been.

'More camp? I don't think I could get any more camp!' he laughed. 'If you look at the *Make It Big* era, that's what I'd call camp. I think there was an awful lot more pelvis movement [at Whambley] but I wouldn't call that camp. I think 1984 was quite camp for a lot of people. The funniest is the "Last Christmas" video cos we've got all our friends in it. Everyone's got long hair. And everyone shouldn't have long hair. There's nobody in that video that looks like they ought to have long hair. Cos long hair should grow down, right? In the whole of that video everyone's hair is growing out. It's unbelievable. Everyone's got this hair that's got a life of its own.'

Although he'd privately set himself a goal of making the big leap up to the same level of solo success in America as Michael Jackson, Madonna, Prince and Bruce Springsteen – the names that now dwarfed his Class of '82 contemporaries – it was yet to happen.

'I don't have the status of celebrity in America that I have over here,' he said. 'It's not a big deal. Some places spoil me but I'm not on the level of a Bruce Springsteen.'

I'd asked him if he could ever see himself doing a Tom Jones and playing Vegas in twenty years' time – he'd recently been there with Kathy.

'No, I can't imagine myself in twenty years' time playing Caesar's Palace. Kathy spent all night playing the slot machines but I went straight to bed. I can't get into blackjack or any of that. It's not like when I was a kid and I used to put some money on the Grand National because I didn't have any money and it would have been nice to have some. They gave us a huge suite. If they'd known I was only going to spend about fifty dollars they might not have done.'

George was certainly no skinflint. When we were out of an evening he'd pick up the drinks bill or dinner ('I reckon I must have bought everyone's drinks in here,' he observed wryly after one Brown's monster of a bar bill headed his way) and he even forked out for a bunch of friends – including Nanas Sarah and Keren – to go to Richard Branson's Necker Island. He was, of course, impossible to buy for. Posh white wine was an apparently safe option but then you assumed he could always buy a better bottle himself – and what if you got one he hated? One time I bought him a blue vinyl 12-inch of Sheila & B Devotion's 'Spacer' but then panicked it wasn't enough of a present so took it home with me again.

Politics was supposedly of less interest to *No.1* readers so again these quotes never made it to print, but there was a General Election coming up and George was feeling more ambivalent than before. Wham! had got a lot of stick for miming at a striking miner's benefit at the Royal Albert Hall (though the money and profile raised by them appearing was the real point of the exercise). In the Thatcher years it was assumed that those pop stars with flouncy hair and Yohji Yamamoto suits were all dyed-in-the wool Tories while only Red Wedge supporters like Weller and Billy Bragg were in the Kinnock camp.

'Whereas I voted Labour with total confidence last time, I don't know what to do now,' he said. 'I think I'll vote Labour simply on the arms issue [something he'd address again in 2002 with 'Shoot the Dog']. I don't know if it's the best thing in the immediate future to have a Labour government but I know that any government that is making a real black-and-white decision on that is a good thing. It's a real shame that they cocked things up for themselves so badly last year. But, really, I think it's down to having such an extreme right-wing government. You're bound to get an extreme left-wing reaction. Even if the majority of the Labour party doesn't want that. When a country has moved as far to the right as we have, it needs easing back into the middle. People are too scared of being told it's totally wrong. Red Wedge and extreme left movements, for me, although I think their hearts and ideals are in the right place, I don't think they take human nature into account. I'm afraid I'm very much a moderate. But the Tories will get in again. I have no doubt about it. The rich are getting richer – which is a very embarrassing thing for a rich person to say.'

There had been plans to work with Michael Jackson but they'd recently fallen through.

'Basically, when we talked about it it was supposedly an anti-apartheid thing,' he said. 'Honestly, I'm quite disappointed about the whole thing. I think what happened was, we had the meeting and I was stupid enough to mention it to Julie Burchill. Not that she wrote anything bad but she mentioned it in her piece in *The Times* and the next thing you knew it was all over the papers that I was supposed to be doing it. It must have looked to him – especially considering his status in America compared to mine – that it was an opportunistic thing I was trying to do. As it turns out, I'm glad it didn't happen because on top of the Aretha thing it would have looked bad. Although if the proceeds had gone to the Africa fund that would have been good. He's not crazy though. I only met him for about three quarters of an hour but he seemed very sweet and much more of a balanced person than you would imagine.'

George later told me that as he and David Austin left the meeting at Neverland they looked back and in the hallway MJ was in front of the mirror practising his dance moves. The man in the mirror in full swing.

It would be another five months till his solo album was finally ready. At this stage the opening track was intended to be what finished up as the final closing track – 'Kissing A Fool'.

'That's a song that I've been writing for about two years,' he said. 'Then I changed it and it became this new ballad. Now I don't know what to do with the old song. Don't hold me to this but I think the album title is *Kissing A Fool*. No, not "Kissing a Fall". F-o-o-l. I'm not kissing Mark E. Smith! Anyway, that's what I think, although I'm not sure. I might have another blockbuster track that comes out in the next two or three months.'

Three months later, on my twenty-fifth birthday, he popped along to Il Siciliano where we were celebrating and took me out to his Mercedes to listen to a new song that he'd just finished, 'Faith'. The guitar break in the middle was still absent so it was only about three minutes long but it most definitely got the thumbs up. Another blockbuster track.

I did get a call from him on the day that I finally got my mitts on the album for *No.1*. That night June asked me to stand by my phone at home and he called to go through it track by track. Apart from wishing that both 'Hard Day' and 'Hand to Mouth' hadn't been wasted as B-sides I didn't have anything much of import to add. Four US Number 1 singles on the trot and over twenty-five million sales worldwide would suggest he'd got it about right, although for me his third solo album, Older, in 1996, is still his greatest.

No next step would have been complete, of course, without a party. Wham! had always served up good ones with an entertaining array of guests. For *Make It Big*, *No.1*'s Karen Swayne had even bumped into Frankie Howerd who had complimented George on his lovely teeth. For the 'Faith' one it was to the Savoy with everyone from pop stars of the day like Curiosity and Mandy Smith to the fantastically poodle-haired rock/soap combo of Brian May (George was a massive Queen fan, particularly the albums *A Night at the Opera* and *A Day at the Races*) and Anita Dobson.

As luck would have it, the Saturday it fell on was Halloween so our lot decided it must be fancy dress and turned up as a bunch of red devils. On arrival, we realised we were the only ones to have got this memo, but only security got the hump. One was heard to remark: 'I don't care if they have got a ticket, if I see one more red devil they're not coming in!'

Find of the night was Britain's most celebrated Madam, Cynthia Payne. Her life had already made it to the big screen at the start of that year with Julie Walters in Terry Jones' *Personal Services* but now she had another young actress in tow for the evening. My final memory of the night was Madame Cyn banging on the doors of Brown's as she hollered at the doorman: 'I'm Cynthia Payne and this is Emily Lloyd. She's playing me in a movie!'

Naturally they let them in forthwith.

14

PRINCE SAYS KEEP IT COMING

I'll admit it, I was slow to Prince. In typically Johnny-come-lately fashion, it had taken till 'When Doves Cry'. A *Top of the Pops* clip, cropped of beginning and end still gave us Prince on a purple motorbike, Prince naked in a bath with doves flying hither and thither and Prince coming down a spiral staircase from nowhere. But it was in those last moments before it dissolved into a squiggle of eighties video graphic effects and back to the studio audience that it really got me. No longer just clips from his forthcoming debut movie, *Purple Rain*, this was Prince in his fedora and fishnets in a whited-out studio surrounded by an assembled gang of musicians. This was a group like no other I'd seen. A man in surgical blue scrubs and shades; a woman with massive quiff, Regency brocade fawn long coat and lace undies; a drummer with stand-up kit dressed like Mozart on his way to the races. All dancing and dipping and playing as one. It was *The Muppets* meets *The Warriors* meets the Blitz. It was The Revolution.

I was yet to make it to the big city when London received its first royal visit. Three pounds to get in, Prince at the Lyceum in 1981 wearing fishnets and flasher's mac on his *Dirty Mind* tour has since become a touchstone early-eighties London gig; up there with Luther at the Dominion and Grace Jones' One Woman Show on Drury Lane. The difference being that whilst those two were the hottest tickets in town, Prince barely pulled in enough punters to half fill the room.

London would have to wait five long years before it got the chance to make up for such slack attendance. There was one headline-making smash-and-grab visit when he nipped into The Grosvenor in 1984 to trouser a BPI Best International Artist award, dwarfed by his personal bodyguard – the massive, snowy-haired Chick Huntsberry – and not best impressed when Frankie's Holly Johnson introduced him as someone with whom he'd had sex over the phone.

Really, Prince had no need to travel. If the new MTV generation of British pop acts had sussed you could get a three-minute pop promo to tour the world for you, Prince took that ninety minutes further. With a clear vision and the brassiest of necks, he got Hollywood to come to his home town and shoot *Purple Rain* – his little 7 million dollar Oscar-winner that grossed more than ten times that and did the same job for him on an epic scale.

Like *Saturday Night Fever* six years earlier, I was dumbstruck by the results. That look on the faces of the Minneapolis First Avenue faithful, resplendent in guyliner and New Wave haircuts, as The Kid hits the opening chords of 'Purple Rain' brought a similarly gobsmacked response from row K of the Warner West End at the London press screening. Pete Barrett was tickled pink to see me wiping a tear from my eye but, hey, this was emotional stuff. His Royal Complicatedness had finally given band members Wendy & Lisa their due by playing their song *and* he'd stopped taunting them with that pop-up toy monkey.

There were of course times at *No.1* when we took the mick out of Prince. The little fella. The first time he graced our cover in

February 1985 it was as his Spitting Image puppet with a 'Puppet Master Prince' cover line and a Martin Townsend interview with his former guitarist Dez Dickerson – he of the Kamikaze headband – who had given way to the incomparable Wendy Melvoin at the end of the 1983 *1999* tour.

Dez had never really been down with some of his boss' 'out there' stage gear. Like when Prince appeared in what Dez referred to as his gerbil suit (please let there be a song in those legendary song vaults of his called 'If I Was Ur Gerbil') clearly displaying the Nelson family jewels. Dez also wasn't mad keen on some of the fruitier lyrics. He insisted to *No.1* that he only ever mouthed the words to 'Sister' – a bouncy little number about incest. Natty headband or not, Dez clearly had to go.

The following month, March 1985, I was in Australia with Spandau when MTV broadcast Prince and The Revolution's *Purple Rain* tour from Syracuse. I was used to seeing Tone and the boys striking a few rock poses in front of the screaming Melbourne hordes, catching a few teddies and popping on a bit of Tchaikovsky to get the crowd going before launching into 'Highly Strung'. No disrespect to the Spands, but what was now emanating from my TV set was on a whole different level to that; indeed to anything I'd ever seen.

At times, it was hard to pinpoint just exactly what was going on. One minute Prince was sliding down a fireman's pole, the next he was off for forty winks (we'll call it winks) under a purple blanket. There was a long conversation with a big white flapping sheet, standing in for God, which he conducted from his piano stool whilst playing his exquisite gospel lament, 'How Come U Don't Call Me Anymore?'. When Prince was done with that he went and sat in the bath. There were lacerating guitar solos, heavenly falsettos and astonishing pirouettes and splits in life-threatening high heels, whilst behind him The Revolution – Wendy, Brown Mark, Bobby Z, Lisa Coleman and Dr Fink – did their rock solid musical thing whilst delivering immaculately drilled dance moves as tight as anything James Brown had to offer. I was simultaneously electrified and exhausted watching it.

What any good obsession needs, though, is company. By the time Prince finally put us out of our misery and returned to London in the second week of August 1986 I'd found a fellow believer. Paul Rutherford loved Prince to bits. Whilst Frankie were officially in the middle of their comeback with 'Rage Hard', most of the talk at our *No.1* FGTH photo shoot was of Prince. And if it wasn't Prince it was of another of his First Avenue beneficiaries, The Time's Jimmy Jam and Terry Lewis, whose musical transformation of sweet little Janet Jackson on her *Control* album was enough to knock even big brother Michael for six, going on to sell 14 million copies around the world.

Press tickets for Prince's three Wembley Arena shows were unsurprisingly in scant supply. I'd not risked a freebie and instead had hurried to the box office to buy four myself. Off we went – me, Paul, Polly Strettell and Jacquie O'Sullivan – in a state of high excitement. And high was exactly where we were sitting. I'm not sure it was possible to get four tickets further from the action. Way up in the top of Double Z, peering down the mile-long aircraft hangar that is the Arena we were at least two postal districts away. But even as a dot on the stage, there was no mistaking what he was delivering.

In a revamp as radical as Bowie switching mid-US tour from *Diamond Dogs* rock opera to *Young Americans* stripped-down soul a decade earlier, Prince binned baths, poles and billowing sheets for a simple chequered stage and a soul revue line-up that gave starring roles to two former minders – Wally Safford and Greg Brooks – and The Time's Jerome Benton as his three stooges. The Revolution were even sharper and funkier, supplemented by a horn section, but just to prove all you really needed was a bit of floor space and a mike stand, Prince took it further back to basics grinding his equipment and teasing us 7,000 onlookers with a deliciously extended version of 'Head'.

Of course, once bitten there was no way that just one two-hour taste of His Royal Canary Suited and Bootedness was going to be enough. Word was starting to get around that unlike most pop stars who tended to clock in for a couple of hours, do a gig then get on with the partying, Prince was more partial to playing – and then playing all over again. After what we'd just seen it hardly seemed feasible. Still, there was a Warner's after-show being thrown in his honour at Busbys on Charing Cross Road. But how to get our paws on the hottest ticket in town? What we needed was a guy on the inside. Or gal.

As luck would have it, when she wasn't busy delivering her own musical take on James Brown with Brilliant's reworking of 'This Is A Man's World', June Montana had got herself a bit of extra work helping her mate Taryn over at WEA. Sometimes that meant just answering phones, other times a bit of a vinyl mail-out. But amongst her duties for this particular week was putting Prince after-party tickets into envelopes. It was the perfect crime. With a little sleight of hand and her always impressive 'don't fuck with me' face firmly in place should anyone challenge her, June deftly redirected some precious invites for all three after-parties in our direction.

The first night at Busbys proved to be a bit of a trial run. After a lifetime starved of Prince live we were only beginning to learn the ropes. Would he do a couple of numbers? Would there be hits or B-sides or covers? Would it be the whole band? Would there be guest stars? Could it be Madonna?

We weren't fast enough back from Wembley to get right down the front at the club, and at first I'm not sure we were convinced that anything more than some purple tribute act would be standing behind those microphones set up on the stage. But appear he and The Revolution did for an hour-long jam that included one guest star – Ronnie Wood – and one Rolling Stones song – 'Miss You' – that Prince declared he wished he'd written.

It was pretty damn special seeing them in a more intimate setting but, greedy fuckers that we were, we reckoned we could do better. The free bar had been a distraction, and even in a room of about 300 people, we still hadn't managed a clear eyeline. The second night's after-show was at Richard Branson's Kensington Roof Gardens, a top-floor nightclub complete with live flamingos. Since we didn't have any more Wembley tickets, we made sure we arrived on the dot. There was a tiny stage, essentially on the same level as the dance floor, with the equipment already set up ready for action. Sod the free drinks, Paul, Jacqs and June set up our stall a nose length from his keyboards stage right and remained rooted to the spot, ignoring all distractions.

It's a testament to just how dazzling that *Parade* line-up was that I'd completely forgotten, until someone recently reminded me, that Eric Clapton was also somewhere on that tiny stage that night. We were all too wrapped up doing little 'rain come down' hand movements over Prince's fingertips as he noodled away on his B-side fan favourite '17 Days'. From the back of Double Z to right slap bang under their noses in the space of forty-eight hours was quite the journey. But for all the OhmifuckingGod-ness of being there, what was really thrilling was watching Prince and The Revolution all appearing to have an absolute ball. What with the hired muscle, years of no-shows and lack of interviews it was easy to imagine that Prince was a bit of a cold fish – or at least someone as disconnected from the rest of us as Michael Jackson. These after-shows revealed another side to him (although how anyone who does a rendition of 'How Much is that Doggy in the Window' in his main show could not be suspected to have a sense of humour, I don't know).

The following year, I interviewed Jill Jones, who had been in and out of Prince's life personally and professionally as far back as the *Dirty Mind* tour when her mum managed support act Teena Marie. Jill sang backing vocals and made video appearances on 'Lady Cab Driver' and '1999' and delivered a fairly wobbly performance in *Purple Rain* as jilted Jill, the First Avenue barmaid ignored by The Kid. She thought Prince was funny too.

'People say: "We want an interview with Prince," said Jill. 'I say: "Go and check out *Under the Cherry Moon* [his slapstick heavy second movie]; you might learn a lot." Prince has got a good sense of humour and the humour in *Cherry Moon* is his humour.'

The sight of Prince running along the race track in his high heels as Christopher Tracy at that movie's climax nearly gave Rutherford a coronary when we saw it a couple of weeks later over the bank holiday. But even that just made us love him more.

There were disappointments to follow. The summer of 1987 *Sign 'O' The Times* tour should have seen 40,000 of us basking in His Peach and Blackness at Wembley Stadium. Mere days before he was due to play, it was discovered that the set with all its ramps and alleys and hoardings, which had already played round Europe, didn't actually fit. The fact that Simon Mills at *Sky Magazine* was (quite rightfully) crowing that he'd already seen the show in all its glory in Rotterdam didn't help.

Sign 'O' The Times had taken us a whole lot further down the road, and the hype that accompanied its impending release built to unprecedented levels. Usually when it came to reviewing new albums, magazines would be sent a copy through the post or by bike to contemplate at their leisure. For *Sign* we were individually summoned to WEA's press office where we had eighty minutes to listen to the four sides and then swiftly draw our conclusions. For *No.1*, where space for critical analysis was minimal, that didn't make much odds, but I felt for Paolo Hewitt one floor above us at the *NME* as he scratched his head after just one earful to see where the hell Prince was coming from with something like 'The Ballad of Dorothy Parker'.

George Michael was another who was respectfully baffled by some of *Sign*'s material when we talked at that time. George had his doubts even on the *Parade* tour when he told me one night at Zilli's, another Aldo eaterie, that he felt it was cheating audiences to only do thirty seconds of one of your biggest hits, as Prince had done with 'Little Red Corvette'. Now with *Sign* we got into a debate over Prince's use of vari-speed, which I'd said I thought he didn't like.

'It's not that I don't like it,' said George. 'I really like the vari-speed but I think it's overused. I just feel that the album is terribly self-indulgent. I tell you another thing I realised listening to that album – and it's something we'll all have to watch out for – is that now that compact discs are definitely going to take over it's very easy to skip tracks. If one track doesn't grab you you just flick on to the next one. There's stuff on that album that I really can't be bothered to listen to. I don't like "Hot Thing" or "It".

'The album is all attitude. It's great attitude and it's really sexy, but I don't think the music backs it up. I think "Strange Relationship" is great and "Sign 'O' The Times". It would have made a much more impressive single album. If he could get the amount of brilliant melody that he's got on some of the earlier stuff and combine it with that imagination he would make an absolutely stunning album. But it was very brave. It remains to be seen how the album will do.'

It didn't sell like *Purple Rain* (roughly 22 million to *Sign's* 4 million worldwide) but posterity is resoundingly in Prince's favour. Hailed by many publications as the album of the year, it became the album of his career – all the more extraordinary for the fact that he played every last note with the exception of the live recording of 'It's Gonna Be a Beautiful Night'. In the upper constellations of greatness, an artist can just occasionally hit on such a hot streak of inspiration that they take a whole decade with them, reinventing and re-energising themselves and everyone around them as they go. Bowie did it in the seventies and the likes of Mott the Hoople, Lou Reed, Iggy Pop and even Luther Vandross felt the benefit. And in the eighties, it was Prince; and whether you were Vanity 6, The Bangles, Sinead O'Connor, Chaka Khan or even Sheena Easton, he sprinkled some extra stardust.

Like Bowie, Prince ended up providing the most far-reaching, all-encompassing and artistically satisfying body of work of his decade. From *Dirty Mind* to *Sign* he flitted from filthy funk, power and electro pop through anthemic rock, psychedelic funk, folksy and 1930s balladeering to lean, incisive, soulful social commentary.

Neither sold the most records of their eras, but 100 million plus actual sales is an elite club that the big hitters of future generations can only marvel at.

Starved of any live sightings in 1987, we feasted on Prince's offshoots instead. We already knew Wendy & Lisa, Sheila E, Vanity 6, Apollonia 6, Susannah Melvoin and The Family and we'd even warmed to a remoulded Sheena Easton, but it looked like the best of all might be upon us when Jill Jones finally stepped into the spotlight. Her first single, 'Mia Bocca', featured a video by Jean-Baptiste Mondino so gorgeous that the weekend before she was due to fly in to do UK press we'd watched nothing else. The Laughing Stock crew in Wapping were literally hauled out of their beds so we had an excuse to watch it again. Rutherford declared it the best video he'd ever seen, which delighted Jill, a Frankie fan.

'I think it's the best quality video there's been in a long time,' she said, despite the annoyance that MTV was deeming it too racy to broadcast. 'I think that's just funny. I'm proud of it. If I were in bed with twenty guys then I'm sure they'd show it because it would be expected from the Prince regime. I wish people would start to see things artistically rather than just looking at and praising trash. But in anything if you go against the grain, you pull through in the end cos you're not just conforming to other people's ideals. Frankie were a band that went against the grain. You really have to. So I'll keep doing things the way I want to do it.'

Catching a few rays on the roof of WEA whilst reclining in a little black Azzedine Alaïa dress for *No.1*'s photographer, the Jones was already an old hand at ducking all the relationship stuff about her and Prince but was still far more open than the rest of Team Paisley Park when it came to other aspects of his work and family life. The way she told it, theirs was more of a paternal thing (perhaps the implications of that are best not dwelt on but she'd been raised in Ohio by her mum and grandparents with no dad on her birth certificate).

'Prince has been more like my dad,' said Jill. 'I can't bully him. He's the only one. He just looks at me in the studio when I go in and it's chaos. He's stable, giving me good advice, always hearing my new adventures: "So what's new with you now?" He keeps saying me and his dad are a lot alike. It's true. Me and John L [jazz pianist, John L Nelson, whom Prince had given a co-writing credit on 'The Ladder' and 'God' on *Purple Rain*] have a great time. His dad is one of the most wonderful men I've ever met, besides Azzedine. Older men are my friends more. I have a good feeling with them.'

There's some debate as to whether the album's stand-out track, 'Baby You're a Trip', which opens and closes it, was one that Prince gave her or that she wrote about him or even about someone else. They share credits on four other songs and there's an unreleased Prince demo of 'Trip' that has since surfaced. She told me she'd written it and looked a little hurt that I might be suggesting that the line about a star-struck little fool could be referring to her.

'Someone asked: "Are you his girlfriend?"' said Jill. 'I said: "Seriously, would I have hung round this long without being credited with something more than being just another girlfriend? That's crazy. For that song [the person] was even crazier than Prince is in relationships. I've seen Prince in his relationships. I wouldn't want anything to do with that.'

She had a boyfriend who was back in New York looking after her dogs, which were peach-and-white bichon frise. The first, Koo Koo, was a gift from Prince (and a future song title for Sheila E).

'My dogs rule my house.' She laughed. 'Prince gave Koo Koo to me on the *1999* tour because I was sort of bored with the tour. I sang and danced and did things but I wanted something else so I said I really wanted a dog. He was like: "Jill, are you crazy? A dog on tour?" So he surprised me cos I was like moping around. Now I've told him I want a horse. Prince said: "Why don't you change the 'r' to a 'u' and you'll have a house."'

Of all his camp, Jill seemed the most like a female version of him. She wasn't a fan of the term protégé.

'In a way I wish they would say I was more equal,' said Jill. 'I feel like I'm not going to be such a burden. This all takes a bunch of people. Maybe one day they'll get it.'

Back in Ohio, before her mum moved to LA with her and remarried, she'd been the only mixed race child in the whole town.

'It was such a small town,' she said. 'I lived with my grandparents while my mum was travelling doing modelling and singing. I was the only mixed kid. It was the strangest thing. I got more stick from the black kids than the white kids. They would throw rocks at me sometimes. The only times they were nice to me was if I let them brush my hair. But the white kids would go: "You little n****r." I pulled one kid right off the merry-go-round for that.'

The Jones was certainly her own boss. After we'd chatted and done photos, I went with her to a Radio One interview and then back to Soho so she could pop in on the Richmond/Cornejo shop run by one of our gang – Kim Hunt – who'd also spent the weekend lapping up her 'Mia Bocca'. How dress-shopping with *No.1* journalists fitted into WEA's overall press schedule wasn't abundantly clear, but she did it all the same.

In a world where even something as magnificent as The

Revolution had already come to an end (replaced by the New Power Generation), she was well aware of the shifting dynamics around her purple playmate.

'Each person has to be in charge of their own destiny,' said Jill of all the hangers-on. 'If they're hanging on, suddenly they are removed from the situation – in a funny way. It's not that he gets rid of a lot of people. They just can't hang any more. You feel them when they walk in the room. I know when someone's about to leave. I can feel it. I'm sure it hurts them a little sometimes. But desperate people frighten me. I don't like desperate people. It's scary to be around them.'

That summer she was due to open for him on the US leg of the *Sign 'O' The Times* tour. She was already three songs into a second album and had been out in Amsterdam watching the show and gleefully eying up his ramps for her own use. Whether she wasn't watching everything else close enough or the sands had simply shifted once again, I don't know for sure, but come summer she was also gone; written out of the next Prince chapter.

By 1988 I was even starting to have dreams about Prince. Rutherford had very sweetly given me his vinyl copy of *The Black Album* when he'd got hold of one after the crashing disappointment (essentially more grist to the mill!) of it being withdrawn at the eleventh hour. A UK fan club called The Revolution, run by a generous soul called Camille, had sent me a cassette of out-takes from the proposed triple album (initially *Dream Factory*, still with The Revolution, *Crystal Ball* and the vari-speeded *Camille*) and one track 'Joy in Repetition' with its strung-out, funked-up grind about a club where a live band that played a song called 'Soul Psychodelicide' (a little bit behind the beat) had penetrated deep.

A quick side note on why Prince was the gift that kept on giving for fans. When we lost him (way too soon with George and Bowie) in 2016, YouTube was flooded with concert rarities. Amongst them was a live audio jam of one song that lasts a back-breaking fifty-nine minutes – that'll be The Revolution playing 'Soul Psychodelicide'.

My strangest Prince dream was one where Prince is standing over me playing 'If I Was Your Girlfriend' and I'm in a pair of monogrammed blue and black flares. He then gives me Cat's – his dancer – tutu to wear, but I've forgotten to put any pants on and my erection keeps raising it up, much to the alarm of the audience.

A trip to LA at the start of 1988, ostensibly to do a feature with Jermaine Stewart in Disneyland for *No.1*, ended up coinciding with Rutherford working on his solo stuff with former Prince co-writer André Cymone who told him that the 'Suck up food and heat' line from 'Bob George' was Prince being his mum. Paul was also mates with Jody Watley who recounted a visit to Prince at Paisley Park where fantastically he disappeared and reappeared five times in completely different outfits before they even made it out the door.

As the year built too, too slowly towards the now desperately awaited summer *Lovesexy* tour, there were more treats and even the occasional fall out. When the 'Alphabet St.' video landed on my desk, I raced all the way to Wapping in my lunch break to share it with Ruthers for the first time. Another lunchtime Paul bunked off his own recording session with ABC (where they were recording 'Seduction' and 'Cracked Wide Open') so we could catch the *Sign 'O' The Times* movie in its all too brief one-week residency at the Dominion Theatre.

Our one Prince flashpoint was when I admitted to quite liking Sinitta's 'Cross My Broken Heart' single.

'I'm gonna write to Prince,' threatened Paul, appalled. 'He won't let you buy his records now!'

There had been a happy new addition to our purple clan. I'd met Alice Temple a few times when she was hanging out with Boy George and Fat Tony and I was knocking about with Jane Goldman. We bumped into each other again one Sunday morning at a preview of *Sign 'O' The Times* at Warner West End (where else?). Alice was talking to a tramp who was lying on the pavement outside the Hippodrome.

'Have you been up all night?' asked Alice.

'I've been up for twenty years!' said the tramp.

Suitably fuelled by eighty-five minutes of Prince and Cat at full throttle, we headed back to mine to pore over my treasured out-takes, the Channel 4 *Parade* tour (with its mysterious close-up of what looks like a fanny but is actually Prince's armpit), a WEA VHS of singles promos that someone had kindly sent my way and anything else I could think of. Alice did a great Wendy impression (and had a bit of a crush). She'd been hanging out with Bobby Z and his wife, Vicky – who was brilliant at prompting stories about Wendy, Prince and Madonna when Bobby was trying to be a little more discreet. Alice also turned me on to Stevie Wonder – 'If you love Prince, you will love Stevie!' – who I was shamefully sketchy on from his early seventies glory years so she sweetly made me a great mix tape.

The countdown to 1988's *Lovesexy* tour seemed to take forever, but finally Monday, 25 July came around and with a roar of his white Thunderbird with Cat and Sheila E. lounging in the back for

'Erotic City' it was Wembley Arena here we go again. Blessedly, this time in the round and with no need of binoculars. Any lingering regrets for that lost *Sign 'O' The Times* tour were parked as Prince and his positivity-laden New Power Generation delivered 130 minutes that ranged from the unexpected (*The Black Album's* 'Bob George') to the saucy ('Jack U Off') to the sublime ('Anna Stesia').

The biggest surprise of the night, though, was saved for the aftershow at Camden Palace. It looked like Cat was officially the belle of the crystal ball as Prince kicked off a two-hour second set by getting everyone to sing 'Happy Birthday' to her. But then, four songs in, he peered down to the left of where I was standing and picked someone out in the crowd. He'd already handed Mica Paris a tambourine to tap along to 'Forever in My Life' and now he fancied a bit more.

'You sing, don't you?' he said with a sly smile. Then with just enough of a pause for the enormity of what he was suggesting to sink in, they were into 'Just My Imagination' with Mica beaming and blushing in equal measure and totally delivering the goods. Less successful was a repeat performance from Ronnie Wood. 'It's not a piano you know, Ronnie!' laughed His Royal Polka Dottedness as Prince strapped on his sexy sky-blue guitar and Ronnie fumbled about.

Actually, there was one more surprise that night that would take another twenty-seven years to reveal itself. Somewhere in the Wembley auditorium was a super-hot Barry girl in Alphabet letter tights called Katie. She'd done a bunk from her mum and dad's house in South Wales and hot-tailed it to London on her own for her first ever Prince concert. That's as good a first place to (almost) meet your future wife as I can think of.

The rest of the week followed a pattern that Prince fans around the world would become familiar with over the following decades. Every night was a fresh hunt round London for that precious after-show gig. Could it be the I/D party at the Empire Rooms, or maybe he'd pop up with Curtis Mayfield at Dingwalls? How about the Limelight? Cat and Mico Weaver (NPG guitarist) were spotted at Café de Paris on the Wednesday. In the office, Burschey and Bell tried to convince me that it was worth a trip to the Mean Fiddler in Harlesden on the off-chance that The T-Birds were really Prince in disguise.

Thanks to the incredibly sweet and supremely statuesque Alison Brunjes who was part of the Sigue Sigue Sputnik crew, I got to see him at Wembley again on my actual birthday. Since the after-show party jam he'd now added a 'Blues in C' interlude and a much-talked-about grand piano medley, which that night blissfully delivered 'The Ladder', 'How Come U Don't Call Me Anymore?', 'Condition of the Heart' and 'Raspberry Beret' – every one an ace. Even then I wanted more. My next night's Prince dream had me being presented with a very special copy of 'Glam Slam' that when you flipped it over had a never-ending list of covers on the B-side: the Prince equivalent of Willy Wonka's everlasting gobstopper.

Later Prince treats would come in the shape of a couple of *No.1* interviews with Wendy & Lisa, who were as smart and sexy and funny as you could possibly have wished for. I even got to play Ms and Ms (our variation on Mr and Mrs) with them.

'There's only one person who Lisa has ever thumped,' said Wendy. 'With very good cause. I shouldn't say who but hallelujah.'

She smiled. 'You can guess who . . .'

Happily, they eventually made up and would work with him

again on his *Musicology* album in 2004 and were also there for his stunning BRITs return visit in 2006.

My Prince obsession reached such dizzying and random heights that I even sorted my pension plan on the advice of one of his most fleeting protégés: a girl called Ashe, whom he'd met in London and who I duly interviewed for *No.1* for any scraps. But seriously, who else would you ask for sound financial advice except someone vaguely connected to Prince? I should have given Sheena Easton a bell about my ISA.

As for meeting him, sadly I never got the call to Paisley Park. It's probably for the best. I'd surely have put my foot in it or broken out in a cold sweat. If I was slack-jawed at Geldof, it doesn't bear thinking about how I'd have coped with just me, Prince and a couple of Jehovah's Witnesses.

Instead, our only encounter was when I was DJing. It was 1995 and The Artist Formerly Known As had 'Slave' emblazoned on his cheek and was over to collect a Best International Male BRIT award for his one and only UK Number 1 – the independently released 'The Most Beautiful Girl in the World'.

I was DJing at Brown's and being post-BRITs, it was packed. Usually my weeknight sets on a Tuesday would be played out to a pretty much barren dance floor with all the merriment going on in the upstairs or up-upstairs bar and just the occasional sortie downstairs from Tara Palmer-Tomkinson to request George Michael's 'Fast Love', which she would wait for, dance to, then bugger off back from whence she came. Tonight, though, there was barely room for Tara to shake a tail feather. The dance floor was so rammed that it took me a few minutes to spot the stellar presence sitting just a few feet away with a minimal crew as he checked out everyone's best moves.

Then the thunderbolt struck. It's The Artist Always Incontrovertibly (Whatever He's Got Written On His Cheek) Known As Prince. Look, he's checking out the dance floor and holy cow now he's checking out the DJ. I'm the DJ. TLC's 'Creep' is nearly done. What am I gonna play next? Do I play one of his? What have I even got of his in my record bags? A quick shufty. Three very well-worn 'Kiss', 'Get Off' and 'Alphabet St' 12 inches. No, not cool. I mean, they're all very cool but not when he's right there. I could play '♥ or Money' (the 'Kiss' B-side) but then that might clear the dance floor. Shit. I play a Prince record in front of Prince and it clears the fucking dance floor. WTF?

This internal monologue could have gone on a whole lot longer but T-Boz, Chilli and Lisa Left Eye were almost done. I hastily slapped on an old Brown's banker, Brandy & Monica's 'The Boy is Mine', and started frenetically flicking through the remainder.

That's when I spotted one of Prince's crew getting to his feet and with a nod of his head purposefully begin to make a beeline in my direction.

I'm not averse to the odd DJ request. Sometimes it can liven things up – on the proviso, of course, that you've got the bloody record. As Prince's suited person sidled round the side of the booth and fixed me with his beady eye, I braced myself for some rare Sly or Staple Singers request or something else I hadn't got, like Public Enemy.

A large paw slid smoothly into his trouser pocket and produced a fold of notes with a brief, easy-to-follow message: 'Prince says keep it coming.'

I nodded sagely. In all honesty, I would have run all the way to Tower Records and back to get him 'The Smurfs Sing Christmas' if that had been his heart's desire. But considering my bags were bulging with pretty much nothing but TLC, Brandy, Destiny's Child and Salt-N-Pepa, being asked to play more R & B divas wasn't a tough ask.

'Prince says keep it coming.' It was the easiest thirty quid I ever made.

15

DOWN TO EARTH

Pop can't stay still. Much though the artists, fans and journos might love it to, the glory years are as fleeting as seasons. *No.1* mag had caught a good wave in 1983 just as Duran, Wham!, Spandau and Culture Club came to the boil. A year later, we had the Brucie bonus of Frankie Goes to Hollywood. Then that Christmas something unexpected happened that pretty much scuppered that class of eighties pop.

For all its honourable intentions – and genuinely life-changing results – Band Aid was not great for pop. The spectacle of chart rivals suddenly being all buddy-buddy, rubbing shoulders wasn't an entirely new one. Mick Jagger's there hanging out with The Beatles when they did their *Our World* live broadcast of 'All You Need is Love'. Bowie and Bolan are clearly pals when the former went on the latter's TV show *Marc* to muck about and duet. But for all that, as a fan, you still made your choice: Beatles or Stones, Bolan or Bowie, Spandau or Duran. The Christmas 1984 cover of *No.1* sported two hitherto unthinkable double acts: John Taylor with Tony Hadley and Paul Weller with Boy George.

The reality of course was that all these pop folk did meet up because they were all appearing on the same TV shows, be it backstage at *Top of the Pops* in White City or Euro festivals in San Remo or Montreux. But even so there were many who were most particular about the company they kept. Kevin Rowland forbade Dexys from fraternising with the other chart acts; Spandau had an argy bargy with Frankie about all their piss-taking at the Thompson Twins' summer party at Stocks; and Paul Weller got very uppity with the Style Council's graphic designer, Simon Halfon, having anything to do with George Michael and Wham!. It was all very handbags at dawn, but it gave the fans a clear sense of identity and all those pop stars their edge.

From Band Aid onwards it got harder to keep track of who was with whom. Duran's guitarist Andy Taylor essentially became a gun for hire, guesting with rock stars like Billy Idol and Michael Des Barres once he'd decamped to LA. George Michael popped up on not one but two Elton John records ('Nikita' and 'Wrap Her Up'). And Tony Hadley surprised even his fellow bandmates when he materialised in front of 80,000 Queen fans in Auckland doing 'Jailhouse Rock' with his new pal Freddie Mercury in a post Live Aid love-in.

Sting referred to Live Aid, when I interviewed him in Denver soon after it, as 'one of the best days for rock and roll we've ever had.'

'It was a wonderful warm feeling of camaraderie,' said the former Police frontman. 'We all used to live this cellular life where you never really meet your peers. That's all changed since we made "Do They Know It's Christmas?" and did Live Aid because you actually had to be in the same room with these people. I met Boy George in LA last week and he came to see the show and it was like we were old friends. The British rock industry is so bitchy. You hate everybody. I hate the Style Council, hate Billy Idol, hate fucking Depeche Mode. All of that. But this record brought us together.'

Group hugs aside, this all-in-it-together approach spread everyone a little too thin, and as they all became victims of their own success and spent less time minding the shop back home, others snuck in. Norwegian pop trio a-ha spotted the gap in the UK market and pouted their way most effectively into teenage hearts. The more mainstream British pop acts that followed in the slipstream of the classes of 1982/'83/'84 found it harder to keep afloat. Pretty faces like Nick Kamen (off the back of one Levi's ad and a brief patronage by Madonna) and Patsy Kensit with her Eighth Wonder boys gave *No.1* a few cover opportunities, but the emphasis had changed. Pet Shop Boys, The Smiths and New Order were the ones making the great pop records, but they weren't delivering on the pin-up front. Which is why, when the dust had settled on our Wham! goodbyes and Prince dance sessions, *No.1* mag was left with the puzzling choice in 1986 of Bon Jovi or Europe?

As a pop fan, this perplexed me greatly. How could we be expected to have our usual *No.1* fun with a bunch of poodle-haired, uniformly dressed, adult-orientated rock acts?

It was a dilemma that coincided with *No.1* being appointed with a new editor, Alan Lewis. Where previously Phil McNeill and Lynn Hanna had both had a keen eye and ear for pop looks and pop sounds, dear Alan had spent the past few years polishing the optics running his own family country pub. He'd started out at *Melody Maker* in the seventies, and then edited *Sounds* and pop spin-off *Noise*, but Alan was much more partial to tales of riding shotgun with Sammy Hagar, *Bullet*-style, through the streets of San Francisco or sixties soul music, than the latest trendy haircut.

An early features meeting where we were encouraged to bring along new ideas saw myself, Karen, Debbi, Max, Panos and Burschey pushing hard for whichever Duran member we could spirit back from some far-flung part of the globe to once again grace our front page. Whilst Alan insisted now was the time for Joey Tempest and 'The Final Countdown'. As Team Duran pulled a collective face that suggested someone had just dropped their dinner, Alan shook his head in despair at our sniffiness.

'It's simple bigotry!' he declared.

Relations between the old guard and the new ed were slow to improve, despite Burschey's skills of diplomacy as the deputy ed, especially where I was concerned. A trip to Belfast with Eugene Manzi to interview The Communards was greeted by an unequivocal critique sitting on my desk the morning after I filed my copy.

'Your Communards feature is as dull as the pictures, i.e. very,' typed Alan. 'Surely our readers don't give a toss about politics in Belfast or censorship in America or the band's business relationship with their record company. They <u>would</u> have been interested in hearing more about the nuances of a gay duo supported by a girl band and a backing singer who's more butch than the leader. Or where Jimmy gets that awful haircut. Or indeed anything of a human, personal nature rather than the band's totally unremarkable views on Ian Paisley etc. Please remember who we're writing for!'

I repaired to the Bloomsbury Tavern for an early liquid lunch. But it was hardly Alan's fault. The pop charts were short on pop and I was suddenly (shamefully, when you think what an ace job it was) short on enthusiasm.

The only real saving grace in chart terms came once more from London's club scene. Curiosity Killed the Cat were more Notting Hill/Chelsea than Soho but they certainly knew their way around the Wag as well as being on the periphery of the Laughing Stock. The first time I met their drummer Migi Drummond's Spanish mum, Ana, one Sunday morning after a long night at their family home in East Sheen, I opened the kitchen door and she told me to fuck off.

'Oh sorry, I thought you were the dog,' she explained. It was reassuring to know I wasn't the only one with an eccentric mother.

At either end of 1986 I saw Curiosity play at the Wag and Ronnie Scott's, but although they had a loyal west London posse, there was no indication that they were about to become our next teen sensation cover stars. They'd managed to get Andy Warhol to guest in the vid for debut single 'Misfit' but if anything, that just made them a little less teen-friendly.

January, though, was always a good month for fresh contenders to blossom once the Christmas big-hitters had been binned. For Pet Shop Boys, 'West End Girls' had found its way to the top at the second attempt at the start of the previous year, and as we slipped into 1987, Curiosity watched with slight amazement as 'Down to Earth', their second single, shuffled slyly up to Number 3. Before they knew it, there were screaming girlies waiting for them outside Capital Radio.

The drill hadn't changed much since Spandau days. Now it was Phonogram PR, Linda Valentine, directing us through the mayhem. She'd already been kicked and had her hair pulled by a few of the more lairy fans on a previous visit when they mistakenly assumed she was one of their girlfriends, so she wasn't hanging about.

'You're going to have to be fast with pictures,' she told our photographer as we sped after her boys up the Euston Road to Capital. 'Couple of frames. No one's going to pose.'

She was right. Simply keeping the band's arms and legs safely in their sockets and making sure Ben kept a firm hold on his trademark back-to-front Greek fishing cap were the priorities of the day as the first wave of screams came rolling past us and onto the boys. As we hopped over a bollard and dashed through a handy side entrance past the chaos already engulfing the main reception, Jane Goldman suddenly appeared shaking her head.

'I've come to deliver something to a fucking press officer then got caught up in all of this,' said Jane. She'd also been on the receiving end of some fan aggro. There had been a story about her in the *Mirror* linking her with Jonathan Ross, who she'd just started dating. 'I've received death threats in *Just Seventeen*. Four readers rang up and said: "Tell that Jane Goldman she better watch out cos we're gonna kill her cos we love him!"'

The Capital Radio interview was conducted inside a glass goldfish bowl, which was handy for the hundreds of fans stuck outside pressed up against the windows. We learned that Ben liked house parties with a bit of go-go and Trouble Funk, that he didn't wear aftershave ('au naturel'), that he was still denying any sauciness with either Paula Yates or 'teenage temptress' Mandy Smith and that, really, he wasn't going out with anyone right now, honest guv (big squeal from outside). Migi did admit to having a model girlfriend, Emma (Woollard, who I'd met in New York). 'Whispers' had correctly reported a few weeks before that he'd wooed her away from *Rumble Fish*'s Matt Dillon, which was a creditable effort.

'Mile High' and 'Curiosity Killed the Cat' got an airing and there was just time for Ben to step in and do today's weather report and Julian the traffic.

'It is still dry and quite warm,' intoned the Volpeliere. 'But the cloud will not do what it's told and disappear so we won't get quite so high as we thought earlier in the day.'

Getting high was certainly on the Curiosity to-do list. Max Bell was greatly amused when he interviewed them for *No.1* one Friday evening at their rehearsal studio and there were all sorts of coded references to putting in calls for some 'oobie-doobie-do'. Then again, maybe they were just big Sinatra fans.

For me, Curiosity were the last new pop stars who really did the business in my time at *No.1*. Good-looking lads that they all undoubtedly were, Ben had something else that made you watch him. Those gangly limbs took on a life of their own, like he was being operated by a slightly wasted puppeteer, as he rasped his way through his tales of crazy sheep noirs and funky answerphone messages.

A few months later, I was back at Mike Prior's photo studio being played a cassette of what sounded like Michael Jackson out-takes (complete with eeeks, squeaks and shamones) by a couple of exceedingly confident cropped blond twins with Grolsch bottle tops on their trainers, but for all their enthusiasm Bros never did it for me. At a Saturday afternoon matinée of theirs at Hammersmith Odeon I was tapped on the knee. Looking down to see their seven-year-old target audience staring up at me, I realised it was probably about time to get my coat.

George Michael had identified the paucity of new pop riches a few months earlier in one of our interviews.

'Really, the whole Wham! and Duran thing has been spawning people that are very visual ever since with gradually less and less musical back up,' said George, talking about both Eighth Wonder and Nick Kamen. 'It's already produced less and less sales. Everything goes in cycles.

'There's more immediate and more genuine excitement about

Curiosity. Ben is not a classically good-looking guy. He's just someone who has a lot of charisma and style. But I can't say I'm very excited by this whole situation of a lot of re-releases [in movies like *Stand By Me* and Levi's ads] and the amount of energy that is being spent on artists who are the same age as the record company bosses, simply because they're on a bit of a nostalgia trip. In America, especially with the huge success of Genesis now, everyone seems to be saying: "Let's go back to the seventies." But rather than trying to bring out a seventies' attitude – or even late-sixties' – in young musicians they're just going back to those old people.'

Be it Genesis or Bros, Alan Lewis was clearly no more captivated than I was. He headed off to oversee the *NME*, who were going through their own changes, and *No.1* was greeted with a new – or in my case, old and extremely familiar – face: former *MM* features ed Colin Irwin.

Colin had been given an exciting new remit to lick *No.1* back into shape, helped by a few parting notes on the current personnel by Alan. Keen to share, he called me into his office.

'Basically, I've been told by the powers that be that if I want they are perfectly happy for me to sack you,' said Colin.

In the shock of that moment, I can't say I registered all the specifics but I think Alan's personal assessment of my contribution to the mag was pitched somewhere between 'absent' and 'off his gourd' and there was a feeling by the publishers that it was time to get rid of the 'dead wood' and 'refresh'.

Luckily, being the generous gent that he is, Colin reckoned I might still have something to offer and promised to get the best out of me. On the proviso that I took this rocket up my arse seriously, he suggested I stuck around then promptly offered me my own column in the mag.

To be fair, this was probably long overdue (the rocket, not the column). As far back as early 1986 I'd been given a concerned ticking off by Sade. I was meant to be in Paris getting some quotes from her in response to some half-arsed tabloid concoction (she was extra newsworthy having just won a Best Newcomer Grammy) about walking off-stage saying, 'Hang on to your love [a song title of hers], I can't hold on to mine' – as she and Spike were supposedly splitting up. Back in her dressing room after the first night's show, she vented her spleen at Fleet Street but then quietly sat me down to say that while most of our lot clearly enjoyed the odd indulgence, I looked like I was taking it a bit too far. I was touched by her bothering to take the time to have a word when she no doubt had 1001 more important things to deal with. Then off I went with the rest of our mob for another big night out.

Even I could see that work and play didn't always mix. Not long after Bananarama moved into their adjacent houses, poor Keren from the Nanas (why was it always Keren?) was fairly nonplussed to find me speeding in her brand new kitchen in the early hours after I'd popped round to see the Faheys but found them all to be out. On another occasion, I woke the day after the *Absolute Beginners* party on someone's sofa (it turned out to be Dagger's). I phoned the office with the excuse: 'I don't know where I am!' Once I'd established I was still in the right country, I headed not to *No.1* but to Groucho's where I kept a box of fave VHSs in the upstairs TV room (*Get Carter*, *Performance*, *Grease*) and got an early start on my Friday night. It was also Dagger who came across me one night in New

York at the Palladium, standing on one leg, sporting elephant ears and a trunk.

'This man is a respected music journalist!' he exclaimed, with a shake of the head.

Most unnerving had been the moment interviewing Rutherford when I hallucinated that there was a policeman in a brown waste-paper bin sitting next to Paul.

'Ever since I took that 2-CB I keep seeing people standing in doorways that aren't there,' I explained, which didn't seem to bother Paul unduly.

In fact, the most bizarre moment of that ecstatic year of 1986 had been the taking of 'that 2-CB', done as the research guinea pig for no lesser mag than *The Face*. A couple of months before my twenty-fourth birthday, the lifestyle bible had run a four-page article about the rise of MDMA and interviewed a cross section of partakers – me being one of them – under the headline 'The Agony and The Ecstasy'. The writer, Peter Nasmyth, had met me in Soho and apart from my confounding him by not wearing soft strokeable clothing (my cashmere polo neck must have been in the wash) or having a Moonie-like permagrin, we'd chatted about my various adventures, with his main conclusion being that I was possibly trying to attach more cultural importance to who was taking it (I claimed it was ten of the main pop groups of that time – five of whom had liked it) than he considered valid in 1986.

Still, apparently pleased with the piece, the magazine then planned a follow-up in which new variations of the drug could be roadtested. I was handed a lengthy instruction leaflet concerning this 2-CB, originally used in California in the psychiatric community in the seventies during therapy, and told to report back with my findings. Unfortunately, all that went out the window (including the leaflet) when I was presented with the little devil on my birthday. Already fairly larupped, I quickly popped it down my gullet and off I went.

For the next ten or so hours, I found myself travelling through the Limelight, Wapping, Il Siciliano and God knows where else in a considerable pickle. There were hours of hysterical laughter followed by strange desert-like winds blowing around me and then a period when my body went so completely floppy that I couldn't even take off my T-shirt.

The long and short of all this was that, despite my former ed's concerns, by 1987 E and I had essentially parted company. There are only so many times you can say to yourself: 'Ohmigod, I have never felt this way before' until you remember that actually you felt exactly this way just last Friday. And Thursday. And Monday.

I had reached my ecstatic optimum. It was time to move on.

16

EVERYBODY NEEDS GOOD NANAS

I have many, many photos of Miss Jacqueline O'Sullivan. Yet the snapshot that best sums up our early years as partners-in-crime sadly doesn't exist. We're back to that Wham! farewell party at the Hippodrome and Jacquie is wearing a twenty-foot inflatable giraffe on her shoulders, like an American footballer, with a glint in her eye reminiscent of a marauding bull about to charge.

That giraffe caused a lot of trouble on the Wham! dance floor. In fact, it's probably fair to say that once Jacqs had wrestled it from its moorings and got amongst 'em all, that dance floor never really recovered. I don't know what was funnier – accessorising with a massive inflatable, the ensuing destruction or that look of fierce intent on her face. O'Sullivan, live and dangerous.

Jacqs and I first met on a Saturday bank holiday morning in Bournemouth in 1984 when she was a Shillelagh Sister, gagged and bound and waiting for her close-up. *No.1* was doing another of its spoof photo love stories – like Madonna's, another that never actually made it into the mag. The shoot by Neil Matthews sounds a lot raunchier than it was. Less fetish and more Four Go Mad on the Beach with the other three Shillelaghs rescuing their lead singer with a couple of water pistols from the clutches of two very spivvy-looking rockabillies who just happened to be Jacqs' and Lyn Halpin's other halves – The Polecats' Phil Bloomberg and Boz Boorer

– lending a hand. The idea was, of course, much like the Nanas pushing around their 'Cruel Summer' truckers, that the girls not the boys triumphed.

Actually, drawing that comparison makes me think I shouldn't have been quite so surprised when one Monday night in early February 1988 Jacqs rushed up to me at Brown's and announced: 'I'm joining Bananarama!'

I hadn't seen that coming. In fact, it was only a couple of hours since I'd watched the original three stealing the show at the BPI awards (as the BRITs was known then) doing 'Love in the First Degree' with a bunch of extremely well-oiled dancers at the Royal Albert Hall. At no point of that Bruno Tonioli-choreographed routine had I thought: 'You know what? Lose the Fahey and bring in the O'Sullivan.'

Siobhan had married Eurythmic Dave Stewart the previous summer and she'd aired her frustrations with the Stock/Aitken/Waterman approach to hit-making – massively successful though it had been with the Nanas – for a while. When it came to promotion for the last Bananarama single of that year, 'I Can't Help It', a heavily pregnant Shuv had excused herself from interviews saying she had nothing much to say. So I guess I should have rumbled something was up.

But still, Jacqueline?

Jacqs hadn't been singing much since The Shillelaghs' CBS deal had petered out after their first two singles had failed to dent the charts. She'd started to get together another band with Phil Bloomberg called Max Attraction but most of her time was either spent holding down a receptionist job at an advertising agency off New Oxford Street called Leagas Delaney with her mate Sally

Brazill, working on the door of a Monday night fetish club called Skin 2 behind the Astoria, or arsing about with me and the rest of the Laughing Stock.

Then one day out of the blue came a call from Stock/Aitken/ Waterman's Pete Waterman, who'd worked with her momentarily on The Shillelaghs, asking her if she'd like to make 'a lot of money very quickly'. She assumed it was as a backing singer so went down to PWL, met Pete and then the next thing Nanas' manager Hillary Shaw was appearing out of the shadows like Michael Aspel doing *This Is Your Life,* and Bob's your uncle – Jacquie you're the new Nana.

It wasn't a total shot in the dark as far as the other two were concerned. Jacqs knew Sarah and Keren from being out and about, although of the three she probably knew Siobhan the best. All were Wag regulars and their paths had crossed as far back as Blitz and early Spandau and punk gigs. But it's one thing being on nodding terms in a nightclub and quite another being catapulted into the middle of Britain's most successful girl group.

It placed me in a curious position too. By then I'd already known Sarah and Keren for five years, although we'd hung out much less since Mel and I parted company. They remained the funniest group to interview, but I certainly wasn't spending anything like the amount of time with them that I spent with Jacquie.

Almost from the start of the Laughing Stock days Jacqueline and I had been thrown together. Whatever the occasion we were the last ones awake, the last ones to leave. If there was 'going on' to be done at the end of a night out, one of us would drag along the other like a kid with a favourite toy. One Sunday in particular I remember being in a beer garden in East Sheen, more snakebites had been ordered and Jacqs held me firmly by the hand and said: 'You're mine.' No one had ever come right out and picked me first before – not even in rounders. I was chuffed.

It was never a girlfriend/boyfriend thing. One time when I was tripping I was convinced Jacqs had turned into a girl I knew at kindergarten. The only catch being I've never been able to remember that girl's name – or if she actually existed. But that's how far back my knowing of her seemed to go.

Anyway, now one of my closest mates was entering into some sort of pop star agreement with some other old mates and I was in the middle doing my bit to reassure all parties that they would get on absolutely fine. Oh, and interview them, by the by, seeing as how that was still my job.

My 1988 diary fortuitously covers many of the ups and downs of Jacqs' early Nana days more comprehensively than any journal I'd ever written. And there were plenty of both.

Three nights after Jacqs' big bombshell, I heard back from June Montana, who'd bumped into her, that Jacqs was already having a bit of a panic. She was zipping off to Germany next week to do her first telly. Then America. Then South America. It was a bit of a 0 to 60 in ten seconds. But the TV promo went off fine. Jacqs forgot a few of the words to 'I Can't Help It' (she'd never owned a single Bananarama record in her life) but all three of them just laughed their way through it. Then they went out and got drunk in true Bananarama fashion.

It must have felt a bit like it does for *X Factor* winners – except without the six months of preparatory build-up. Two days later, she was starring in her first Bananarama video ('I Want You Back') and doing her first *No.1* cover interview.

The vid, directed by Nanas' favourite Andy Morahan, was a

three-day spectacular. I arrived mid-afternoon on day one to find half of Busbys nightclub's regular Do-Dos crowd being lined up in the car park of some south London industrial estate whilst a self-invited Philip Sallon drilled them all in a dance routine of his own making. Buffalo gals and boys were going round the outside, up the inside and all around the houses whilst stylist Paul Lonergan was weeping with laughter at the spectacle.

Meanwhile upstairs trying on a series of seventies' outfits that took her back to her first nightclubbing days down the Bandwagon in Kingsbury (minus the girls' blacking up as The Supremes bit), Jacqs was quieter than usual. For a few minutes, it felt awkward talking to her as we worked our way through some standard *No.1 Intimate Details* questions ('Anyone ever stick your head down the loo at school? Can you remember your first snog? Did you ever want to be an air hostess?'). Then the penny dropped that my actual job that day was not about the mag, it was about helping her enjoy this mind-bending shift in fortunes. Wigs were donned, vodka was imbibed and Jacqs embraced the madness.

I shed tears of pride when she made her first appearance on *Going Live* that April, but was surprised when a couple of days later I discovered she still hadn't signed any actual contracts. After an unexpected late night back at someone called Olga's house in Fulham, Jacqs confessed she was worried about performing live with the girls – 'I know what I'm like,' she said, in between comparing record sales with a Hall and Oates backing singer called Myra. 'I'll take over.'

The greatest worry, apart from how to play it as the new girl, was the tricky old dynamic of three. Someone was always going to be the odd one out, especially when you had two people, like Sarah and Keren, who had been friends as far back as junior school. There were times when I know even Siobhan could find herself on the outside of such a strong bond, but I guess that's life. From Sarah and Keren's point of view they were letting someone completely new and unproven on board after they'd already put in seven years of work and were about to have an entry in the *Guinness Book of Records* – ousting The Supremes as the world's most successful girl group – to show for it.

A warm-up tour in Tokyo that June – those live dates they'd been limbering up for for the past five years – allayed a lot of Jacqs' fears. All three of them found an hour of non-stop singing and dance routines fairly knackering but singing live was where Jacquie O – as the girls had fabulously dubbed her – knew she delivered. She didn't stint on the nightlife either, particularly when some of the Laughing Stock happened to show up on modelling assignments.

It's traditionally the police who are in charge of sniffer dogs but in those days, Jacqs had a nose as unerring as any bloodhound and a pair of peepers as sharp as Sherlock's. I once saw her spot a micro-dot on a duvet made up of hundreds of similarly tiny spots and then spend a couple of minutes pretending to keep looking for it because she was embarrassed how quickly she'd pinpointed it.

In Tokyo, everyone was told that acid was both impossible to find and expensive.

'I just went up to this weird-looking girl in a nightclub, asked her if she knew where you could get anything and she gave me a microdot,' Jacqs told me on her return. While Sarah and Keren sensibly got some shut-eye for the following night's show, Jacqueline and mates Swiggy and David treated their hotel's residents to a few vigorous Olympic events up and down the corridors (this was the year of Flo Jo) with a couple of breakfast trolleys as well as liberating a giant teddy from a nearby store.

Poor Hills Shaw was run ragged. Fit models were bonked and a brief dalliance with one of pop impresario Simon Napier-Bell's latest post-Wham! duo, Blue Mercedes, occupied a couple of evenings – although in all honesty Jacqs had far more of a laugh with Napier-Bell.

Back in London, she sweetly treated me to a meal at Il Siciliano and a night at Zanzibar as she brought me up to speed on the not inconsiderable amount of work she'd been putting in. Not only was there Mr Blue Mercedes and that nice model who she'd left in Japan, but also a new flatmate Dan who was lead singer with another new club band, Nasty Rox Inc., managed by Dave Dorrell, who were also enjoying success in Japan. Big in Japan really was a phenomenon for less successful UK acts, as well as a band name.

Creatively, Jacqs was also keeping herself busy. She'd been writing stuff for herself but had also notched up two writing credits with the Nanas. She explained to me how their hit-making process worked. Firstly, S/A/W would lay down various backing tracks, then the girls would select one they liked. After that they would all work on the melody, come up with some lyrics, think of a title, and there you had it – another hit in the can.

There had been whispers about collaborating with others. Sarah told Paul Rutherford one night that they fancied working with ABC after he told her how much he'd enjoyed it with Martin Fry and Mark White. S/A/W threw a wobbler, though, when the girls tried to put some time aside with Madonna and Elisa Fiorillo producer John 'Jellybean' Benitez.

There were more random pop star nights back in London. A

hunt for a party at Sade trumpet player and Stuart Matthewman's brother Gordon's flat saw myself, Jacqs, Fat Tony and Boy George traipsing up and down Stockwell Road in the early hours of a Tuesday morning. George was ringing people's doorbells and hollering up.

'Hullo, this is Boy George and Jacquie O'Sullivan is down here too!' Sadly no one was impressed enough to let us in.

On a couple of occasions Bros entered the frame. At the opening of Aldo's new restaurant, Signor Zilli's, which would become our new unofficial HQ, Matt Goss presented Jacqueline with a red rose. Not long after at Benihana, a favourite celebrity Japanese restaurant in Swiss Cottage, Jacqs spotted the Goss again as we presented her with a cake before she headed off to America for a couple of weeks' promotion.

'I wish I was married to one of Bros!' declared Jacqs as loudly as possible as she cut the cake. In actual fact, she was far too busily engaged in lobster races across the grill with Paul Rutherford to contemplate a showbiz marriage. Although she had got one more tabloid surprise tucked under her Tokyo Disneyland hat ˙ . . .

My diary entry of 23 November is unequivocal: 'I'm sorry but this time O'Sullivan has gone too far – Paul from *Neighbours*!!'

It had all kicked off the night before when Sade had thrown an after-party for the end of her *Stronger Than Pride* tour. Quite how Stefan Dennis aka Paul Robinson had come to be at a Sade party I have no idea, but Jacqs had seen him the previous Sunday when both Nanas and *Neighbours* had found themselves on the same bill of the Royal Variety Performance, and he'd clearly scrubbed up well enough for her to have another gander.

By now, on top of my pop journo duties, I had landed an interesting new role as O'Sullivan boyfriend vetter. I'd already spent a few evenings round hers thwarting her poor besotted flatmate Dan's best efforts to have some quality alone time with her, which we instead filled with video sessions in her bedroom of favourite *French and Saunders* episodes ('Whatever Happened to Baby Dawn', 'Star Pets') and the movies *Hope and Glory* and *Prick Up Your Ears*. But an Aussie soap star was a new one.

Neighbours was by now a full and functioning part of *No.1*'s pop roster – mostly because of Jason and Kylie (their Number 1 duet 'Especially for You' was upon us), but just about everyone from Ramsay Street was having a crack at pop stardom in their wake. Hence Stefan with a butch George Michael 'Faith'-style biker's jacket casting aside Paul Robinson's sensible suits and snarling 'Don't It Make Ya Feel Good!'

I was far from optimistic. Still, the night after their night before I got the Bat signal to head to Il Siciliano. So myself and Jacqs' oldest confidante, Jo Hargreaves, settled in for a selection of vino followed by sambuca and vodka through straws (supposedly got you pissed quicker) whilst the Dennis did his best to regale us with some entertaining tales. We then repaired to Signor Zilli's where *No.1*'s Paul Bursche, in his new capacity as a Phonogram press officer, was entertaining US rockers Cinderella and kindly sent a couple of bottles of champers our way (perhaps it was the Dennis leather jacket).

The night ended with a nip into Brown's for a bit of a strut to INXS before returning to Il Siciliano where all that was waiting for us was a paparazzo who got his pic of the pair of them on the corner of Old Compton Street. When I woke the next morning and popped on the telly there was Stefan on *Open Air* up in Manchester, having made his 7 a.m. alarm call. So at the very least he had stamina.

The one thing I'm pretty damn sure Stefan didn't mention on our first night out was the existence of a Mrs Dennis. Thanks to the previous night's pap, that soon changed – although it was still hardly front page news. By Christmas, it's fair to say things were on the wane. The pair of them spent the festivities down in Somerset with relatives of his, but as Jacqs put it on the phone: 'I'd never do that again.'

Which brings us to 28 December. The middle bit of that post-Christmas, pre-New Year when things can sometimes go askew as folk race back from family commitments to see what other fun is left to be had.

I'd been down in the countryside waiting for some sort of intervention by the London mob. When that failed to materialise, it was the next train back, a quick pit stop at mine on the Grays Inn Road for beers and snakebite-making kit, then round to Jacqs' flat on St Augustine's Road in Camden where she and Polly were already beavering away making masks and generally keeping themselves entertained.

Jacqs had been given a telly by the record company as a Christmas gift so naturally after *Brookie* we sat down to watch the *French and Saunders* special. That was the first of the night's surprises. I'm not sure if Sarah and Keren had any inkling about what was to come but from the slack-jawed, boggle-eyed expression on Jacquie O's face, I know the last thing she expected to see on a quiet night in with a couple of pals and a dab of this and that was Lananeeneenoonoo. Dawn and Jennifer's spoof doco of a day in the life of Bananarama was so spot on – from the vomiting out of cabs to the nervous new girl glances to the tricky studio recording sessions microphone pecking order etiquette – that Jacqs was convinced they must have been hiding in a broom cupboard watching. The fact that she was being played by Jo Hargreaves' old mate Kathy Burke made it even more surreal. It was a proper out-of-body experience.

Giddy from the excitement of this unexpected induction into comedy history, we continued apace with the night. Larson cartoons were pored over, *The Cotton Club* was on the telly and Siedah Garrett's 'K.I.S.S.I.N.G' made sure the wooden floorboards got a good pounding for Jacquie's long-suffering downstairs neighbour.

It was close to midnight when Stefan Dennis turned up on her doorstep.

To be fair, on a night of surprises, it wasn't entirely unexpected. He'd been calling the flat from about 11 p.m. and no number of bogus voices – 'Simper, you answer it!' – had managed to put him off. In the end, there was a ring on the doorbell and there was Mr Robinson and his mate Max. Max I immediately warmed to. There's a *Far Side* cartoon where a hippy knocks on someone's door looking for an address and is confronted by a creature with webbed feet, elephant's arms, a hoover appliance for a mouth, an elongated neck and a revolving helicopter blade as a hat. 'Oh wow, déjà vu,' is the hippy's response. That was Max's favourite, I can't remember Stefan's.

Anyway, more snakebites were had, wigs were worn and a couple of hours later Max decided it was time for them to call it a night and left. Unfortunately, Stefan had other ideas. That's when he stormed the ramparts and scuttled back in through her bedroom window.

Earlier in the evening, Jacqs had told Poll and me quite categorically that it was all over between her and her Aussie playmate and although a woman has the right to change her mind, it didn't sound a lot like that was what was happening as the pair of them tried to resolve some communication problems in the bedroom while Poll and I waited for the whole thing to be swiftly dealt with so we could get on with our night.

A thump and a crash was the first indication that something was up. The second was Jacqueline shouting 'Paul!' The only person who answered to Paul from our lot was Rutherford so it had to be pretty serious. Now, my track record of rescuing damsels – or indeed anyone – in distress was pretty much a blank sheet, so as I hesitantly made my way through to the bedroom I wondered what the hell was coming next.

As it happens, what I was greeted by was a slightly groggy-looking Stefan. He'd apparently made the fatal mistake of not heeding Jacquie's request to leave when she first broached it. Lest there be any more confusion, and to put a stop to any amorous intentions, she'd then punched him in the face and kneed him in the bollocks at which point, much to her annoyance, he'd fallen into her wardrobe. This was where I came in.

Not knowing any of this, I simply had one thought: Paul Robinson from *Neighbours* is going to thump me. I'd had a similar experience a few years before at one of the *No.1* birthday parties at Busbys when gargantuan DJ Steve 'You Wot' Walsh's minder had taken unkindly to me doing 'wanker' signs behind his boss' back while he performed his execrable version of 'I Found Lovin''.

'You think you're pretty funny, don't you?' said the minder when he confronted me on the staircase.

'Comparatively,' I replied. At which point he flattened me. What amazed me most in that instant was not that I was now lying on the floor but that my adversary was telling me to get up.

'No,' I said, as reasonably as possible. 'You'll just hit me again.'

Staring now at the slightly dishevelled soap star in front of me, I realised I had to do something to defend my mate's honour. I could try to hit him, but I didn't want to rile a wounded tiger (wallaby) because he'd no doubt hit me back. Or I could try measured disappointment. One guy looking another guy in the eye and going: 'Mate, it's time to leave.'

I didn't have the brass neck (or the inclination) to call him mate but I did plump for the second option, and as the front door closed quietly behind me, I realised all my body parts were still assembled in the correct order and that I was in the same upright position as before my tentative suggestion. And with that we carried on with our night.

17

WE'LL ALWAYS HAVE PARIS

I needed to say goodbye, with some reluctance, to *No.1*. Five years is a long time in pop and it felt even longer when I reflected on everything I'd been lucky enough to cram into it. The parties, the press trips, the lunches, all garnished with the chance to quiz your favourite pop stars, see them in action and only occasionally have them wanting to knock your block off.

I wasn't the only one of the original *No.1* gang to leave. Phil McNeill had started up a lad's mag (not that kind) for IPC called *The Hit* taking Martin Townsend and Deanne Pearson with him. Lynn Hanna had left to start a family. Mark Cooper headed off and expanded his music portfolio somewhat to heading up BBC music. Anne Lambert reverted to maiden name Annie Woods and became one of *EastEnders*' most popular writers. Karen Swayne decided that as we'd started on the same day (and nearly been sacked on the same day) we should also leave on the same day as she eyed up a tasty job in New York on the US version of *Smash Hits*, *Star Hits*. Debbi Voller and Paul Bursche had provided *No.1* with its first office romance and wedding and while Vole stuck around a little longer, Burschey had swapped sides and was now working alongside Linda Valentine and Bernadette Coyle in the Phonogram press office.

Hats off to Paul. If there's one job that sounded like mighty hard work it was dealing with music journalists on a daily basis. We were a demanding lot. If it wasn't a phone call for more freebie vinyl or lunches or press trips it was us showing minimal interest in anyone on the record company's roster that we either didn't know personally or wasn't Madonna, Michael Jackson or Prince. Burschey dealt with all of this (and us) with good grace. None more so than the night of the 1989 BRITs.

This was, of course, the year of the infamous Sam Fox- and Mick Fleetwood-hosted ceremony – the shambles to end all shambles – where the presenters, performers and award-givers had not a Scooby what was going on. 'And now the Four Tops,' was Fleetwood's introduction and out popped Boy George. Piss poor that it was, as a car crash it was hilarious to watch. The *No.1* crew were in a box and had got stuck into the free bevy so were in extremely good spirits by the time we moved on to the official BRITs party – essentially a very large room stuffed with the night's top pop talent for us to pester. I had an uneasy encounter with Womack and Womack whose 'Love Wars' was a firm favourite. In the days before phone cameras, there weren't a lot of selfies done so it was all about autographs scribbled on whatever menu, napkin or notebook you could find. My proudest was Doris Hare from *On the Buses* at a Frankie Howerd Royal Variety lunch.

'I'm sorry, but we don't do autographs,' said Cecil Womack firmly but politely. 'It's against our religion.'

Considering *No.1* had recently run a competition to win signed copies of their latest 12-inch – 'Baby I'm Scared of You' – I found that strange. But with a quizzical eyebrow I let it go and barrelled onward. It was at this point that Burschey had the misfortune to bump into me. As he tells it I seemed fairly together, possibly because he was nearly as pissed as I was.

'Come along to the Polygram after-party when you're done here,' he said in his usual genial way. Then wandered off to keep an eye on his various acts.

It seemed rude not to. I'd had many a merry night with the Bursche, and the Phonogram roster was still a good one. There was Tears for Fears, Dexys, ABC, Wet Wet Wet and my very favourite band of the time, INXS.

I had a bit of previous with INXS. In the early days of *No.1*, Phonogram had organised a Paris junket to see the band play – no need to write anything – then 'get to know' them at a slap-up dinner afterwards. This was pre-'Need You Tonight' and 'Never Tear Us Apart' INXS. Frankly, I knew nothing of their work but a trip's a trip, even if it was Paris. You see, I also had a bit of previous with Paris.

A few months before I'd been to France's capital for a *No.1* Spandau cover shoot that coincided, somewhat tenuously, with that aforementioned Gary Kemp birthday party celebration. It had not gone well. The first night was spent trawling round several night-clubs that Dagger and various band members deemed not trendy enough. Then we found Les Bains Douche, a club that was trendy enough but where our photographer, Iain McKell, promptly had all his camera equipment nicked.

There was admittedly a cracking party in Kemp Sr's honour on the Sunday night bolstered by the surprise appearance of an exceedingly merry Siobhan Fahey who I hit the dance floor with, aided by a generous supply of whisky bottles on every table. It all went tits up again the following day when, due to a mix-up at the hotel, I missed my flight and had to spend the night at Charles de Gaulle Airport with fellow journo Louise Court where we were nearly choked to death when some bright spark let off a tear-gas pellet.

All of which I was regaling press officer Bernadette Coyle with on the INXS jaunt as we headed merrily into the centre of Paris.

'Worst of all was this fucking awful hotel that was basically in the equivalent of Watford,' I explained. At which point our journey continued. And continued. Until forty-five minutes later, we'd driven out the other side of Paris back to that self-same godforsaken hotel.

The gig itself was fine. There were drinks. They seemed a decent enough combo. Nothing mind-blowing but solid Aussie rock. So onward to dinner. I can't recall how much the Hutchence and the Farris brothers moved amongst us but I was sitting next to former *Sounds* reporter and tabloid TV bulldog Gary Bushell. Bloody Marys were ordered. Then more Bloody Marys were ordered. Then I went to the loo.

Over the years, I've had a happy knack of being able to kip pretty much anywhere, however uncomfortable it might be and whatever I might have taken. Many's the night at the Wag when there would be a knock on the toilet door from the kindly cloak-room attendant to wake me from a snooze. It therefore didn't entirely surprise me when I suddenly awoke in my cubicle with a start after having briefly rested my eyes.

What surprised me more was that I emerged from le pissoir to discover that the once bustling restaurant was now completely deserted with the lights off.

Furthermore, it had also been locked up. I spent the next half hour wandering up and down through the kitchens, around the various floors, desperately searching for an exit and shouting for help in rubbish O-level French, to no avail. Eventually, I found an open window on the second floor. Not on your nelly, I thought. It was another half hour before I conceded that this was the only option. Tentatively, I eased myself out onto a tiny ledge then leapt/fell the last part, landing on my alcoholically anaesthetised arse. Just to stick a cherry on top of the whole disaster, my morning alarm failed to rouse me and the rest of the junket, presumably having forgotten I ever existed, flew home without me.

So yes, bit of previous with INXS. By now, though, I had seen the light and was a devoted and enthusiastic fan. Something that I think was rapidly dawning on Burschey as he saw me fall through the doors of his exclusive after-party and make a beeline for him with a battle cry of 'Where's the Hutchence?!'

Rapidly recalibrating the situation, Paul did a quick scan of the room to check where said precious rock god was ensconced then directed me in the opposite direction.

There were other things to distract me. The dance floor, I noticed, was empty, so I started by rectifying that. Another Phonogram signing at that time were young rock hopefuls Then Jerico who had finally made it into the charts with their bit of flouncy anthemic rock, 'Big Area'. I had some knowledge of lead singer Mark Shaw as he'd once copped off with a mate of mine, Kate McIlwain, who had delighted in informing me that his real name was Mark Tiplady. There was something about the Shaw's exaggerated rock poses that tickled me. A touch of Jagger strut, a modicum of majestic Bono sweep. Mark liked a mike stand spin and a microphone twirl, and if a scarf could be draped and waved hither and thither then so much the better. I had neither microphone nor mike stand but I did have an old hankie. As 'Big Area' hit the decks, I hit the floor and delivered my solo interpretative dance of Mr Tiplady in his pomp.

Quietly pleased with my efforts and having worked up quite a thirst, I headed for the free bar where I saw Burschey talking to some bloke.

'What's your name, sonny? I asked. As respectfully and swiftly as possible, Paul introduced me to Wet Wet Wet's manager, Elliot Davis. Having little more to add to their interrupted conversation I waved cheerio and collected a couple more drinks before resuming my hunt.

Rather like an *It's a Knockout* event, it was now just a question of how many obstacles I had to negotiate before reaching the finishing post. Phonogram had recently had a big hit with an American singer, Robin Beck, warbling the new Coca-Cola theme, 'The First Time'. She was quietly minding her own business, talking to Burschey and others, when I took a bit of a shine to her and belligerently tried to persuade her to take to the dance floor to get a piece of some of those crazy moves I'd demonstrated earlier. She wasn't sold on this and after politely knocking me back for the umpteenth time I grumped off in a huff.

I was very close to giving up on my mission and putting Burschey out of his misery, when suddenly lo and behold, I saw him. There in front of me was the snake-hipped, leather-trousered, tousle-haired eighties equivalent of Jim Morrison, lounging casual as you like in a booth, unattended.

We've all seen those slow-mo action sequences where something terrible is about to happen. The hero lets out a low strangulated 'Nooo!' as he or she tries to avert the oncoming disaster.

So it was with Burschey. He couldn't have been more than a few paces away but the angles were against him and before he knew it I'd made it and hopped on board Michael Hutchence's lap whilst prodding a finger and telling him with great certainty over and over again: 'You are the greatest rock and roll singer in the world. Yes you are!'

Paul reliably informs me that it was the last time a Phonogram BRITs after-party ever made the mistake of combining journos and talent again. There seemed no better way to bid adieu to my *No.1* days.

18

RAISE YOUR RUMP OFF THAT SEAT

It was all very well Jacqueline making fabulous pop videos, swanning round the globe and wrestling soap stars but, truth be told, I had other plans for her. Selfish git that I was I wanted her to be in *my* pop group.

All those long weekends of misbehaviour when we'd invariably be the last two standing, sitting or snuffling had got some of our lot thinking.

'Why don't you two do something together?' they said, possibly just to prise us off their sofas.

It sounded an excellent idea to me. We were surrounded by folk who were pop stars or photographers or models or stylists. I knew Jacqs could sing and I was sure I could do, well, *something*.

Of course, like 15 million other kids who tuned into *TOTP* I'd harboured dreams of stardom. When I wasn't raising an eyebrow as Roger Moore I was perfecting my Geldof scowl or crashing Jam chords on my tennis racquet. Tucked away in my study at school, I wrote some terrible lyrics on a variety of subjects.

Moaning about not wanting to go to university (and sounding like I didn't much fancy a job in Fleet Street either), there was 'University Blues':

> I'm sitting here in Sherborne Mews
> Just sitting in Chaucerian moods
> Troilus looms and Macbeth fades
> It is so pointless what they said
> Cos if I leave now they're no use
> In Fleet Street's world of typed abuse

A trip to London for my initial NCTJ interview and examination had given me a chance to vent my inner 'A Bomb in Wardour Street' Weller when I happened to see the fairly grisly aftermath of a stabbing near the Dominion Theatre:

> Walking down the Tottenham Court Road
> I saw a body – losing blood
> Two men were helping – others stared
> It needed no clairvoyant to see no one really cared.

It needed no clairvoyant to see my influences either. And then there was 'Threesome':

> Tele
> Vision
> No Communication
> Alienation
> Save Me

I can shed little light on this one. Had I been disturbed by a Peter Davison-era episode of *Doctor Who*? Were we doing Ezra Pound in English Lit? Or was the tuck room telly simply on the blink?

Later in Cardiff, I attempted to move things along by buying a bass guitar. Apart from learning the riff to The Police's 'Bring On the Night' not a lot else happened with that. Instead I met Dagger and Spandau in Tiger Bay, realised that there were already plenty of folk out there who were actual proper pop stars, put the whole thing on the back-burner and became a journalist instead.

Still, after five years at *No.1* it felt like it was time to have another crack at it. I took a deep breath and handed in my notice to Colin Irwin, who, being lovely, made all the right encouraging noises whilst no doubt thinking I was nuts.

I'd have probably agreed with him if it hadn't been for Pet Shop Boys. Thank God for Pet Shop Boys. Up till their mid-eighties arrival, the journey of pop journo to pop star was hardly a well-trodden route. Both Geldof and Chrissie Hynde had written a couple of reviews for *NME* at the start of their careers but, as far as I knew, no writer had gone fully native and made a success of it till Neil Tennant.

Of all the other writers on rival pop mags, Neil was the one I used to see out the most. He never mentioned any pop aspirations and Lord knows what they thought at *Smash Hits* when he chucked in his prestigious deputy ed's job, but it didn't take him long to prove he'd made the right decision.

Pet Shop Boys' second single, 'West End Girls', had been that great January sleeper but it was its gorgeous lush follow-up, 'Love Comes Quickly', that for me sealed the deal. Not only were they making great pop records but there was a wit and attention to detail. Their first video compilation, *Television*, and first pop annual, *Annually*, were typical multimedia bonuses and that was inspiring. There was a logic (at least as I saw it) that if you devoted your life to writing about pop you might also have a certain aptitude for making it.

Anyway, that was my theory and I was sticking to it. Whenever anyone stared at me like I was stark staring mad when I told them I was leaving my fantastically cushy job at the ripe old age of twenty-six for a life of uncertainty, I just smiled enigmatically and said: 'You know, like Pet Shop Boys.'

Had I communicated these lofty ambitions to Jacqueline? Not exactly. I was quite aware of how ridiculous it sounded:

'Dear Jacqs, please can you bin off the most successful girl group in the world and come and try your luck with me. I have a Casio and a Fostex 4-track and not much clue how to use either of them.'

Meantime, Jacqs was still enjoying being a Nana. The demands of performing and partying had caused the odd stress and strain as they ploughed on from country to country. But on the whole, Jacqs had had a fine old time, particularly in the company of the girls' wardrobe department – their old pal (and mine) Miss Melody O'Brien and Taboo DJ Jeffrey 'Hinto' Hinton.

The biggest drama had occurred the night before the tour began when Jacqs was still in London. A few of us decided to give her a bit of a Wapping farewell. Supplies were gathered for this special occasion and all seemed fine as we settled down to watch the 1972 Elizabeth Taylor, Michael Caine and Susannah York movie, *Zee and Co*. I think Liz had just announced that she would be wearing some 'top clobber' when someone remarked on the unusual metallic taste in their mouth. Was anyone else feeling it?

Yes, they were. In a sudden panic, we realised that the Es we'd swallowed – and just swallowed more of because the first one didn't seem to be working – were in fact acid. Even the shortest trip would be nothing shy of eight hours discombobulation. It was already well past midnight and Jacqs' car pick-up for her flight to Montreal was at 6 a.m. Someone had read somewhere that the only way to negate the effects was to eat raw bacon and star fruit so that was how she spent the last few hours limbering up for the biggest tour of her life.

Thankfully, Jacqs is made of sterner stuff than most and having somehow negotiated that tricky first hurdle, the US dates that followed had plenty of highlights. Siobhan sweetly sent her red roses in New York and came along to the show with Dave Stewart (or 'thingy' as Jacqs called him when she phoned *No.1* to give us an update). Other famous faces in the audience included Al Pacino and Raquel Welch. Sadly, Prince, who was rumoured to be attending on a number of occasions, was a no-show, reportedly hard at work on the *Batman* movie soundtrack. Jacqs did meet Peter O'Toole in LA, though, who, apropos of nothing, tried to offload a baby that he was holding onto her. By now more *My Favourite Year* than *Lawrence of Arabia*, Jacqs said he looked like the top of his head had been chewed by a dog.

Despite such glamorous encounters, she was also missing home, so I promised to send the occasional Red Cross parcel of *Far Side* books, audio tapes and anything else I could think of. A Duran boat trip and album launch in London Docklands proved to be just the ticket. Apart from doing a running commentary for her on the day's events, I got John Taylor to send his taped felicitations and Nick Rhodes to burble on about art ('My favourite is a French artist called Jean Cocteau but I like a lot of different periods – Pop Art, Surrealism and a little bit of Impressionism') whilst Deanne Pearson asked Le Bon why he was talking in a ridiculous transatlantic accent, at which point he turned his back on her.

The only hiccup came when I left my tape recorder running for a bit of the band performing 'The Reflex' and an overzealous security guard turfed me out with a threat of more damage if I continued to take the piss.

There was an extra addition on the end of that cassette that had nothing to do with Duran. That Sunday afternoon Prince session I'd enjoyed with Alice Temple had unexpectedly produced something more than just our mutual purple love fest. A couple of months later I'd called her when *Purple Rain* was on the telly and she told me she was doing backing vocals with a guy called Eg.

'He said my voice was really good,' said Alice, sounding pleased as punch. 'It's the first time I've heard it properly on tape.'

Alice had a lovely voice, menthol dreamy, cool and mournful. Eg White had been in the boy band Brother Beyond (and would go on to write and produce some of Adele's early hits like 'Chasing Pavements' and pen *Pop Idol* winner Will Young's career reviving 'Leave Right Now') but he'd bailed early on BB and was now having a lot more fun recording with Alice in a makeshift studio in his west London home. So much fun, in fact, that the pair of them had even found some time for me.

I was a bit stuck. Since leaving *No.1* I'd been doing a bit of songwriting with Alex Godson. Al had done a great job coming up with some sexy bass lines to accompany my vocal efforts hummed hopefully into my 4-track, but he had a lot on his plate. He'd pretty much finished with Eighth Wonder but was demoing with a gal called Keeley as well as working on solo numbers for June and Rutherford and even a collaboration with Living In a Box's Richard Darbyshire for Elisa Fiorillo, singer of one of our favourite recent dance hits with Jellybean, the transplendent 'Who Found Who'.

Impatient git that I was, I decided to look around to see if anyone else could help me get something on tape that would so knock Jacqs for six that she'd turn her back on all those cute teddy bears and even cuter lads being slung at her on tour and instead climb on board with me.

'Nothin' Else On Her Mind' had been inspired by something Jacqs told me one night at the Wag about a mutual friend who had started taking heroin because she felt she was being excluded by her old mates, so what else was she gonna do? Pretty much anything except take heroin, seemed the logical answer, but I guess we all have our moments. After singing along at home to a lot of early Stones' blues numbers like 'Play with Fire' and 'No Expectations' I'd come up with my own approximation. Bolstered by Eg and Alice's great harmonies and Eg's fabulous guitar licks, I managed to do my best Jagger impression in the central heating cupboard under his west London staircase and off went the tape to hopefully tickle Jacqs' fancy Down Under.

To my immense relief she loved it but not enough to jack in a world tour on the strength of three minutes and fifty-eight seconds of bluesy warbling from me. I had to be realistic. I needed a plan B.

19

PUT ON YOUR SLIPPRY FEET

So, if I hadn't got Jacqueline, who and what was this imaginary group of mine?

I knew from many a conflab with Dagger on Spandau and Lee on Pride and Sade that I needed my pop manifesto. Who did this group represent and what did it stand for?

This was a time of Nirvana and Take That, neither of which I assumed was my target audience.

A name would be a start. I thought Feet Don't Fail Me Now! Bit of Funkadelic, an exclamation mark, like Wham!, and just a suggestion that at any minute everything might fall flat on its arse.

I'd had dinner at Bahn Thai in Soho back in May 1988 with David Johnson, who I'd not seen in years, but whose pop cultural savvy I trusted. I needed a grown-up. He immediately told me that was a rubbish name because, from a journalist's point of view, it had a built-in *Fail* right in the middle of it. I'd written the lyrics for a song called 'Slippry Feet', which I hoped like 'Wham Rap!', 'Chic Cheer' or 'Boxerbeat' would set out my stall. David said call the group that.

'Slippry Feet Theme' was an ode to all those independent women I'd encountered in clubland from Le Beat Route girls through to the Laughing Stock lot. Women who took no shit and who weren't about to waste an evening being hung up on some lad when they could be hitting the dance floor and raising hell instead.

Take your hands out your pocket
Raise your rump off that seat
Say bye bye to that bar boy
And put on your Slippry Feet

Slippry Feet should be a dance group like KC and the Sunshine Band or Chic, fronted by me if you please, but with floating members. 'David Lynch in a disco' was the tag line. Twisted, with a bit of pizazz.

Twin Peaks, which first aired in the UK in 1990, was a big influence. As was *Blue Velvet*. If I was to front this thing it would have to be as someone like Dean Stockwell's nightclub host Ben, singing showbiz laments to an audience of Isabella Rossellini, Kyle MacLachlan and Dennis Hopper with his little canister of helium. Ten years past Blitz Kids, we were onto the Blitzed Kids.

As for who would be in this band, early notes decree that everyone else should be fairly ancient (to make me look younger?). A drummer of Charlie Watts' vintage, a 'quiet' keyboards player in a mask and a large female bass player, described as 'roomy' (clearly I was spending too much time reading *The Silence of the Lambs*). Since I hadn't actually got my shit together enough to put an ad in the *Maker* and start auditioning this band, I decided to concentrate on finding a manager instead.

A manager could galvanise all this; a manager would get things done.

Optimistically starting at the top, I reckoned it was a toss-up between the two whose ethos and results I admired the most – Steve Dagger and Lee Barrett. Mrs Simper suggested Queen's manager Jim Beach, who she'd improbably met at some drinks party, but I imagined he was fairly busy looking after one of the world's biggest rock bands. Dagger and Lee also both had plenty to be getting on with. Spandau were on a bit of a sabbatical (in fact a lot of a sabbatical, though they didn't yet know it) but Steve was also managing Tony Hadley's solo career, not to mention Gary and Martin Kemp's and Patsy Kensit's acting commitments.

Meanwhile, Lee had not only an internationally successful Sade but an early, pre-Bush Gavin Rossdale band, Midnight. So it was a no from both of them. Typically, they were still generous with their advice.

Lee's big thing was 'parallel strands'. Rather than just keeping all my eggs in one basket with a demo, I needed an array of different things to 'carry the word of mouth and conversation on'. He suggested three strands: a record company to pay for more studio time, some live PAs and a video promo.

'PAs are worth doing to get rid of nerves, even if they're just down in the village in Wiltshire,' said Lee. 'Also, you then bring so much more back to the studio with your vocal. Sade did things like play in St Albans when she was demoing so she knew all the songs inside out when it came to recording the album and performing on shows like *Loose Talk*.'

Before I could get to any of this – or Dagger's fantastically comprehensive breakdown of all my record company deal options – I still needed a manager.

John Tinline had been around the scene for a long time. He'd done Spandau's PA as far back as The Makers and Dagger had often appreciated his dry, more experienced take on the music business in the band's early formative days.

Now he rather fancied following in the footsteps of Steve and the rest of them. Which was how, after a couple of beers with him at some Christmas bash, I found myself at the start of 1991 singing along to Alex Godson's 'Slippry Feet' backing track in my front room like an *X Factor* contestant.

Four minutes and five seconds later I nervously awaited the judge's verdict. John later told me that although he hardly thought he'd witnessed the Second Coming the fact that I was prepared to make such a numpty of myself (I'd imagined I was just going to play him the song on my 4-track) had worked in my favour.

'Well, you can carry a tune,' was all he'd say that night.

John didn't know it but that in itself was a massive relief. At the recommendation of June Montana and her flatmate – The Dream Academy's Kate St John – I'd been religiously going for singing lessons in Marylebone with a wonderful lady, Jean Marshall, who taught at the Royal College of Music.

I was in no doubt that I needed these lessons but the initial prospect was terrifying. As Jean went up and down the scales with me for the first time, I stumbled after her like a blindfolded child trying to pin the tail on a donkey. Any notes I happened to hit were more luck than judgement and by the end of it I was sure I'd detected the odd sliver of pain in her otherwise indefatigably cheery countenance.

More daunting even than the substantial mountain I clearly had to climb, were the moments that top and tailed each lesson when one pupil would be finishing up and another arriving to begin.

Not one to stand on ceremony, Jean would invite the new arrival into her small practice studio above the Piano Forte shop and there you would stand waiting your turn, wishing yourself invisible, whilst a wonderful singer like Neneh Cherry, Kate or June knocked it out the park. Then, when there were only five minutes of your own lesson still to go, there would be the dreaded tap on the door from your successor, who in turn would stand silently by the window, looking out down Marylebone Lane, no doubt wondering how much longer they were going to be subjected to me murdering 'Sally Gardens' or 'Raglan Road'.

God bless Jean. Like John, she kept her initial misgivings to herself. 'Basically you were doing everything wrong,' she later told me sympathetically after some tiny breakthrough had finally been made. Thanks to her perseverance, by the time Mr Tinline rustled up someone to collaborate on some new material, Jean had miraculously put me back together in some sort of working order.

My new songwriting partner was to be Andy Carroll, a former member of Habit, the band once managed by Oliver Peyton. To my great good fortune, Andy liked the vibe (yes, we did use such terms) of 'Slippry Feet Theme' and 'Nothing Else on her Mind' and was prepared to give it a go.

As with all fledgling projects, when money is scarce it was a question of fitting around Andy's other musical commitments and grabbing cheap studio time whenever and wherever. To make it more intriguing, Andy enlisted the services of a gunslinger guitarist called 'Mad Dog' Gendler. A man who, Andy explained, when supplied with sufficient rocket fuel would give my tracks all the vim and vigour necessary with wah-wah, acoustic and whatever else he had in his armoury.

When he hauled his axe into Andy's Kensal Rise studio, looking a little like Stig of the Dump, I realised that Paul Gendler and I were already acquainted. Before entering his wild-man-of-rock phase, Paul had been a neatly coiffed, wedge-haired member of Modern

Romance. Although we never actually met, he'd been on the other end of the phone line when their band leader Geoff Deane gave me a call at the *Maker* HQ offering some suggestions on how my face might be rearranged after my sniffy review of one of their singles. All of which amused Mad Dog greatly and he became a welcome addition to the team.

The other major breakthrough came in the early hours of a May Sunday morning.

'What am I doing?' said Miss Jacqueline O'Sullivan, in answer to someone's question. 'I'm thinking of going in with Paul Simper.'

The words I'd been longing to hear. Three years into her Banana-rama adventure, the outlook was a little less rosy. These things are never clear-cut but I think singing live was what Jacqs most enjoyed doing with the girls – it was when they actually needed her the most.

Jacqs also wanted to write. I'd worked on a lyric with her that she'd started about Elvis' last days called 'Trauma Room No. 1' and there were two Nana songwriting credits – including the single 'Love, Truth and Honesty', when they were still working with Stock/Aitken/Waterman – that she was pleased with. There would later be a kerfuffle when Jacqs' credit for that single mysteriously vanished from subsequent pressings of the *Greatest Hits* album. Pete Water-man very decently stood by Jacqs over her contribution and everything was eventually sorted. In the meantime, their latest album, *Pop Life*, recorded with former Killing Joke member turned dance producer Youth, which took most of 1990 and 1991 to record, had no O'Sullivan credits whatsoever.

What had probably swung things finally in my favour was the day that preceded Jacqs' early morning announcement. Sitting in

Andy's studio on the Saturday afternoon listening to playback, we shared a bit of a moment as that gloriously sassy twang of hers brought everything to life. With Jacquie O in the mix Slippry Feet made a lot more sense. A disco Sonny and Cher, I reckoned, albeit without the domestic abuse.

So now as a duo it was back to Lee's tick list. Simon Withers, one of the original Blitz Kids, had kindly agreed to make our pop promo. Apart from designing clothes, Simon had been responsible for the stark Fritz Lang-inspired expressionist lighting of Spandau's early live shows, which we both loved. So something on a similarly shoestring budget that created its own little world, like *Twin Peaks* with its backward-talking midgets and velvet-curtained rooms. A dive into my box of masks, wigs and cardboard cut-outs of Tony Montana and Hannibal Lecter hopefully provided us with the props, and John Tinline's PA company out in Park Royal provided the studio for planet Slippry Feet.

We were yet to see any record companies but, thanks to Simon, we had at least acquired our first famous fan. Being married to Siobhan Fahey's sister Maire at the time, Simon's brother-in-law was Eurythmics' Dave Stewart. Dave had got Simon involved with some state-of-the-art video installation he had set up at his and Siobhan's Seven Dials apartment in Covent Garden. Something that involved computerised lights in the carpet with sensory triggers that reacted to your weight or your heartbeat and with which Dave had alarmed his neighbours by demonstrating with a sixteen-foot-high image from some Japanese porn movie. When he wasn't busy with all of that, Simon was trying out various camera lenses for our video shoot and, to get him in the mood, he put on a couple of our tracks.

'I thought I was alone in the house,' said Simon. 'Then Dave walked in and said: "Turn that right up." He thought the tapes were fantastic and said to tell you that.'

Ideally this is the moment in the story where Dave Stewart whisks Jacqs and I off in his Rolls Royce to sign a hefty deal before jetting us to celebrate with Mick and Jerry in the South of France. Sadly not.

Nonetheless, praise from a Eurythmic was better than a poke in the eye. More practically, though, our next port of call was Dagger, who had offered to furnish us with a breakdown of all the record companies we should see. The number of options had diminished significantly since he'd first so successfully run rings around them all with the Spands at the start of the previous decade, but there were still about ten to choose from. And as it wasn't that long since he'd negotiated Spandau's move from Chrysalis to Sony, he'd had dealings with all of them.

Dagger started with a general point of order.

'You can say anything to any of them because they all lie to each other,' he explained. 'When you say you've already dealt with so-and-so they are never going to know whether you have or not.'

Once we'd digested that nugget, these were the edited highlights of his UK music industry hit-list, circa 1993.

Top of his list were Sony, EMI, London and Mute.

'Sony have just had a couple of really bad years in the UK. No British signing has sold internationally the way that Paul Young, Wham! or Sade did. But if MD Paul Russell is behind you, he'll push it all the way – release the single again and again till it's a hit, like Bros.

'EMI has a bit more English reserve. The doorman at EMI still really runs the company. On the American side SPK is the bright new, very pop, very efficient, very successful company. They've got shitloads of money and have done very well with Wilson Phillips, Vanilla Ice and others. I've spoken to Clive Black, who's head of A & R in the UK, about you. He signed Marc Almond and Tasmin Archer – unusual but good pop signings. The wild card at EMI is Dave Ambrose who's a lunatic but signed Duran and Sputnik and made EMI sign the Sex Pistols. So he's got a track record and there's always a chance he might come up with another great band. London Records is Roger Ames and Tracy Bennett. They love the scam and the chase – kidnapping two of Duran from a Holiday Inn and following Blue Rondo to a South American festival in Salisbury. Tracy's good and he loves the wind-up.

'Mute is the only real independent left and this might be up Daniel Miller's street. The track record of Depeche Mode and Erasure speaks for itself. The only problem with a licenced label can be that you are with different labels all over the world. Spandau had that problem with Chrysalis who had wound up the likes of France and Germany with promised Pat Benatar and Debbie Harry tours and all they got was five blokes [Spandau] in kilts.'

He was less enamoured, at least where Slippry Feet were concerned, with Virgin, WEA, Polydor, MCA/Geffen, Island and Phonogram.

'One of the drawbacks with Virgin is that they have never been very good at developing pop careers. They can do one album like *Dare* or *Colour By Numbers* and that's it. Also, more and more of their departments are being taken over by EMI. Polydor was once described by Bryan Morrison of publishers Morrison/Leahy as 'a fucking madhouse', but the interesting person in A & R there is

Feargal Sharkey who has just joined them and must be mad keen to sign someone good.

'WEA: the problem is it was set up as Atlantic to sell US products in Britain and it tends not to work the other way round. It's like a door that just opens one way. Now that MCA have bought Geffen they've become a big international company. David Geffen was the first star A & R man. John Lennon, Joni Mitchell and Elton John all signed to him in the early seventies. The big question is, would they understand Slippry Feet? The senior A & R at Phonogram is Dave Bates who is a solid, respected A & R. What you don't want is a young trendy because they don't understand how to develop a group. Guys like Pete Tong are used to a dance record they've found going in at Number 4 then disappearing after a few weeks. They've become stars through doing this but groups threaten that. As for Island, unless Chris Blackwell is completely into it himself there's no point. He only comes back from Jamaica for two months of the year, sacks all the A & R men and goes away again.'

His verdict on BMG, a merger of RCA and Ariola/Arista was the most succinct: 'Two big inefficient record companies merging to make one big inefficient record company.'

We got an early meeting with Rob Stringer, head of A & R at Sony, who Burschey had also briefed me on now that he had moved from Phonogram's press office to Sony. Rob's main signings had been the Manic Street Preachers, bands like Flowered Up on the Heavenly label and an EMF-ish group called Bedazzled. 'So he's not looked at anything like you're doing, which I see as being to your advantage.'

After listening to three tracks, Rob said he was more impressed than he expected to be and was interested that Dave Stewart was a fan ('just don't let him produce you!'). John duly reported all this back to Lee Barrett who thought this response sufficiently encouraging that we might get signed just from this.

In the end, it was Polygram who were the first company to put their hands in their pockets and pay for more demos. But as time dragged on, it was clear that we needed to deploy the tried and tested third strand of Lee's battle plan – a live showcase. If we could get all the record company folk under one roof with a partisan audience, maybe we could crack this. Lee's initial suggestion of a couple of local village halls in the wilds of Wiltshire had been upgraded to something a little more glamorous.

Raymond Revuebar in Soho was admittedly the faded, seamier side of glamour but considering both Jacqs and I had spent most of our adult lives in one West End dive or other, it felt about right. Advertising its wares in blazing red neon three storeys high as 'The World Centre of Erotic Entertainment', the Revuebar (owned, as most of Soho was, by porn king Paul Raymond) was into its 'twenty-ninth sensational year' when we came along. It was also home of the Boulevard Theatre, a 350-seater, which when it wasn't tits ahoy had been the venue for the *Comic Strip*'s first live shows and was later where Eddie Izzard honed his stand-up.

In terms of the two ends of the spectrum that this venue was used to offering, Slippry Feet's show probably fell somewhere in the middle. In terms of titillation, we were short on full-on nudity but we did have a large inflatable banana and a drag queen.

The banana was for the song 'Cock-a-Hoop'. A cautionary tale about a promiscuous old rooster falling foul of the ever-escalating HIV epidemic, which sadly reflected the increasing number of losses around us. In the summer of 1991, two absolute diamonds had gone in the space of a month – Joe Batty and club DJ and Department S singer Vaughn Toulouse. Suddenly too many friends were swapping nights on the town for bedside vigils at hospitals like St Mary's in Paddington. That October, new figures showed that more people in America had died from AIDS than were lost in Korea and Vietnam.

Dexterously manoeuvring both the banana and some hoops – we were nothing if not literal with our stage act – in a bit of bawdy shadow play were club legend Sue Tilley – more widely, though less gallantly, known as Big Sue – who worked as a DHSS officer in Camden by day and on the doors of the Wag and Taboo by night, and actor Steven Brand, Jacquie's boyfriend, who'd enthusiastically thrown himself into our nonsense.

The drag queen was John Derry-Bunce Esq., a pal of Sue's who we'd met out and about and at Susan's Mornington Crescent council flat where she hosted boozy Sunday afternoon sing-alongs. John gave us his best sashay for 'Come Here You Great Big Beauty' – our one mid-set ballad that was inspired by an unfortunate mix-up on my holiday with Joe, Paul, Miranda and Polly in Mykonos.

We'd befriended a couple of girls who worked in a local M&S in Canterbury. Having paddled out to sea on our lilos we were avidly listening to one of them giving us the inside scoop on all the latest sandwich ranges when I suddenly spotted a large wave heading towards us.

'Come here you great big beauty!' I hollered at it. Unfortunately, at the exact moment that our M&S gal's slightly larger sister rolled into view on her lilo. It's not that easy to convince someone that you were directing your comments at a wave, but I did my best.

The other main comedy element of the show was our encore,

'Ridiculous'. Now nearly thirty, I still hadn't managed to extend any relationship beyond the three-month mark. There was always a reason of course – usually telly, music or movie-related. Like the date who didn't get why I watched nothing but *French and Saunders*. Or the gal who wasn't that keen on Wham!. Or the one who turned up so pissed to see *The Silence of the Lambs* (admittedly on my fourth viewing), that I ducked down low in my seat when she staggered off to the Ladies so that I could watch the rest of the movie in peace.

> However long I spend my time on it
> Whatever way I try to look at it
> This love thing
> I look ridiculous

Whilst Jacqs was resplendent in shimmering gold with her goddess-like crown and a fancy Sam McKnight hairdo, 'Ridiculous' would be my cue to attempt a hell-for-leather quick change into something suitably preposterous. Hired from the treasure trove that was Islington's Costume Studio, I managed an Elvis outfit, wedding dress, a 'Je m'appelle Raquel' *Corrie* T-shirt, scarf and skirt, and a green foam dinosaur.

A decent number of record companies turned up and made suitably encouraging noises to John, Lee and Dagger. I was personally thrilled when Tony Hadley took the trouble to pop backstage afterwards to congratulate us. Other friends were more confused (though possibly not that disappointed) when they ended up in the Revuebar's adjacent strip show by mistake. As for the posse of Japanese businessmen out on the town for a good time who ended up catching our show instead, I can only hope that John Derry-Bunce gave them food for thought.

In the hope of rounding up all those A & R who had missed that Friday night show, we followed it up with a Christmas one at Camden comedy emporium, Jongleurs, a night most notable for Les Dennis taking a wrong turn into our after-party and being pounced on for a photo op by Sue Tilley.

It was still a slow old process. Management fell by the wayside. After investing in our first two shows and early demos, John Tinline magnanimously let us go our own way as we explored other options. Other writing partnerships developed, first with Phil Bloomberg and Patsy's brother, Jamie Kensit, on two more disco ditties, 'Staying Up' and 'SCREAM', and then with photographer/ producer Oli Maxwell. Oli had already done a backing track for a most excellent Phil Dirtbox poem, 'The Buzz', which Phil would perform along with plenty of others whenever he had a captive audience. I saw him collar Michael Hutchence (for once, not my fault) and Paula Yates on one late night, and another time he riled Woody Harrelson into angry action on a supposedly quiet night in Soho House.

Jacqs and I had our own crack at 'The Buzz', adding some snippets from *Jaws* and turning it into a B-52s beach party. Still on a movie bent, Oli had another instrumental whose bass line was reminiscent of Roy Budd's *Get Carter* theme. I didn't need to be asked twice to come up with a tribute to one of the film's lesser lauded characters in my all-time favourite movie. Edna Garfoot, played by Rosemarie Dunham, was the landlady of the local Newcastle B & B who Michael Caine's Jack Carter passes the time with when he's not busy smashing gangster's faces through car windows, having phone sex with Britt Ekland or flashing Edna's neighbours whilst touting a shotgun.

> It was fun while it lasted
> Sort of dead fantastic
> Playing bed and board with you
> I was wary of your barrel.
> Dug your hips so narrow
> On the phone you rapped so blue
> Oh, your lids are so heavy
> Hands so rough and ready
> I should have guessed our love was bruised.
> Know you're hardly sentimental
> Jack's not short for gentle
> Now my blouse is ripped in two
> And you've got dead eyes on you
> Dead eyes so blue

Soon after, I collared *Get Carter*'s director Mike Hodges at an ICA screening of *Pulp* – his follow-up movie to *Carter* with Caine – and gave him a tape of 'Jack'. To my utter joy he later called me saying he loved it and asked if there was anything he could do to help. The only thing I could think was to ask if he'd mind indulging me by doing an interview about directing *Get Carter*. I was imagining a little half-hour chat somewhere over a coffee. Instead, he came round my flat and cheerily answered every fanboy question I could think of over the course of an afternoon, before sending me corrected handwritten notes of my transcripts and a two-page treatment of his still-aching-to-be-made *Get Carter* sequel, *Jack's Back*. He even posed by my *Get Carter* poster from Julia Marcus in my stinky old bedroom.

My favourite *Get Carter* story of his was when he took his devout Catholic mum from Salisbury to the movie's big London premiere.

'She sat next to me at the premiere and up to that point I'd thought: "Well, this all seems perfectly normal,"' said Mike. 'Watching with my mother, as the film unfolded, I began to think: "Jesus, what can she be thinking?!" At the end of it the lights went up and the audience reaction was amazing. My mother just turned to me and said: "Very interesting."'

Apart from The Best Afternoon of My Whole Damn Life, the reality of our situation as we approached December 1993 – more than two years since Jacqs had left Bananarama and five years since I'd left *No.1* – was that Slippry Feet were still no closer to a deal.

That my mother should be the catalyst to change all that still confounds me.

Hoping to hype things up again, we laid on a third showcase at Leicester Square's Maximus disco, formerly the home of Leigh Bowery's legendary mid-eighties Thursday night carnage, Taboo. Naturally, Mrs Simper would be in attendance, and as with our first show at Raymonds Revuebar, she would be dining first with her country posse at Signor Zilli's in Soho.

This was all fine and dandy. Whilst Jacqs and I busied ourselves with the costumes, props and dancers down the road, Mrs S could get on with knocking back the Chianti Classico and generally lording it in Soho.

It wasn't till she was waiting for her profiteroles to arrive that she suddenly spotted George Michael. George was another Zilli's regular and on this occasion was quietly tucked away in a corner with a couple of mates, minding his own business. Or so he thought.

Blithely ignoring the counsel of various members of her coterie to 'leave him be', 'best not disturb him', 'he's entitled to his privacy' etc, Mrs S rose purposefully to her feet and, with a last dismissive swish of her napkin at the various killjoys, bore down on her prey.

'I'm Jean Simper,' she announced as George's fork paused mid-air. 'Now, are you coming to my son's show?'

In truth, we had invited George so it was just possible that he had some idea what this rather imperious woman in her best twin-set was referring to. All the same, she had rather caught him on the hop.

'I'm actually working this evening,' he said, quite possibly a fob-off but also, as he was in the process of setting up his own record label whilst his war with Sony rumbled on, possibly true.

'Never mind that,' said Mrs S. 'He always goes to yours.'

She had him there. My love of Wham! and George as a solo artist had in no way diminished. Whether such devotion on my part demanded a reciprocal favour on George's was more of a moot point.

Still, an hour later, as we took to the stage with our pom-pom brandishing backing dancers – Jody, Bayo, Emma and Siobhan – in the glittery bowels of Leicester Square, there he was: George flipping Michael, drink in hand, and behind him, lurking like Luca Brasi in *The Godfather* sticking it to that band leader – Mrs S.

After the show, the traditional huddle of pop managers had gathered at Signor Zilli's to assess what had gone before. Lee Barrett couldn't contain himself.

'That's it,' he exclaimed, pointing a finger skywards, like Sir Isaac

Newton with his apple. 'That's the missing ingredient – Mrs Simper. Mrs Simper works!'

The very next day, we had our first national press piece. The *Daily Star*'s Linda Duff had caught wind of it through another journo, Julia Kuttner, and so off we went to Kettner's champagne bar for a photo shoot in wigs and finery whilst Linda decreed that we were just what George's new record label was looking for.

'The group combine bawdy lyrics with techno and camp styles and could be next year's answer to The Pet Shop Boys [sic]' declared the next day's paper.

All of a sudden, Sony, who had at least put some money into the Maximus PA, became very interested. Not only that but on the publishing side of things another memorable character entered the fray.

Steve Dagger had told me many stories about Bryan Morrison. One half of publishing giants Morrison/Leahy who had snapped up George Michael and Wham!'s publishing on the strength of a short burst of 'Careless Whisper'. Bryan was an industry legend. In the sixties, he'd managed the Pretty Things and Marc Bolan, later he'd published everyone from Pink Floyd to T-Rex and The Jam.

When Dagger was first ushered in for an audience with Bryan back in 1980, he was in the penthouse suite at One Hyde Park. Now he'd relocated a little further north towards Paddington, where he'd taken up residence in another very Bryan address, Number 1 Star Street. The performance that came with it was equally impressive. When we were shown into his offices, all we could see at first was an imposing desk and a high-backed chair. Then, with a perfectly timed swivel, there was Bryan in front of us, like a classic Bond villain, puffing on a very large cigar.

His shtick was much the same. He'd told Dagger that Spandau were going to be e-normous (in spite of the tiny detail that he'd not actually seen them) and once he'd taken us through his impressive roster of talent, he said much the same for Slippry Feet. He was particularly taken with a new song we'd written with Bloomberg based on a Chopin prelude. 'Funny (Yesterday Tonight)' presupposed what might happen if two best friends one night had a moment of weakness (we hadn't) then immediately regretted it. The chorus being: 'Wish it was yesterday tonight.'

Bryan reckoned this had something of the class of George's 'Careless' line about guilty feet having no rhythm, which had also made him sit up and listen. It was hard to tell from just the one meeting how much was Bryan coolly blowing cigar smoke up our behinds, but we left feeling like a million bucks. Our lawyer, John Kennedy, let us know that there were also more meaningful noises coming from Sony. Deal-wise it looked like 1994 was finally to be the one.

The second Friday of that January, I received an excited phone call from Burschey. He'd just been in a meeting with Sony's A & R all present.

'It's all agreed,' he said. 'They just said it: "We're going to sign Slippry Feet."'

If there was one thing Dagger in particular had been insistent on it was that ours should be an album deal.

'It has to be,' said Steve. 'If it's just for, say, two singles and that week you come up against a Madonna Christmas single, you're fucked.'

The offer that came from Business Affairs at Columbia was not an album deal. It was, it said, an initial commitment of two firm singles (A and B sides) and an advance of £17,500 for both singles based on a collective recording budget not to exceed £20,000.

John Kennedy's advice to us after we'd been in to see him was downbeat but pragmatic.

'I do not like it and am happy to take your immediate decision which is that we should reject it outright, but you must be aware that of course if you turn this down you are taking a chance that a better deal will be available elsewhere.

'Please do not misunderstand me, I do not think it is a good offer . . . but I do want you to stop and reflect for a moment that you could be turning down £30,000, which may not be available again . . . Having said that, if we can get Sony to an album deal, I would hope that we can equal and/or better the proposal elsewhere.'

So as we moved into February we rejected it. The same month Bryan Morrison offered us a one-year publishing deal with three one-year options: £30,000 on signature; £15,000 on album release; £10,000 on first single going Top 10; and £10,000 on first album going Top 10 in *Billboard* or *Music Week*.

Then it all went very quiet. Through March. Through April. Very, very quiet indeed.

It was May before we discovered our A & R man at Columbia – the guy who'd offered us our deal – was in rehab.

There had been an incident in Bournemouth (where else?) at the record company's annual conference. These record company conferences weren't always lively affairs. I'd been to one in Eastbourne in the early days of Eighth Wonder where the group had to show their faces and press the flesh, and from Patsy and Alex's reports I had a far better time back at the hotel with the mini-bar and a club sandwich.

At this one, though, our A & R guy had really gone for it. Cutting out the middle man he'd busted into the hotel room of his dealer, grabbed a big bag of powders and hot-tailed it back to his own room where he remained holed up for the next three days until some sort of intervention was made.

All of which makes for a great story, but was of little help to Slippry Feet. As it was explained to us, if the guy who was making the deal is nowhere to be seen, there ain't no deal.

Clearly in the music industry these things happen. Recreationally in clubland, these things happened. So there was little point us tearing ours, or anybody else's, hair out.

Bryan Morrison came up with some money for a summer show at RAW, the nightclub off Tottenham Court Road run by Oliver Peyton and his sisters, Catriona, Marie and Siobhan. I got to wear my dinosaur outfit; our dancers, Jody and Bayo, got to do their best Bananarama dance moves with Jacqueline; and friend and lifelong Spandau fan Tracy Bullock seized her moment and went in for a surreptitious squeeze of the Hadley arse – who was once again in loyal attendance – when he wasn't looking.

After that (the show, not the arse squeeze), the Morrison publishing deal also disappeared into the ether. We heard that Dick Leahy wasn't impressed with the flyers we'd made featuring pictures of famous folk who'd attended previous Slippry Feet shows with one of our song titles underneath. Les Dennis' was 'Come Here You Great Big Beauty', Tony Hadley's was 'I Get Excited' and George's was 'Ridiculous'. Personally, I think the disappearance of Bryan had a lot more to do with the record deal falling through.

The cavalry did come valiantly over the hill one last time for the group in the heartening shape of another Bullock. Tracy's husband,

Ade, a music biz accountant who had also been a good friend and supporter of the group for years, decided to give it a go. With his company, Frank Productions, he found the money for three new demos, 'Horny Hairy & Handsome', 'Could Be Raining' and a new version of 'Funny'.

We'd already visited Raymond Revuebar, but it's little sister club Madam Jojo's proved ideal for a Christmas and Easter extravaganza with more dressing up. The second show, which incorporated both myself and a long-suffering Ade dressed as teddy bears, and was then followed by a stripper, sadly ended with me throwing a massive paddy. A new song, 'Distraught (Thinking About)' was bumped in favour of the lady popping interesting things up her fanny, and for some unfathomable reason I blamed this all on Jacqs.

There were hungover apologies the following day but this was now the spring of 1996. Regretfully (particularly for Ade who, like John Tinline, had invested a goodly amount of time, energy and money into the group) Jacqs and I decided it was time to call it a day.

Should we have stuck with it? Friends pointed out that Army of Lovers and Scissor Sisters both found decent audiences touting fairly similar goods. But like The Makers, and unlike Spandau, we never really got beyond our partisan friends and family audience.

Thanks to an exceedingly dedicated Jacqueline fan, Kurt Pagan Davies, a gorgeous CD and booklet of twelve of our demos ended up being released in Japan five years later.

The occasional royalty cheque for sums as big as £1.21 suggests we might have sold one whole copy, nevertheless it does at least exist. I didn't dream it.

Twenty years later, we finally finished that song that had put me in such an ungrateful strop at Jojo's. 'Thinking About', with a verse by both of us, was an ode to Laughing Stock days and all those Fridays into Sundays that got us started in the first place.

We recorded it in north London, appropriately with Phil Bloomberg, and then spent the rest of the day driving round Phil and Jacqs' old Burnt Oak haunts – the Bandwagon, their family's houses, the park where Jacqueline, egged on by her big sisters, had a ruck with some local girl. Then we went for a curry that filled us up for a week.

I can only thank Jacqs for sticking with me through Slippry Feet for so long. I discovered that living life on the other side of the fence I had the potential to be as much of a megalomaniac as any pop star I'd ever interviewed with hissy fits over costumes and sulks over malfunctioning video projectors. On more than one occasion Jacqs needed to point out what a Grade A arse I was becoming.

The only question left was where to next? By the mid-nineties my pop star dreams had evaporated and the joys of pop mag journalism were also on the wane. These were of course the years of Britpop, Spice Girls and Take That. *Smash Hits* was still going, but things were no longer quite the same.

No.1 had been absorbed by the BBC's *Top of the Pops* magazine in the early nineties. I knew its editor from Nanas' days. Peter Loraine had created the brilliant Bananarama fanzine *True Confessions* before applying his same inventiveness to pop mags. It was Peter who bestowed the career defining monikers – Scary, Posh, Ginger, Baby and Sporty – on the Spice Girls. But despite this and making them and Take That cover stars on pretty much a weekly basis, he says there was never any invitation to fraternise once the tape recorder was off. Those days appear to have gone.

Now, unless you are Caitlin Moran (one of the *Maker's* most esteemed alumni), you will not be sitting in the VIP toilet of a Berlin S&M sex party chatting to Lady GaGa for your pop profile while she's having a wee. It's junkets and copy approval and an impenetrable wall of publicists.

Naturally, being the top pal that she is, I again have Jacqueline to thank for where I would end up next.

Jacqs had always had a knack for snuffling out interesting people, as well as other bits and bobs. On the opening night of the upstairs floor at the Wag back in 1986, she'd produced from nowhere a bright-eyed, brown-haired, mega-enthusiastic gal who she informed me could do an amazingly lifelike imitation of a kookaburra's call.

Davina McCall gave us not only her kookaburra, but a gag that involved a lot of running back and forth in front of us, with her right arm crooked like she was holding a rolled-up carpet: 'And that's how you toss off an elephant!'

We've not let her out of our lives since.

It was not Davina, though, but Mike Leigh – another Mike Leigh – who would open up another thrilling, if exceedingly strange, new world to me. When Jacqueline met him at the Edinburgh Comedy Festival, Mike was talking up a show he was a part of back in London, with an old schoolmate, Steve Furst, called The Regency Rooms.

As soon as she returned, Jacqs started harping on relentlessly about how much we had in common. So with some hesitation on both sides – 'What if we're too alike?' – we agreed to meet in Soho's Coach and Horses.

'OK, so what it is,' said Mike, 'is this fictional showbiz legend

Lenny Beige, played by Steve, and Sammy Beige, his manager brother, played by me, putting on various freakish acts in a cabaret revue at this great old supper club off Drury Lane, the Talk of London.'

'Like Woody Allen's *Broadway Danny Rose*?' I ventured. 'Eddie Clark's penguin – the penguin comes on dressed as a rabbi.'

'Exactly that,' said Mike.

Two days later he called me in a state of high excitement. 'We're starting up the Rooms again next week and I've got a new character that I think would be perfect for you. He's a shit magician.'

Little did I know it, but this was to be the start of a whole new journey. One that would take me all the way to the London Palladium where, dressed in just a wig, silver bikini and a crumbling pair of children's roller-skates, I would horrify Simon Cowell, Ant and Dec, and a baying 3,000-strong audience. It was time for my TV life.

EPILOGUE

And finally, just in case you thought I'd forgotten . . . Elton.

You might recall that the last time our paths crossed had not been a happy one. I'd slagged his album. His PR and a fan got upset.

Still, that was 1982. We'd survived a whole millennium since then. It's now the tail end of 2005, England have regained the Ashes for the first time since the eighties and Christmas is just around the corner.

The phone rings. It's publicist to the stars Gary Farrow.

I'd first met Gary in the nineties, in my early DJing days. Various generous folk had kept me afloat with DJ work through the non-platinum Slippry Feet years, none more so than Gary's right-hand woman at his job as vice president at Sony, Jackie Hyde.

Jackie, as Sony's head of entertainment, would book me for countless company and artist events. One minute it would be Gloria Estefan's album launch, the next a posh dinner for the British Phonographic Institute's Man of the Year award at The Grosvenor. Alan 'Fluff' Freeman, John Barry, George Martin, Ahmet Ertegun and Peter Gabriel were all worthy recipients. Also Jonathan King, who's not been mentioned since.

The first time I met Gary in the flesh was at the soundcheck for the Sony Christmas party in Hanover Square. Jackie had got me an early slot and whilst I was faffing about with the cross-fader (never used it) up he popped.

I think it is fair to say of Gary (now Lord Farrow), once met never forgotten. He'd started out in the seventies working at One Step Records – 'The hippest record shop in London' – before getting a job as a runner at Elton's label, Rocket Records. By the eighties he had his own media management company, representing the likes of Jonathan Ross, George Michael, David Bowie, Geldof and Elton. After that, it was on to Sony where he could roar and rampage with the best of them.

'Orright, where's your horns and whistles?' was his opening enquiry. I had no idea what he was talking about.

'Your party whistles! Come on, you've got to 'ave that. Get everyone going! And your horn. Give it some of that!'

I'm afraid my Christmas set remained whistle-free but I must have done something right because a few years later, when Gary ended up marrying my old Cardiff NCTJ mucker Jane Moore, he requested I DJ for their wedding at Claridge's.

Unsurprisingly, considering the combined wattage of their respective careers in music and the media, it was a star-studded affair. His Best Man, Elton, gave a great speech, royally taking the piss out of the groom and commiserating with the bride. In her early tabloid days, Jane had once had to stand gamely at the front gate of Elton's manager John Reid's house in Rickmansworth with a sandwich board round her neck wishing him a happy fortieth from the *Sun* after Elton had sued them for £1 million.

But, back to this phone call.

'What you doing 23 December?' he barked.

Apart from a bit of last minute shopping, nothing sprung to mind.

'Wanna DJ for Elton and Furnish's wedding?'

I checked there wasn't a fault on the line. Elton John and David Furnish's wedding? Their civil partnership? The showbiz shindig of the year?

'Yeah, I've had a word. Told them you did mine.'

I had to admire Gary's logic. I'd played their wedding, people had danced, people had a good time. Elton was there. Bosh. Do the same again.

Over the nightmarish ten days that led up to the event itself, I found myself imagining all manner of mortifying scenarios. Wedding guests like Neil Tennant and Chris Lowe would be asking the groom and groom what big-name club DJ they were jetting in for this very special occasion?

'Oh, it's a mate of Gary's – Paul Simper.'

'Paul Simper?' I imagined Neil politely querying. 'Paul Simper from *No.1*?'

At any moment, I expected to get the phone call from Gary saying, 'Sorry mate, gave it my best shot but they've decided to go with Paul Oakenfold and Fat Boy Slim instead.' Who could blame them?

Instead, two days and counting, I found myself on the phone to David Furnish as I tried to pick my way through the playlist no-go areas and get an idea of what was expected of me in the vain hope that it might calm my nerves. So what not to play, David?

'Obviously, no Elton,' came first off the bat.

'Of course,' I said, kicking myself for the £7.99 I'd just spunked at Play.com ordering his double CD *Greatest Hits*.

'Other guests, Scissor Sisters are fine and George Michael. He always dances to his stuff. [I knew this]. Anastacia might be embarrassed so nothing of hers. Pet Shop Boys – no problem. Let's go for the interesting club mixes where possible.'

I wasn't big on interesting club mixes. I like a record to sound like the record I know, even on the dance floor. But naturally I agreed to everything the Furnish requested and resolved to do a good job, covering as many musical bases as was humanly possible in my midnight to 5 a.m. slot.

The night itself proved to be every bit as fabulous and nerve-wracking as you can imagine. The host of famous faces went on forever. So many that I think the whole Ashes-winning England cricket team were there and I didn't see any of them. Guest acts included all the Billy Elliots and Joss Stone. Then there was a sixties and seventies live hits band – and me.

Considering the genuine possibility that I might properly pee my pants with fear, the one blessing was that it was the band, not myself, that was first up. Having Elton standing right in front of you whilst you essay a piano part can't be the easiest of gigs. To their credit the band delivered their two sets with aplomb. By the time I came on everyone was already far too busy enjoying themselves or sorting their transport home as we moved into the early hours of Christmas Eve to notice an abscence of obscure Balearic dub mixes or some of my more ham-fisted cross-fades. There was an impromptu stage invasion by Kid Rock who pitched in (and immeasurably improved the quality of the mixing) for a couple of records and an Eastern European-sounding woman who pressed fifty quid into my sweaty palm to play some more R & B (Prince says keep it coming).

By 5 a.m. I was back at Windsor and Eton Riverside with my

two bags of records sitting on the platform in the drizzle waiting for my train. Had I atoned for my past misdemeanours with Elton? I hoped *Melody Maker* reader Phil from Lewes would agree I had at least given it my best shot.

THANK YOU

This book is all about right places and right times but mostly right people. So here goes, roughly in order of appearance.

Jane Moore, Anne Ashford and Gary Hurr for braving the inside of that terrifyingly trendy emporium Paradise Garage that led me to Tiger Bay, Bournemouth and, ultimately, Soho – a place I've rarely strayed far from in the thirty odd (and they've been very odd) years since.

Mark Taylor for dispensing the Golden Ticket which delivered me to Dagger. Steve Dagger for throwing open the doors – along with Graham Ball, Lee Barrett and Ollie O' Donnell – on a life I'd never imagined, and taking me along for the ride. Colin Irwin for going to bat for me at the *Maker* and Bob Elms and Kasper de Graaf at *New Sounds*, without all of whom this might have remained a life unpublished.

Maureen Walsh and Lesley Walker for giving me that first vital month to find my feet.

Graham Smith and Lorraine Davies for helping me survive my first full year in London. Their careful tutelage set me up for all that was to come. Graham never quite managed to make me cool, but he did at least make me presentable. Lol, we invented Snake in the Bath.

Phil McNeill for bringing me to my spiritual home on planet pop at *No.1*, even if I never had the good grace to acknowledge it at the time. The whole *No.1* gang for five years' worth of memo(rie)s and Fraser Gray for his *No. 1* photos and answering my phone whoever happened to call!

While we're on photographers: Brad Branson, Mike Prior, Bridget Wheeler, Graham Dexter Smith, David J. and Neil MacKenzie Matthews.

Shuv, Sez, Kez, Melody, Hills and Pete for the laughs. Tony, Gary, Martin, Steve and John for that ticket to the world. Sade, Stuart, Paul, Andrew and Mr Futrell for two Madcap Manhattan (and Parisian) weekends. George, Andrew, David, Pepsi & Shirlie for Whambley and generally Going For It. Patsy K for that one-legged drive. Kate Bush for her kindness. And Bob Geldof for his tolerance.

Exceptionally patient (and generous) PRs and PAs, Eugene Manzi, Fiona 'Fuzz' Grimshaw, Julia 'Juice' Marcus, Chris Poole, Jamie Spencer, Bill McAllister, Mariella 'Barney's!' Frostrup, Linda Valentine and Shiv Bailey.

I started my pop life as a 50p New Romantic but the genesis of this book is indebted to one of my countryside gang. Not only did Giulietta Horner née Edwards sort those Boomtown Rats tickets, she gave me a direct in to Justin Pollard, co-founder and creative director of Unbound. Head of Publishing Matthew Clayton reckoned there might be two tales to tell – the first being My Life in Pop, and here we are.

That the money was ever raised is down to friends, family, pop fans and other most generous souls, with the expertise, guidance and only occasional use of the whip by Unbound's Jimmy Leach and Georgia Odd.

For his wonderful book design – so many requests for the T-shirt and the badges! – Mark Ecob.

If this memoir makes any sense then that is down to these trusted souls who cast an early eye over it – Jungle Julia (this much was poo), Crowther (I did try to add more sex, love), Paul Bursche, Debbi Voller, Peter Loraine, Rae Earl (apologies for that need for a change of Tena Lady!), Deanne Pearson, Karen Swayne, David Johnson (whose comprehensive and generous overhaul brought me far closer to where we are now) and my wonderfully diligent and supportive editor at Unbound, Anna Simpson.

And finally, to Miss Jacqueline O'Sullivan, Paul Rutherford, June Montana, all those Laughing Stock members who gave their blessings and seals of approval and sadly those from within these pages that we've bid farewell to much too soon: Joe Batty, Josie, Ma Burns, Vaughn, Pearl, Pamela, Anne, Swiggs, Brad, Shiv, TPT, David Bowie, Prince and George.

My pantry feels woefully under-stocked without you.

SUPPORTERS

Unbound is a new kind of publishing house. Our books are funded directly by readers. This was a very popular idea during the late eighteenth and early nineteenth centuries. Now we have revived it for the internet age. It allows authors to write the books they really want to write and readers to support the books they would most like to see published.

The names listed below are of readers who have pledged their support and made this book happen. If you'd like to join them, visit www.unbound.com.

Steven Brand

Sally Brazill

Yvonne Breevaart

Richard Broadhurst

Debra Brock

Hamish Brown

Adrian Bullock

Lucy Bulmer

Kate Bulpitt

John Burgess

Jason Burns

Paul Bursche

Michael Bush

Lee Calland

Paul Calvin

Ciro Cancello

Joely Carey

Steve Carsey

Tim Cashmore

Yolanda Castellanos

Nathalie Cauchois

Yolanda Ceveira

Ronke Chalmers

David Lars Chamberlain

Sam Chapman

Vivien Chen

Juan Christian

Kenny Clements

Jacqueline Cliffe

Mo Cole

Lee Collier

Lorraine Collingridge

Charlie Condou

Lucy Connolly

Maria Coole

Steven Corbett

Jon Corbishley

Sean Corentin

Tracey Cormack

Laura Cotton

Louise Court

John Crawford

Adriano Cristino

George Crowther

Kate Crowther

Molly-Jean Crowther

Tania Dalton

Helen Danzey

Joel Davies

Lorraine Davies-Smith

Louis Dawson

Murray Dawson

Greg Day

Alexandre de Brevern

Rachael de Moravia

Hugo Degenhardt

Elliot Denby

Paul Spencer Denman

Peter Denton

Mike Devery

Ruth Devine

Kalbir Dhillon

Emma Doran

Tracey Douglas

JoJo Dye

Rae Earl

Jamie East

Fil Eisler

David Eldridge

David Elliott

Mark Elliott

Jo Elvin

EmEn EmEn

Jamie Emmott

Jude Evans

Mark Evans

Maire Fahey

Niamh Fahey

Anthony Farthing

Luca Ficco

Sean Fitzpatrick

Debbie Fleetwood

Andrew Fleming

Stu Fletcher

Ronnie Franklin

Joe Frost

Julie Fry

Bayo Furlong

Jody Furlong

Steve Furst

Mr Gammon

Nicky Gash

Bernie Gaughan

Lynn Gibson

Mark Goring

Anna Greenwood

Patte Griffith

Annie Griffiths

Sarah Habershon

Edan Haddock

Pip Haddow

Neil Hadfield

Andrew Hale

Sharon Hanley

Agent Hargreaves

Nick Harper

Lisa Harriman

Chris Harrison

Steve Harrison

Caitlin Harvey

Katherine Hassell

Michelle Hather

Cathy Hayes

Norman (Norm Ski) Hayes

Neale Haynes

Andy Healing

Shay Hennessy

Dave Higdon

Silvia Hildebrandt

Iain Hill

Adrian Hird

Michael Hogan

Russell Holborough

Pamela HoneyHeart

Giulietta Horner

Jon Horsley

Lynsey Marie Hoskins

Paul Hoy

Brigette Hughes

Caleb Hughes

Eamonn Hughes

Jack Hughes

Johnathon Hughes

Sali Hughes

Kim Hunt

Gary Hurr

Gillian Hyde

Rachel James

Fran Jepps

David (shapersofthe80s) Johnson

Allison Jones

Chris Jones

Chrysta Jones

Elaine Jones

Lesley Jones

Matt Jones

Sheriden Jones

Kath Jordan

Zoya Kaleeva

Katycoo Katycoo

Lucy Kavanagh

Flea and John Keeble

Lindsey Kelk

Andy Kemp

Gary Kemp

Huw Kennair-Jones

Graham Kibble-White

Dan Kieran

Joanna King

Tim Kirkby

Kenneth Kwok

Colm Lagan

Susi Langridge

Janneau Langridge-Foster

Christine Leech

Mike Leigh

Steve Lewis

Vicky Lewis

Lee Lewis-Davies

Christina Lindsay

Helen Lisle-Taylor

Chris Littell

Dave Little

Amanda Lloyd

Adey Lobb

Plaxy Locatelli

Paula Lockey

Julien Lodge

Adam Longworth

Peter Loraine

Jane Lovatt

Allison Lower

Yolanda Lukowski

Lisa Macario

Ian Macdonald

Polly Macpherson

Daniel Maier

Angela Mancini

Tara Manning

Eugene Manzi

Shane Marais

Joanna Marcus

Julia Marcus

Lauren Marks

Frank Martens

Paul Martin

Alfonso Martín

Rosanna Maulucci

Sebastiano Maziol

Iain McCallum

Rachel McClary

Rachel McCormack

Kate McIlwain

Paul McKee

Sam McKnight

Linda McLean

Ian McLeish

John Mitchinson

Mike & Sally Mooney

Caitlin Moran

Caroline Moran

Rebecca Morgan

Sarah Morgan

Ieuan Morris

Julia Morris

Tabitha Morton

Chloe Moss

Rosie Mullender

Graham Murphy

Paul Murphy

Steven Murphy

George Mylonas

Carlo Navato

Nchallis Nchallis

Sarah Niblock

Andy Nichol

Eric Nicholson

Fi Nightingale

Steve Norman

Stephen O'Brien

Stephanie O'Donoghue

Jacquie O'Sullivan

Lauren Oakey

Nick Oliver

Fizzy Oppe

Emily Oram

Mel Paget

Stephen Pain

Michael Paley

Nick Palmer

Andrew Panos

Tim Parker

Helen Parsons

Jon Peake

Deanne Pearson

Ben Pollard

Justin Pollard

Chris Poole

Andrea Poucher

Martin Power

Tim Price

Paul Putner

Jacqui Quaife

Michael Sholto Radford

Ted Ralph

Eleanor Relf

Michael Repges

Victoria Reynard

Melissa Richards-Person

Anne Richardson

Nicola Ridings

Stuart Rimmer

Davina Robertson

Peter Robinson

Gabriela Rodriguez

Lizzie bloody Roper

Jill Rowe

Jon Rowlands

Roy Russell

Barry Ryan

Liz Scoates

Nicola Scott

Nico Seperas

Tim Sharpe

Hillary Shaw

Mandy Sim

Eleanor Simons

Geoffrey Simper

Heather Simper

Jean Mary Simper

Paul Simper

Dave Skinner

Dan Smith

Graham Smith

Graham K Smith

Pete Smith

Jamie Spencer

Rebekah Staton

Andy Stick

Jordan Stone

Polly Strettell

Karen Swayne

Gabriel Tate

David Taylor

John Taylor

Alice Temple

Lucy Temple

Amanda Thompson

Mitchell Thraves

Sally Tillett

Sue Tilley

Jane Towner

Ian Townsend

Richard Ian Tracy

Jessica Tully

Jacqueline 'Jax Carter' Tunney

Rosemary Turner

Ian Usher

M van Vroonhoven

Beatrice Venturini

Hugo Verelst-Way

Jackie Vickers

David Walliams

Maureen Walsh

Ian Watts, Melissa Caplan

Ron West

Luke Weston

Gary Whalley

Gary Whalley

Hat Whitaker

Terri White

Jennifer Whitehead

Fiona Williams

Shelley L. Williams

Doris Wind

Andrew Winder

Scot Wingenbach

Sue Winter

David Witchard

Sarah Withers

Simon Witter

Jenny Wood

Arthur Wormwell

Marvin Wormwell

Yvonne Yuen